Understanding and Using Microcomputers

Steven M. Zimmerman
College of Business and Management Studies
University of South Alabama

Leo M. Conrad
Imagineering Concepts

West Publishing Company
St. Paul New York Los Angelos San Francisco

Library of Congress Cataloging-in-Publication Data

Zimmerman, Steven M.
  Understanding and using microcomputers.

  Includes bibliographies and index.
    1. Business—Data processing.   2. Microcomputers—
Programming.   I. Conrad, Leo M.   II. Title.
HF5548.2.Z58   1986   650'.028'5416   85-20293
Softcover: ISBN 0-314-93528-2
Hardcover: ISBN 0-314-98566-2

Copy Editor: Rosalie Koskenmaki
Text Design: The Quarasan Group, Inc.
Cover Design: Bob Anderson, Computer Arts, Inc.
Artwork: Alice B. Thiede, Carto-graphics
Composition: Clarinda Company

Registered Trademarks

Access 1-2-3 is a trademark of Novation, Inc., **Anadex** is a trademark of Anadex, Inc., **Apple I, Apple II, II+, IIc, IIe, Apple III, Apple DOS** and **Macintosh** are registered trademarks of Apple Computer, Inc., **Business Graphics** is a trademark of Business & Professional Software, Inc., **Business Graphics System** is a trademark of Peachtree Software, Inc., **CPM, Concurrent CPM, MPM-86,** and **CPM-86** are trademarks of Digital Research, Inc., **Centronics** is a trademark of Centronics Data Computer Corporation, **Chart Master** and **Sign Master** are trademarks of Decision Resources Corporation, **Compaq** is a trademark of Compaq Computer Corporation, **Compuserve** is a trademark of an H & R Block Company, **Context MBA** and **Corporate MBA** are trademarks of Context Management Systems, **Crosstalk XVI** is a trademark of Microstuf, Inc., **Data Capture** and **Data Capture PC** are trademarks of Southeastern Software, **DataStar, ReportStar, InfoStar,** and **WordStar** are trademarks of Micropro International Corporation, **Davong Multilink** is a trademark of Davong Systems, Inc., **dBase II, dBase III,** and **Framework** are trademarks of Ashton-Tate, **Dow Jones News/Retrieval Service** is a trademark of Dow Jones & Company, Inc., **Easinet** is a trademark of Esprit Systems, Inc., **EasyLink,** and **Telex** are trademarks of Western Union, **Electric Pencil** is copyrighted by Michael Schrayer, **Encore!** is a trademark of Ferox Microsystems, Inc., **Epson HX-20, Epson QX-10** and **Epson Printers** are trademarks of Epson America, **Ethernet** is a trademark of Xerox Corporation, **F.A.S.T.** is a trademark of Dean Witter Company, **FX-700P** is a trademark of Casio Computer Corporation, **Giraph** is a trademark of Compu Vision International, **GraphTalk** is a trademark of Redding Group Inc., **GraphPlan** is a trademark of Chang Laboratories, **Graphwriter** is a trademark of Graphic Communications, Inc., **IBM PC, XT, AT, PC Jr., PC Net, PC DOS, Topview,** and **IBM 3270** are trademarks of International Business Machines, Inc., **Intel 4004,8008,8086,8087,8088,80286** and **80287** are trademarks of Intel Corporation, **Jazz, Lotus 1-2-3,** and **Symphony** are trademarks of Lotus Development Corporation, **Kaypro II** is a trademark of Kaypro Computer Corporation, **Koala Pad** is a trademark of Koala Technologies Corporation, **MS DOS, Microsoft Word, Multiplan** and **Xenix** are trademarks of Microsoft Corporation, **Multimate** is a trademark of Multimate International, **NEC APC III** is a trademark of Nec Home Electronics (USA), **Ominet** is a trademark of Corvus Systems, Inc., **Osborne** is a trademark of Osborne Computer Company, **PC-1250A** is a trademark of Sharp Electronics Corporation, **PC-8210A** is a trademark of NEC Home Electronics, Inc., **PC Talk III** is a trademark of Headlands Press, Inc., **pfs:File, pfs:Report, pfs:Graph,** and

(continued on page 339)

To our students

CONTENTS IN BRIEF

CONTENTS

3   OPERATING SYSTEMS   67

4   WORD PROCESSING   93

6   DATA BASE   163

9   COMMUNICATIONS WITH CENTRAL COMPUTERS   245

10   LOCAL AREA NETWORKS   265

11   THE INTEGRATION OF OPERATIONS AND DATA FILES   277

12   HOW TO SELECT MICROCOMPUTERS   291

PUBLISHER'S NOTE

This book is part of THE MICROCOMPUTING SERIES. As such it is an endeavor unique both to West Educational Publishing and to the College Publishing Industry as a whole.

We are "breaking this new ground" because in talking with educators across the country, we found several different needs not easily met by just one publication. Those needs are:

1. To teach the principles or concepts of microcomputer use independent of running specific software programs,
2. To teach the skills of specific application software programs, and
3. To create a microcomputer curriculum flexible enough to handle changes in technology or courses with a minimum of change in the teaching materials used.

THE MICROCOMPUTING SERIES is an innovative attempt to meet those needs by closely integrating a machine independent overview of microcomputers (the core text) with a series of inexpensive, software specific, "hands-on" workbooks. Although each text in the series can be used independently, they become especially effective when used together to provide both an understanding of how microcomputers work as well as experience using popular software packages.

We hope THE MICROCOMPUTING SERIES fits your needs and the needs of your students, and that you will adopt one or more of its components for use in your classes. We are also interested in hearing your reaction and suggestions concerning our series and encourage you to share your ideas with us through:

> *West Publishing Company*
> *College Division*
> *50 W. Kellogg Blvd.*
> *P.O. Box 43526*
> *St. Paul, MN 55164*

ABOUT THE AUTHORS

Steven M. Zimmerman and Leo M. Conrad have written together eight books, one major software product, and more than 50 articles in the area of microcomputers. Included in their writings have been texts on quality control, spreadsheets, and business applications on the IBM PC and the Apple IIe.

Steven M. Zimmerman

B.S. Lehigh University
M.S. Columbia University
Ph.D. University of Arkansas

Professor: University of South Alabama. Teaching undergraduate and graduate courses in business microcomputer applications, industrial mangagment, quality control, operations research, applied statistics, and other quantitative analysis procedures in business; 1971–present.

Contributing Editor: H&E Computronics Inc. 1982, 1983.
Vice President and Consultant: A&Z Management Service Inc. 1978–present.
Associate Professor: West Virginia University. 1969–1971.
Instructor: University of Arkansas. 1968, 1969.
President: Mike-O-Neal Motel. 1963–1980.
Assistant Professor: Newark College of Engineering. 1961–1969.
Instructor: Hofstra University. 1961.
Industrial Engineer: Grumman Aircraft Engineering Corp. 1957–1961.

Leo M. Conrad

B.S. Tulane University
B.A. Columbia Pacific University
M.B.A. Columbia Pacific University
M.A. Columbia Pacific University

President: Imagineering Concepts, a consulting firm in microcomputers, public relations, and management. 1956–present.

President: American Society of Technical Writers. 1985–present.
Vice President: CBM Computer Center, Mobile, Alabama. 1985–present.
Educational Director: CBM Computer Center, Mobile, Alabama. 1985–present.
Instructor: Continuing Education. University of South Alabama. 1983.
Instructor: South West State Technical College. 1978–1979.

PREFACE

The growing capabilities and dropping prices of microcomputers resulted in an ever-expanding number of applications. Students today need an in-depth understanding of microcomputers, and the ability to use them. Students can increase their own personal productivity if they learn to use equipment and software.

The nature of our data processing and computer literacy programs is changing in response to the microcomputer revolution. Many varieties of microcomputer hardware and software courses are emerging. Because of these rapid and dynamic changes, we saw a critical need for a new textbook with a new approach to teaching about microcomputers. Thus, we embarked upon writing *Understanding and Using Microcomputers*.

The book and its teaching support package are designed to make learning and teaching about microcomputers easier for both students and teachers. This book is for the beginning student to learn about microcomputers and their use as personal productivity tools. This textbook is written so an individual with no computer background can read and understand it.

The objectives of this text are:

1. To illustrate how and why microcomputers are used in the "real world."
2. To develop personal microcomputer skills so students may increase their own learning productivity in other courses by learning to use:
    a. Word processing programs,
    b. Spreadsheet programs,
    c. Data base programs,
    d. Graphics programs,
    e. Communication programs, and
    f. Integrated and overlay programs.
3. To provide the foundation for a completely integrated series of books which can be used for the entire microcomputer curriculum.
4. To clearly explain the features that are found in general-application software so the student may be better able to select hardware and software. These concepts are then applied to a variety of microcomputers and programs.
5. To integrate each of these components into one complete and flexible educational experience that will provide students with the skills needed for our present technology as well as the broader concepts of understanding needed for adapting to future environments.

The textbook may be used alone. It also may be used as part of *The Microcomputing Series*, a complete learning package consisting of:

1. A core text, *Understanding and Using Microcomputers*. This text is a foundation text. It is neither machine nor software specific. It presents basic microcomputer concepts in a general framework for students to build upon.

2. A series of software specific (MS-DOS/PC DOS) workbooks that you can "mix and match" to meet the needs of your current microcomputer environment as well as your future one, whatever it may be. We are very fortunate to be working with a team of experienced and talented educators in the preparation of this series. They are Steven Ross at Marquette University, Mary Weitzer and Laura Ruff at Milwaukee Area Technical College, and Karen Watterson at Shoreline Community College. Our current group of workbooks (which will be added to as the need arises) include:

- Disk Operating System:
  Understanding and Using MS-DOS/PC DOS
  by Laura B. Ruff and Mary K. Weitzer
- Word Processing:
  Understanding and Using MultiMate
  by Mary K. Weitzer and Laura B. Ruff
  Understanding and Using pfs:WRITE
  by Mary K. Weitzer and Laura B. Ruff
  Understanding and Using WordStar
  by Steven C. Ross
- Electronic Spreadsheets
  Understanding and Using Lotus 1–2–3
  by Steven C. Ross
- Data Base Management
  Understanding and Using dBASE III (Including dBASE II)
  by Steven C. Ross
  Understanding and Using pfs:FILE/REPORT
  by Laura B. Ruff and Mary K. Weitzer
- Integrated Programs
  Understanding and Using FRAMEWORK
  by Karen L. Watterson

Highlights of this text include:

- Chapter Outlines and Goals: The reader is able to look ahead to see the intent of each chapter.
- Micros in Action: Examples of how the application program being studied is used by an actual organization.
- User Windows: Insights into how individuals and companies use the application program being studied.
- Margin Definitions: Each new term is defined in the margin as well as in the text.
- Hardware Requirements: For each type of software package, the needs of each application program are identified so the user is better able to set up a system.

- Hardware and Software Comparison Charts: Selected systems and software packages are compared to demonstrate the variety available and to help in the evaluation process.
- Key Terms: At the end of each chapter the key terms are listed. They are the microcomputer terms that are critical to the understanding of the chapter material.
- Chapter Summaries: These summaries list the important topics and concepts covered.
- Review Questions: These questions help students to focus on the important issues in the chapter.
- Discussion and Application Questions: These questions are used to direct students' outside activities.
- Laboratory Assignments: Laboratory assignments are used to direct students' activities in the microcomputer laboratory.
- Problems: In the spreadsheet and data base chapters, problems have been included to guide students in the use of these programs.
- Glossary: All margin definitions plus additional terms defined in the text are organized into an end-of-text glossary.
- Appendixes: Technical material needed in special situations.
- Cases: Three teaching cases are included as a capstone activity.
- Supplements:
  - Instructor's manual,
  - Test bank,
  - Computerized test bank (available to qualified adopters), and
  - *Teaching Tips Newsletter* a semiannual newsletter will be prepared by the entire writing team with contributions from users of *The Microcomputing Series.*

ACKNOWLEDGMENTS

Many individuals helped in the effort to create this book. Among those helping were an outstanding team of educators who reviewed several drafts of the manuscript. We thank them for their time, their ideas, and their commitment. They are:

Bev Bilshausen
College of DuPage

Lloyd Brooks
Memphis State University

Carol Clark
St. Louis Community College-Florissant Valley

David Cooper
University of Connecticut

Ilene Dlugoss
Cuyahoga Community College

Ben Guild
Wright State University

Don Lyndahl
Milwaukee Area Technical College

Robert Nau
Tulane University

Gregory Parsons
University of South Maine

Floyd Ploeger
Southwestern Texas State University

Tim Robinson
Ramapo College

Arthur Strunk
Queensborough Community College

Jack VanLuik
Mt. Hood Community College

Karen Watterson
Shoreline Community College

The "Micros in Action" feature would not have been possible without: Doug Houston and Carol A. Zimmerman of Doug Houston Real Estate; Bart Johnson of Scott Paper Company; Aubrey Diehl of Schneider Fleming Insurance; Jean King of Jean King and Associates; John Hanley of Burnett-Wilson Inc., General Contractors; Frank Knippenberg of Dean Witter; Robert Moore of Gleem Paint Center; Andres Aviles, Paul Reeves, and Stanley M. Zimmerman of International Software Consultants; and Bryan Nearn of Flautt and Mann Properties, Inc.

Among the many individuals who helped at various critical points in the project were: Warren Beatty, University of South Alabama; Kirt Burdick, Teledyne; Andy Lightburn, University of South Alabama; Gene Shockley, Burroughs Computers; John Coleman Smith, International Software Consultants; and William Walker, University of South Alabama.

The West Publishing Company team of professionals including Tim Reedy, Sharon Walrath, and Richard Wohl among others made the task of completing the manuscript possible. Their help and cooperation added many improvements to the text.

1

Chapter Outline

Chapter Goals

Upon completion of this chapter you will be able to:

Understand how the microcomputer is used in business.

Define a microcomputer from several points of view.

Discuss the history of computers and microcomputers.

Identify some of the social, moral, and legal issues involved with using microcomputers in business.

MICROCOMPUTERS

Business professional (as used in this book): An "end user" of a microcomputer who uses it to solve his/her own problems, and who is assumed to have little or no computer training—in other terms, not a programmer.

Application programs:
A program designed for the business professional to perform a specific business function.

Software:
Programs, instructions that tell the microcomputer how to perform.

Operating system:
The program that directs the flow of data among the parts of the microcomputer, the user, and the application program, often called the disk operating system (DOS or OS).

Documentation:
Narrative supplied with programs to help the user operate the software.
User friendly:
Microcomputers and programs that are easy to use.

The microcomputer is an important tool of the **business professional** because it may be used to increase personal and business productivity. It is an economical and efficient way of accomplishing business tasks.

These tasks include: producing professional documents (word processing programs); making business analyses (electronic spreadsheet programs); maintaining lists of customers, clients, and inventories (data base programs); producing professional presentations (business graphics programs); communicating with other computers (communication and networking); the integration or combining of several of these tasks together (integrated programs); and performing specialized functions such as accounting (specialized **application programs**). There are three levels of application programs:

1. General application programs: word processors, spreadsheets, data base, graphics, and communications
2. Specialized application programs: general ledger, tax forms, statistical analysis, inventory control, quality control
3. Custom application programs: created by a programmer for a specific purpose in a specific organization

The microcomputer, combined with **software** (instructions that tell the microcomputer how to perform, also called programs), is often credited with being "powerful", meaning it has many capabilities to accomplish a variety of "business" objectives.

The microcomputer is a recent arrival on the business scene. We will outline the history of computers and microcomputers. We will also examine the history and future trends of software developed for microcomputers because accomplishing business objectives depends on software.

The microcomputer is a valuable business productivity tool, because programs called **"operating systems"** have been developed to make them relatively easy for the business user to control. The operating system is the controller, similar to a police officer directing traffic flow. The operating system directs the flow of data and instructions among the parts of the microcomputer, the user, and application programs.

Along with the rapid changes and increases in capabilities that have occurred in microcomputers, there are a number of business, legal, moral, and social issues that have developed. We will examine these issues.

The microcomputer may be owned by the company, but it is a personal computer. It is a device used by individuals to increase personal productivity in solving business problems as well as a business productivity tool.

A user of a large central computer system is expected to have some knowledge of how the computer works, how to use the operating system, and often how to program the computer. The microcomputer user expects the microcomputer and its programs to be designed to solve business problems. The microcomputer and its programs and **documentation** are expected to be **user friendly.**

WHAT ARE THE FUNCTIONS OF MICROCOMPUTERS?

The microcomputer helps solve business problems. The microcomputer is a tool for the business professional to use in solving problems. There are several general classifications of programs available for the microcomputer that are particularly valuable to the business user.

1. Word processing
2. Spreadsheet
3. File management and data base management
4. Graphics
5. Communication with other microcomputers
6. Communication with central computers
7. Local area networks
8. Combinations of the above

This list of programs forms the outline of this textbook. It is a list of what we believe is important for you to learn about microcomputers.

Word Processing

A **word processing program** is designed to produce professional documents more quickly and accurately than a typewriter. Its capabilities include:

1. Creating and editing text
2. Printing text
3. Storing and retrieving text

Creating text is typing, editing, and retyping. Printing is producing a **hard copy** in the form specified by the edited material. Storing is saving the text for future use.

Word processing is the production of letters, reports, memos, and other documents (see Figure 1–1). It also includes the use of spelling, grammar, footnoting, indexing, and document assembly capabilities usually found in separate programs. Document assembly programs are often used in legal offices for the creation of individual wills and other legal documents from prerecorded paragraphs.

Spreadsheets

Spreadsheet programs are used for calculation (formula oriented) and presentation of data under the control of the end user. The screen is divided into columns (vertical division) and rows (horizontal division.) The intersection of a column and a row is called a cell.

Figure 1–2 illustrates a manual accounting spreadsheet for posting. Figure 1–3 is the form found on the back of the report you receive from your monthly bank statement. This form is designed to help you balance your checkbook. It, too, is a good application of a spreadsheet. The

Word processing program:
A program designed to aid an individual in the creation, editing, printing, storing, and retrieving of text.

Hard copy:
Text printed on paper.

Spreadsheet programs:
Programs that are used for calculation (formula oriented) and presentation.

FIGURE 1–1
Microcomputer and Printer with Form

(a)   General Journal   Page 1

Date 19XX		Description	Post. Ref.	Debit	Credit
	1	CASH	11	15000	
		OWNERS EQUITY, STACEY CAPITAL	31		15000
		STACEY CONTRIBUTED FUNDS TO THE			
		BUSINESS			
	2	TRUCK	15	4000	
		CASH	11		4000
	2	EQUITMENT	17	1800	
		CASH	11		1000
		ACCOUNT PAYABLE	21		800
		EQUITMENT FOR BUS $1000 DOWN			
		BALANCE DUE IN 30 DAYS			

FIGURE 1–2   A Manual Accounting Spreadsheet

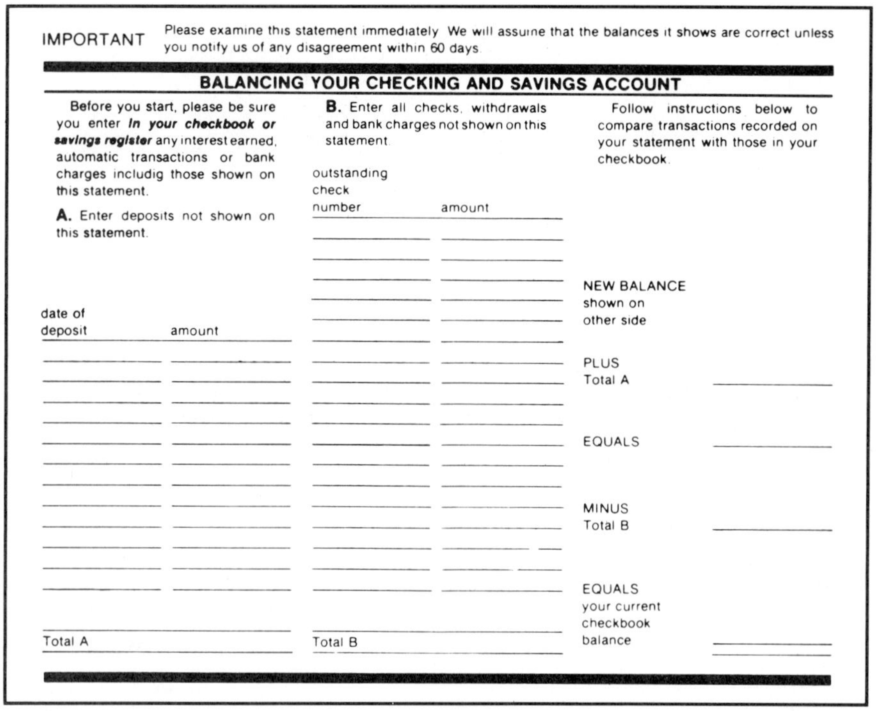

FIGURE 1–3
Checkbook Balancing Form

IMPORTANT	Please examine this statement immediately We will assume that the balances it shows are correct unless you notify us of any disagreement within 60 days

BALANCING YOUR CHECKING AND SAVINGS ACCOUNT

Before you start, please be sure you enter **In your checkbook or savings register** any interest earned, automatic transactions or bank charges includig those shown on this statement.

A. Enter deposits not shown on this statement.

B. Enter all checks, withdrawals and bank charges not shown on this statement

outstanding
check
number   amount

Follow instructions below to compare transactions recorded on your statement with those in your checkbook.

date of
deposit   amount

NEW BALANCE
shown on
other side

PLUS
Total A   _____

EQUALS   _____

MINUS
Total B   _____

EQUALS
your current
checkbook
balance   _____

Total A   Total B

spreadsheet program helps the end user solve common everyday business problems and tasks.

The spreadsheet program user must know how to solve the business problem, but needs only a minimum of microcomputer knowledge to use the program. Any business problem that can be solved with pencil, paper, and calculator may be solved using a spreadsheet program.

File and Data Base Management

File management programs are simple filing programs. **Data base management** may include complete application programs with an objective such as an inventory system or **programming languages** in which many different applications can be created. The business objective, the skills available, the cost of the programs, and the microcomputer available determine which option is better.

File and data base management programs are designed to store, update, and retrieve business information. The entering, recording, recalling, sorting, and using of stored **data** should be controlled by managerial guidelines so that the business objectives of the end user may be accomplished.

Data bases include customer mailing lists, inventory lists, employee records, student records and grades, credit information, etc. Microcomputers, with the addition of data base programs, can be used to manage and maintain business data bases.

File management programs:
Programs designed to store, update, and retrieve business data. These programs are limited to managing simple files with narrow objectives.

Data base management programs:
Programs designed to store, update, and retrieve business data. These programs are not limited to any particular type of application.

Programming language:
A language used by programmers to create, store, recall, and edit instructions to computers.

Data:
Facts that have been collected, organized, and stored.

Data base:
A collection of data stored in your microcomputer, that is used for a variety of business purposes.

Graphics

Graphics may be divided into several classifications:

1. Business graphics
   a. Analytical
   b. Presentation
2. Engineering/scientific graphics

Business analytical graphics programs have the capability of producing bar charts, pie charts, and line type graphs (see Figure 1–4). Business graphics are often used to impress a customer or a supervisor more easily than lists, words, or tables. The data from spreadsheet or data base programs may often be used to prepare graphic presentations without the need to re-enter the data.

Business presentation graphics are graphics that combine art and photography (on the screen) with data for sales and other presentations. The graphics capabilities of the microcomputer include the handling of television pictures and combining them with microcomputer output. Marketing managers will be interested in these capabilities for their potential in advertising. Figures 1–5 and 1–6 are examples of what is currently available.

Engineering/scientific graphics include CAD, computer aided design, CAE, computer aided engineering, CADD, computer aided design and drafting among other similar applications. Figures 1–7 and 1–8 are examples of engineering graphics in use.

FIGURE 1–4
Bar Chart on Screen

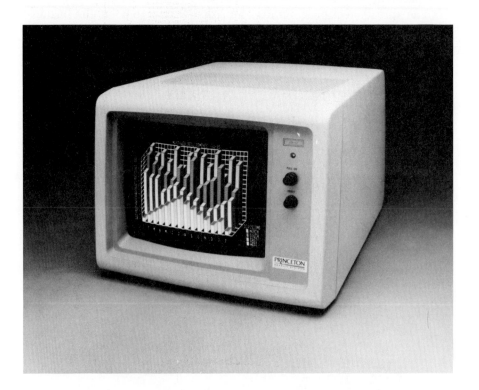

FIGURE 1–5
Digitized Picture and
Microcomputer Output

Other graphics include line charts such as organization charts, flow charts, control charts, and statistical analysis charts.

FIGURE 1–6
Presentation Graphics

FIGURE 1–7
Engineering with a Touch Screen

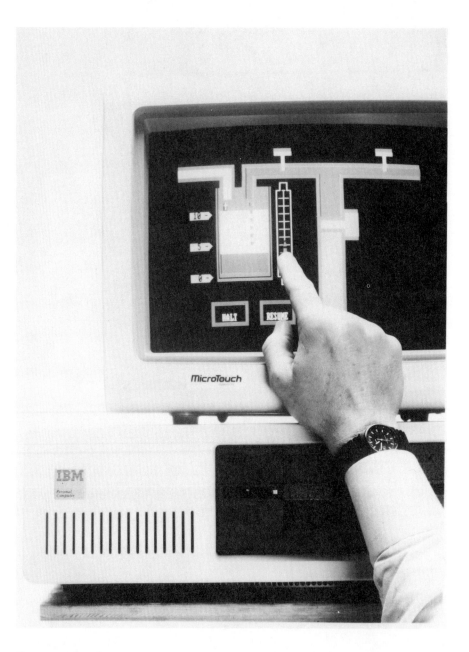

Communication

Communication program:
A program that allows computers to communicate with each other.

Communication programs make it possible for microcomputers to communicate with most computers. They can act as a dumb terminal, i.e., communicate only under the control of an operator using the keyboard, or as a smart terminal that can transfer data files between two computers. The capability to communicate requires a modem (device to connect the computer to a telephone) or a null-modem (device that makes the computer behave as if it is connected to a telephone). Cables and software complete the communication needs.

FIGURE 1–8
Engineering Graphics

Integrated Programs

Integrated programs have different combinations of capabilities available at the same time for selected tasks. There are programs available which combine the features of one or more general programs. Integrated programs often include electronic spreadsheet and the capability to perform graphics. Some programs combine word processing, spreadsheet, data base, graphic, and communication capabilities.

Integrated programs:
Programs that combines the capabilities of two or more general or specific application programs.

Specialized Application Programs

Specialized application programs will help managers who have a need to solve a specific problem. The specialized application program is an alternate tool you may use to solve your business problems. Examples include statistical, accounting, inventory, payroll, real estate evaluation, or project management programs as well as others. Figure 1–9 shows a profit and loss statement produced by an application program on a microcomputer and printer.

A common approach to creating special programs is to design them for a vertical market. A vertical market is a narrow market limited to a specific professional area. Examples of vertical markets are:

1. Accountants
2. Medical doctors
3. Veterinarians
4. Building contractors

FIGURE 1–9
Profit and Loss Statement

```
                        January 3, 1987

                    West Brook Real Estate
                     4151 Bay Lane Road
                    Mobile,Alabama 36605

          P r o f i t   and   L o s s   S t a t e m e n t

Revenue
Number Account        Current Period          Year to date
                    Amount      Percent      Amount      Percent
       ---------------------------------------------------------
6010 Rent Inc        1,760.00      32        4,810.00      28
6020 Evaluation          0.00       0        4,116.39      24
6025 Mgt Serv.       2,701.75      49        2,701.75      16
6030 Capital           571.98      10        2,262.50      13
6040 Interest          364.37       7        1,708.19      10
6050 Consultant          0.00       0        1,000.00       6
6900 Misc. Co          124.00       2          496.00       3
                    -----------               -----------
                    $5,522.10                 $17,094.83
                    ===========               ===========

Expenses

Number Account        Current Period          Year to date
                    Amount      Percent      Amount      Percent
       ---------------------------------------------------------
9100 Maintena         837.47      27        2,139.95      16
9200 Supplies          68.48       2        2,530.32      18
9300 Deprecia       1,286.37      42        5,145.48      37
9400 Interest         577.52      19        2,336.62      17
9500 Operatio         134.90       4          141.06       1
9501 Advertiz           0.00       0           36.30       0
9510 Utilitie           0.00       0          150.00       1
9520 Insuranc           0.00       0          117.17       1
9530 Taxes Re           0.00       0          435.95       3
9532 Other Ta           0.00       0            0.00       0
9540 Professi         133.40       4          240.73       2
9550 Travel (           0.00       0            0.00       0
9560 Local Au          52.70       2          246.33       2
9570 Medical            0.00       0          239.67       2
                    -----------               -----------
                    $3,090.84                 $13,759.58
                    ===========               ===========

Profit              $2,431.26                 $3,335.25
```

WHAT ARE THE COSTS OF MICROCOMPUTERS?

The microcomputer purchase price is less than $15,000. The cost of a microcomputer includes its purchase price, maintenance cost, and operational costs. These costs vary depending upon the location of the purchaser, the time in the life cycle of a microcomputer it is purchased, the source from which it is purchased, the support included in the purchase price, and whether the purchase was cash or credit.

If a microcomputer is purchased when the model is first introduced to the market, you must expect to pay full list price. After the initial sales period the price usually drops and some discounting is available.

From a purchase price point of view, microcomputers are defined as computers selling for less than $15,000. We estimate that the average professional paid less than $15,000 for a "full-featured" microcomputer system between the late 1970s until today. Few units, except for ones with "extra capabilities," sell for more. Figure 1–10 and 1–11 are examples of typical microcomputer systems.

Starter systems have sold for as little as $50. These units, however, often mushroom in price to over $1,500 when their capabilities are expanded.

A "full-featured" system is one that includes most of the accessories available, a printer, and memory capacities equal to the standard of the time. Figure 1–12 illustrates a full-featured system.

"Extra capabilities" refers to state of the art developments when they are first introduced. The extra capability feature of one year is often a standard feature the next year.

The purchase price is not the only cost consideration for microcomputers. Most business microcomputer systems are reliable and have minimal maintenance costs. However, business professionals may protect themselves with maintenance contracts that cover repairs on **hardware.** These annual contracts cost between 10 and 20 percent of the purchase

Hardware:
The part of the microcomputer you can see and feel.

FIGURE 1–10
AT&T 6300

FIGURE 1–11
Compaq Systems

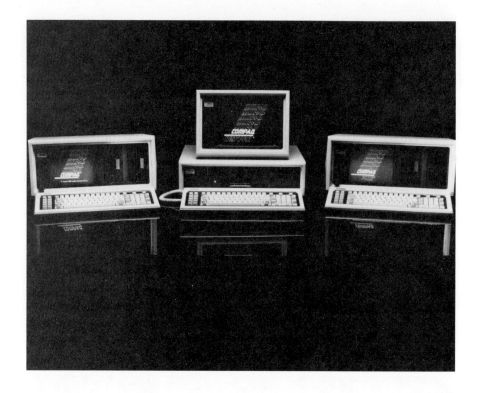

price and are available from local computer dealers. Most problems may be avoided with periodic cleaning and careful use.

The cost of operating a microcomputer system also includes salaries, ribbons, and paper. The benefits obtained in terms of increased productivity means that you can expect the cost of operating a microcomputer to be less than performing the same functions some other way. In chapter 12 you will learn about business evaluation methods called break-even and payback analysis. These techniques compare the cost of two alternate methods of doing a task, and aid you in determining which is best for your needs.

WHAT ARE THE PARTS OF MICROCOMPUTERS?

The microcomputer hardware is the part of the microcomputer you can see and feel. The microcomputer hardware consists of:

1. The computer case (CPU box) contains as a minimum:
    a. A microprocessor
    b. Cards with circuits to control data storage devices
    c. Circuits to communicate with external devices
    d. Chips containing the computer's internal memory
        RAM, Random access memory
        ROM, Read only memory

FIGURE 1–12
Hewlett-Packard's
UNIX System

2. Input devices that connect you to the computer, such as a keyboard, voice recognition unit, bar code readers, etc.

3. Output devices that show you what the computer has done or is doing, such as a cathode ray tube (CRT, screens, monitors), telephone modems, printers, and plotters.

4. On-line memory devices:
  a. floppy disk drives
  b. hard disk drives, fixed or removable
  c. tape recorders

Inside the CPU Box

The core of the microcomputer is the **microprocessor.** It contains the central processing unit (CPU) of your computer as well as other circuits. Usually the capabilities of microcomputers are contained on **cards** or **boards** with special circuits such as ones that control data storage devices or that communicate with devices such as monitors and printers. The memory of the microcomputer, read only memory **(ROM)** and random access memory **(RAM)** is also in the box.

Input Devices

The primary method of input from a human to the microcomputer is through a keyboard. There are many designs for keyboards, but most are similar to that of the typewriter (see Figure 1–13).

Microprocessor:
An integrated circuit on a silicon chip usually less than two inches long and a half inch wide, that consists of the arithmetic, logic, control, and memory units. The remaining hardware supports this chip.

Cards, boards:
Flat pieces of material with printed circuits and electronic components to add special capabilities to the microcomputer. Often called PC (Printed Circuits) boards.

ROM:
Read only memory. Memory with instructions (programs) needed when operating the microcomputer. The user cannot write data into ROM. Sometimes called firmware.

RAM:
Random access memory. Memory used for data and program storage by the user. The user can write and read data in RAM.

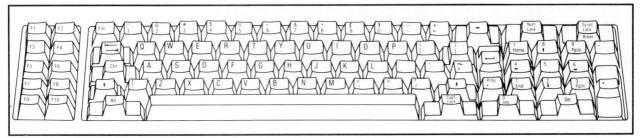

FIGURE 1–13   The Microcomputer's Keyboard

Ouput Devices

The primary method of output from the microcomputer to humans is the CRT (cathode ray tube), also called a screen, monitor, or VDT (video display tube). It looks like a television set (see Figure 1–14). Input and output devices are often called **I/O** devices.

On-Line Data Storage Devices

On-line storage devices are devices that store (record) computer data and programs, but are not electronically an "internal" part of the computer. On-line storage devices are sometimes referred to as secondary storage devices. In many microcomputers these devices are mounted in the same case as the other parts of the computer, but they are electronically connected through special controller boards only. The methods of recording computer information include floppy disk drives, hard disk drives, and large format magnetic tape (see Figures 1–15 and 1–16).

**FIGURE 1–14
CRT**

FIGURE 1–15
Hard Disk Drive System with
Tape Backup

FIGURE 1–16
Two Floppy Disk and Hard
Disk System

THE DIFFERENT SIZES OF MICROCOMPUTERS

The wide variety of sizes, shapes, capabilities, and design among microcomputers makes it easy for the business professional to find a system that fits a particular business need. A microcomputer may be one of four sizes; desktop unit, transportable, briefcase (lap computer), or pocket computer.

Desktop

A **desktop microcomputer** is one that fits on a desk (see Figure 1–17). It may be a "full-featured" unit having all the parts usually found in a microcomputer at any given time. Desktop units may have large monitors, external on-line storage devices, as well as other **peripherals.**

Desktop units have the greatest capabilities because they have the most internal room to expand to satisfy many business needs, by using add-on boards or cards containing additional circuits.

Transportable

The **transportable microcomputer,** sometimes called **portable microcomputer,** is similar to the desktop microcomputer in its capabilities. The transportable is a self-contained package (see Figure 1–18). The parts generally packaged include a monitor, disk drives (both floppy and hard disk), keyboard, and the microprocessor, including external connections for printer and communications. Some units include printers

Desktop microcomputer:
A microcomputer that has the greatest capabilities, most expansion room, and requires a part of a desk for its work area.

Peripheral:
A device such as a printer, bar code reader, or modem connected to a microcomputer to give it special capabilities.

Transportable microcomputers:
Microcomputers that are packaged with most of the features of a desktop, including a monitor.

Portable microcomputers:
Often refers to transportable, and at other times to all computers smaller than transportable.

**AT&T 6300 Desktop System
FIGURE 1–17**

FIGURE 1–18
Hewlett Packard's
Transportable on the Move

while others include built-in modems for communication over telephone lines.

The transportable is useful for professionals who have to travel, for giving sales and educational presentations because it often can be connected to external monitors for group viewing of the contents of the screen, and for users who want a microcomputer that takes up less room, that is, has a smaller **footprint** on the desk.

Footprint:
The amount of space taken on a desk by a microcomputer.

Briefcase

Briefcase computers have "full size" keyboards and are currently the smallest units upon which word processing can be performed (see Figures 1–19 and 1–20). Traveling business professionals may use briefcase computers in airports and on some airplanes. Outside sales people find it convenient to use microcomputer for direct sales support when making house calls.

Briefcase or lap microcomputer:
A microcomputer that fits in a briefcase and/or may be used on an individual's lap.

FIGURE 1–19
**Epson HX-20 Briefcase
Computer**

FIGURE 1–20
**Traveling with Radio Shack's
Model 100**

Pocket

The smaller the computer, the more specialized it tends to be. The **pocket computer** has the most limited memory and capabilities, and it tends to be a calculation and data storage device only. There are some pocket computers with expanded memory that are useful in many business applications where physical size is critical.

Pocket microcomputer: Computer small enough to fit in your pocket.

HISTORICAL DEVELOPMENT OF COMPUTERS, SYSTEMS, AND SOFTWARE

There are four phases to the history of the microcomputer. They are as follows:

- Phase I Pre-microprocessor: Before the development of the Intel 4004 chip.
- Phase II Hardware and Operating System Development: The development of the microcomputer hardware and operating system; computer clubs and creation of the basic hardware.
- Phase III Software Development: The commercial programs needed by the business professional were developed.
- Phase IV Business Use: The use of the microcomputer by business professionals without computer training or background.

Table 1-1 is a detailed time line of the history of microcomputers.

Phase I included the development of computer and electronic theory, and the manufacturing capabilities. The development of the Intel 4004 microprocessor identifies the end of this phase. Figure 1–21 illustrates the size reduction of circuits.

Phase II, Hardware and Operating System Development, covers the period when computer clubs and hobbyists called hackers were responsible for the creation and design of microcomputer hardware and the operating systems needed to make the microcomputers work.

Phase III, Software, saw the development of general, specialized, and custom application programs. The software hobbyists first developed programs for their own use. Many of these programs became the first commercial programs.

Programs were generally produced only for selected microcomputers. The rule, "Find the software, then purchase the hardware," had to be followed carefully.

Among the first programs to become commercially available in the late 1970s were accounting programs such as general ledger, accounts payable, and accounts receivable. Payroll programs came later.

Michael Shrayer developed "Electric Pencil" in 1975 for the Altair and later adapted it for the Radio Shack Model I microcomputer and other microcomputers. Electric Pencil was the first word processor available for microcomputers. Word processing was responsible for a big increase in the use of microcomputers because it is so much easier, quicker, and less expensive to use than typing.

VisiCalc was the first spreadsheet program to be developed (1979). Its existence created a market for microcomputers that had not previously existed. The market developed because VisiCalc could be used by the business professional to solve selected business problems more efficiently than any other method available.

There are many different brands of spreadsheet programs, such as SuperCalc (originally a spreadsheet program that is now an integrated program), Multiplan, and Lotus 1-2-3 (also an integrated program). They are all similar to the original VisiCalc. The capabilities of newer versions of integated spreadsheet programs have added graphics, communications, data base functions, and others.

In Phase IV the business professional came to dominate microcomputer use. The hardware and operating system concepts were developed in Phase II. The basic software, word processing, spreadsheets, and data base programs were created in Phase III. The introduction of microcomputers with packaged business programs, the Osborne 1, and the introduction of the IBM PC in 1981 marked the beginning of Phase IV. You are part of it.

THE HIERARCHY OF HARDWARE, OPERATING SYSTEMS, AND SOFTWARE

Hardware is the foundation upon which operating systems are developed. Hardware and operating systems form the foundation upon which applications program are designed. The hardware of a microcomputer was needed before an operating system could be developed. An operating system is the program that makes the parts of a microcomputer system work as a system. After operating systems became available, **utilities** and programming languages were developed. Application programs were then developed, because it was much easier to develop applications using the operating system, utilities, and programming languages.

Utilities:
Programs that support the operation of the operating system by adding capabilities.

TABLE 1–1
The History of Computers/
Microcomputers

Phase I Pre-microprocessor: Before the development of the Intel 4004 chip.

Before 1800
  Abacus.
1800–1850
  Charles Babbage analytical engine design.
1851–1900
  Allan Marquand electric logic machine.
  Herman Hollerith tabulating/sorting machine.
1901–1925
  The Computing-Tabulating-Recording Company became International Business
    Machines (IBM).
1926–1940
  Benjamin Burack first electric logic machine.
  John V. Atanasoff and Clifford Berry use vacuum tubes as switching units/Iowa State
    College in Ames, Iowa developed the "ABC" or the Atanasoff-Berry Computer. The
    first electronic computer.
1941–1950
  John Mauchley and J. Presper Eckert, Jr. proposed Electronic Analyzer to develop
    ballistic tables for the US Army.
  John Mauchley, J. Presper Eckert, Jr, and John Von Neumann built ENIAC, the first all-
    electronic digital computer.
  The transistor was developed at Bell Laboratories.
  Mark I computer—Automatic Sequence Controlled Computer built by Dr. Howard
    Aiken at Harvard University under an IBM grant.
  Concept of stored program developed.
1951–1955
  UNIVAC 1—First commercial computer to become operational.
  IBM-650; planned production of 50/over 1000 were sold.
  FORTRAN (FORmula TRANslator) computer language developed.
1956–1960
  COBOL (COmmon Business Oriented Language) computer language developed under
    the leadership of Grace Hopper.
1961–1965
  President John F. Kennedy dreams of space flight. Creates NASA, National Aeronautics
    and Space Administration.
  BASIC (Beginners All-purpose Symbolic Instruction Code), 1964-developed at
    Dartmouth College by John Kemeny and Thomas Kurtz under a National Science
    Foundation grant.
  Operating systems developed.

**Phase II Hardware and Operating System Development: The developement of
the microcomputer hardware and operating system; computer clubs and
creation of the basic hardware.**

1966–1970
  Intel received commission to produce integrated circuits (ICs) for calculators.
  Intel built microprocessor 4004; Ted Hoff, Stan Mazer, Robert Noyce, and Federico
    Faggin were the project team.
1971
  Intel developed 8008 microprocessor.
1972
  Gary Kildall wrote first programming language PL/1 for Intel's 4004.
1974
  Intel 8080 developed.
  Microcomputer disk operating system, CP/M, developed by John Torode and Gary
    Kildall
1975

(continued on following page)

TABLE 1–1
(Continued)

The MITS Altair went on sale—the first microcomputer in kit form based on the 8080 microprocessor.

Bill Gates developed MicroSoft BASIC for Altair.

Many computer clubs started across the nation.

Dick Heiser opened The Computer Store, the first retail computer store in Los Angeles.

1976

IMSAI started shipping first computers.

World Altair Computer Conference held (first microcomputer conference).

Apple I demonstrated by Stephen Wozniak.

CP/M (Control Program/Microcomputer)—disk operating system for MITS Altair went on sale.

Michael Shrayer developed *Electric Pencil, the first word processor for microcomputers.*

Phase III Software Development: The commercial programs needed by the business professional were developed.

1977

Computerland opened first franchise in Morristown, NJ.

Apple introduced Apple II.

Commodore introduced PET computer.

Tandy-Radio Shack introduced TRS-80 Model I microcomputer.

1978

Apple added disk drives.

1979

TRS-80 Model II introduced by Tandy.

The word processing program WordStar released by MicroPro.

VisiCalc, the first electronic spreadsheet produced by Personal Software.

Source—national data base for electronic mail and other information services was started.

CompuServe opened its computer for use by microcomputer users for information services, electronic mail, etc.

1980

Hewlett-Packard released HP-85.

MicroSoft developed PC-DOS, the operating system for IBM PC.

Dow Jones News/Retrieval Service opened to Apple computer users.

First LAN, Local Area Networks available.

Phase IV Business Use: The use of the microcomputer by business professionals without computer training or background.

1981

Osborne Computer Corporation introduced Osborne 1 with packaged software.

Xerox released 8010 Star and 820 computers.

IBM introduced IBM PC, personal computer.

1982

Apple III introduced.

1983

IBM introduced PCjr.

Osborne Computer filed for reorganization.

DEC introduced the Rainbow personal computer.

Apple introduced Macintosh

1984

IBM PC AT introduced.

AT&T entered microcomputer market after divestiture.

Laser printers introduced for microcomputers.

1985

IBM PCjr. production discontinued.

AT&T introduced the UNIX-PC -multi-using, multi-tasking Personal Computer with network capability.

Many firms introduced local area networks.

Procedures developed using special hardware and software systems to increase the
amount of internal memory.
Development of 10,000 band modem.
Future trends: The productivity of microcomputers continues to increase. Costs fall while
capabilities improve.
Applications such as artificial intelligence, laser disks, optical cables and disks,
emulation of special devices, voice recognition, voice synthesis, networks, multi-user,
multi-tasking, optical character readers, and others continue to develop.

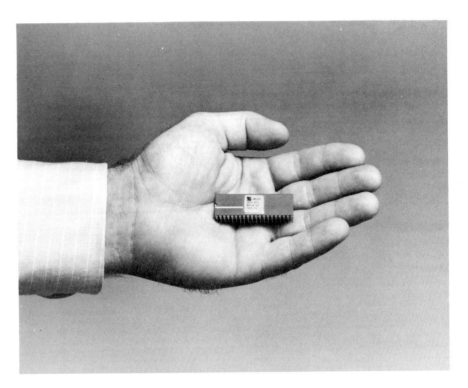

FIGURE 1–21
The Size of Memory Circuits

An overview of the **hierarchy** of hardware and software is shown in
Figure 1–22.

Hierarchy:
Classification or grading of a group
or set from high to low.

You have now learned about the development of the many hardware
parts of a microcomputer. Disk operating systems underwent concurrent
development.

DISK OPERATING SYSTEMS

*The disk operating system is the program used to make all the parts
(hardware and software) of the microcomputer work together.* Computer
users, usually through programs, send instructions to the disk operating
system, which then directs the hardware how to carry out the given instructions (see Figure 1–23). The disk operating system is what makes
your computer hardware, printer, monitor, keyboard, disk drives, tape
recorder, and software work together as a system.

FIGURE 1–22
**The Hierarchy of Hardware,
Operating System, and
Software**

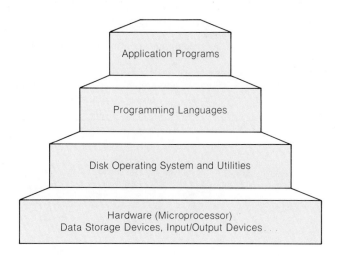

Each part of the microcomputer system must react with split-second timing to accomplish different tasks. A good operating system makes the task of getting useful results from a microcomputer look easy.

The more popular operating systems found in microcomputers include:

1. Apple-DOS, Apple Disk Operating System used on Apple computers.
2. CP/M, Control Program/Microcomputer—popular business operating system used by many independent manufacturers.
3. MS-DOS/PC-DOS, Microsoft Disk Operating System/ Personal Computer Disk Operating System used on the IBM PC and look-alike family of microcomputers. Currently the most popular among independent manufacturers.
4. TRS-DOS, Tandy Radio Shack—Disk Operating System used in various forms on the many Radio Shack microcomputers.
5. UNIX—The multi-user operating system developed by Bell Laboratories.

A family of microcomputers is defined by the operating system used. Application programs created to work on one member of a microcomputer family will often operate on most microcomputers using the same operating system.

COMPUTER LANGUAGES

Computer languages have been developed to fit different user needs. To program (give instructions to) a microcomputer, a computer language is used. The objective in designing a computer language is to create a lim-

FIGURE 1–23
The Disk Operating System
Directs the Flow of Traffic

ited language that human beings can relate to, and that a computer can understand so that a set of machine language instructions may be generated. Humans speak English, French, and other similar languages. Microcomputers speak with on and off switches, a binary number language. The computer language bridges the gap between human and **machine language.** Computer languages are often classified as **assembly languages, low level languages,** and **high level languages.**

The most popular microcomputer language is **BASIC,** Beginners All-purpose Symbolic Instruction **Code.** The original version was developed at Dartmouth College by John Kemeny and Thomas Kurtz as a teaching language. The version of BASIC on today's microcomputers has many capabilities beyond the original language. BASIC's popularity can be traced to its relative ease of learning and its added capabilities.

Standards defining the acceptable statements in BASIC and other languages are maintained by ANSI, American National Standards Institute. The standard is not complete because of the rapid changes in hardware, capabilities, and software in the microcomputer industry. There are many "dialects" of BASIC which vary greatly.

Instructions written in a computer language may be converted to machine language using a compiler or an interpreter. A compiler is a translator program that takes the near English code and translates it into a set

Machine language:
A formal system of signs and symbols including rules for their use that convey instructions to a computer.

Assembly language:
A language that is close to machine language and may be easily converted using a special program called an assembler.

Low level language:
A computer language near machine language.

High level language:
A computer language near English.

BASIC:
Beginners All-purpose Symbolic Instruction Code.

Code:
The use of symbols or numbers to represent letters, numbers, or special meanings.

of machine language codes all at one time. If there are any **syntax** errors, such as misspelling a word, the compiler will not be able to complete its task. All such errors must be eliminated at this step.

An interpreter is a program that translates a line of near English code into machine language, executes the line of code, translates the next line, etc. This type of language is slower but easier for the development of new applications because it helps with error elimination.

Some of the languages available on microcomputers are shown in Table 1–2.

LEGAL AND ETHICAL ISSUES

Legal and ethical questions abound. Currently the legal and ethical issues of the most concern to the microcomputer user include:

1. Ownership of programs
2. Ownership of data
3. Data security
4. Misuse of data

Ownership of Programs

It is easy to copy programs for backup and other purposes. However, when a program is sold, you purchase the right to use it on a single computer or in a single location. You do not purchase the right to re-sell it or give it to your friends (see licensed agreement, Figure 1–24).

TABLE 1–2
Microcomputer Languages

Language	Application	Compiled	Interpreted
Assembly*	Used to create machine language programs.		
BASIC	Found on most microcomputers.	X	X
C	Structured programming language; Can perform many tasks that would normally require the use of assembly-machine programs.	X	
COBOL	COmmon Business Oriented Language; For business programs such as accounting.	X	
FORTH	FOuRTH generation language; Business, scientific, process control, robotics. Contains a resident assembly language.	X	
FORTRAN	FORmula TRANslator; Engineering and science applications.	X	
LOGO	Education; Uses graphics for programming.	X	
PASCAL	Simple and structured for general applications.	X	X

Assembly is almost always available on microcomputers. It is generally the language used to create high level language compliers and interpreters.

It is estimated that as much as 80 percent of the software being used in corporations and by individuals was not purchased legally. The software has been copied in violation of the licensing agreement. There are no accepted solutions to this problem, and now that you are entering the world of computers, it has become your problem.

Whatever the legal resolution of unlicensed software copying is, you should do everything in your power to act within the law. You would not like to lose your job and destroy your career by stealing a piece of software.

FIGURE 1–24
Software Agreement

Rawhide Software
1163 Napoleon Road
Bowling Green, Ohio 43402

RAWHIDE ™ LICENSE AGREEMENT

READ BEFORE OPENING: CAREFULLY READ THE FOLLOWING LICENSE BEFORE YOU OPEN THE SEALED PACKAGE. OPENING THE SEALED PACKAGE CONSTITUTES YOUR ACCEPTANCE OF ALL TERMS OF THIS LICENSE. IF YOU DO NOT AGREE WITH THEM, PROMPTLY RETURN THE SEALED PACKAGE UNOPENED TO RAWHIDE SOFTWARE AT THE ABOVE ADDRESS OR TO WEST PUBLISHING COMPANY ("West"), 50 WEST KELLOGG BOULEVARD, ST. PAUL, MINNESOTA 55101, AND YOU WILL HAVE NO FURTHER LIABILITY.

1. License. Rawhide Software ("Rawhide") grants you a non-exclusive, non-transferable limited license to use, copy and permit others to use the copyrighted software contained on the diskette in the sealed package, together with the accompanying copyrighted user documentation (collectively, "Software"). All use must be in accordance with the terms of this License. Title to and ownership of the Software remains in Rawhide.

2. Limitations.

a. You may use the Software solely for educational and instructional purposes in connection with a college-level course for which a West text is the approved textbook (the "Course").

b. You may permit enrollees in the Course to use the Software.

c. You may copy the Software for use in connection with the Course but you may make only that number of copies which is reasonably necessary for such use.

d. When you copy the Software, you must also reproduce the machine-readable copyright notice on each copy and affix a reproduction of the copyright notice contained on the enclosed diskette on each copy.

YOU MAY NOT USE, COPY, MODIFY, DISTRIBUTE OR TRANSFER THE SOFTWARE, IN WHOLE OR IN PART, EXCEPT AS EXPRESSLY PERMITTED IN THIS LICENSE.

3. Term and Termination. This License is effective when you open the sealed package and remains in effect until terminated. You may terminate this License at any time by ceasing all use of the Software and destroying the Software and all copies you have made. It will also terminate automatically if you fail to comply with the terms of this License. Rawhide may terminate this License one year after its effective date by giving you notice of termination. You agree to cease all use of the Software and to destroy the Software and all copies upon termination.

4. No Warranty. NEITHER RAWHIDE NOR WEST WARRANTS THE PERFORMANCE OF OR RESULTS THAT MAY BE OBTAINED BY USE OF THE SOFTWARE. THE SOFTWARE IS PROVIDED "AS IS" WITHOUT WARRANTY OF ANY KIND, EXPRESS OR IMPLIED, INCLUDING THE WARRANTIES OF MERCHANTABILITY OR FITNESS FOR A PARTICULAR PURPOSE.

5. Limitation of Liability. Neither Rawhide nor West shall be liable to you for any damages, including direct, incidental, special, consequential or any other type of damages, arising out of this License or the use or inability to use the Software.

6. Proprietary Rights. You acknowledge that the Rawhide ™ name, the names of the Rawhide programs and the Software (including all support materials) are copyrighted, trademarked or owned by Rawhide as trade secrets and/or proprietary information and that all such matter shall remain the exclusive property of Rawhide.

7. Governing Law. This Agreement will be governed by the laws of the State of Minnesota.

YOU ACKNOWLEDGE THAT YOU HAVE READ THIS LICENSE AND AGREE TO ALL ITS TERMS. YOU ALSO AGREE THAT THIS LICENSE IS THE ENTIRE AND EXCLUSIVE AGREEMENT BETWEEN YOU, RAWHIDE AND/OR WEST AND SUPERCEDES ANY PRIOR UNDERSTANDING OR AGREEMENT, ORAL OR WRITTEN, RELATING TO THE SUBJECT MATTER OF THIS AGREEMENT.

Ownership Of Data

Software belongs to the developer and designer. Data belongs to the individual or institution that collects it. To enter a data base without the consent of the owner, to view, copy, or damage the information in any manner, is neither moral nor legal in most instances. State and federal laws addressing the unauthorized entry of individuals to data bases are under development.

Data Security

Data security systems and procedures are difficult to create and maintain. It is said, "Whenever a better security system is created, someone will come up with a method of breaking the system." Many individuals will earn their living creating and maintaining data security systems.

Misuse of Data

Data is a valuable asset of a business. Data may represent power to earn money and control the activities of individuals. Data may also harm individuals when used wrongly, by error or by intent. Government data bases have long been a concern of individuals who worry about possible invasion of privacy.

Increasing capabilities of microcomputers mean that individuals and businesses are able to maintain their own data bases. Many problems will be created by the proliferation of electronic data bases.

As a manager or user of a data base you have a responsibility to use the data in a professional manner. The laws on how these data bases can be used and the responsibility of the owners are just now being written. You will be judged by their standards once they are implemented. You have the opportunity and obligation to participate in the development of these standards.

SUMMARY

You have been introduced to the uses of the microcomputer in business. The microcomputer has been defined from several points of view. Some of the social, moral, and legal issues associated with the use of microcomputers have been reviewed.

The aspects of the microcomputers that you have been introduced to include:

1. The microcomputer is a business tool.
2. The microcomputer purchase price is less than $15,000.
3. The microcomputer hardware is the part of the microcomputer you can see and feel. The parts are:
    a. The CPU box: microprocessor, cards, and memory
    b. Input devices

c. Output devices

d. On-line memory devices

4. The different sizes of microcomputers makes it easy for the business professional to find a system that fits a particular business need.

5. There are four phases to the history of the microcomputer:

Phase I Pre-microprocessor

Phase II Hardware and operating system development

Phase III Software development

Phase IV Business use.

6. Hardware is the foundation upon which operating systems are developed.

7. Hardware and operating systems form the foundation upon which application programs are designed.

8. The disk operating system is the program used to make all the parts of the microcomputer hardware and software work together.

9. Computer languages have been developed to fit different user needs.

10. Some legal and ethical questions are:

1. Ownership of programs

2. Ownership of data

3. Data security

4. Misuse of data.

KEY TERMS

Application programs
BASIC
Business graphics programs
Business professional
Code
Communication programs
Data
Data base
Data base management programs
End user
File management program

Hard copy
Hardware
I/O
Machine language
Microprocessor
Operating systems
Programming language
Software
Spreadsheet programs
Word processing program

REVIEW QUESTIONS

1. Why is the microcomputer a business tool?

2. What are the three levels of application programs?

3. What is the function of programs, that is, software?

4. Why is the microcomputer a personal computer?

5. What does a word processing program do?

6. Give some examples of the output of a word processor program.

7. What are data base programs designed to do?

8. What is the difference between data and facts?

9. Give some examples of the output of a business data base management system.

10. What do business analyical graphics programs do?

11. What are the limits of microcomputer communications?

12. Why would a manager select a specialized application program?

13. Identify the costs associated with the purchase of a microcomputer.

14. What is a "full-featured" microcomputer system?

15. Why should a business professional consider the purchase of a microcomputer maintenance contract?

16. What are the physical parts of a microcomputer?

17. What is the relationship between the microprocessor and the CPU?

18. What is a microprocessor?

19. What is RAM and ROM?

20. What is a PC-board?

21. What is the primary method of input to a microcomputer?

22. What is the primary method of output from a microcomputer?

23. What are some methods of recoding computer information?

24. What is a peripheral?

25. What is a briefcase computer?

26. What are the four phases in the history of microcomputers?

27. In what phase did John Torode and Gary Kildall develop the first disk operating system for microcomputers?

28. What was the first word processor program?

29. What was the first electronic spreadsheet program?

30. What events signaled the beginning of Phase IV?

31. What is the hierarchy of a microcomputer system?

32. What does the disk operating system do?

33. What is the importance of families of microcomputers based on operating systems?

34. What is the objective of a computer language?

35. What is a compiler and what is an interpreter?

36. Identify some legal and ethical issues.

37. What is the estimated amount of illegal software being used?

38. Who owns software? Who owns data?

39. What is the responsibility of the manager/user of a data base?

SELECTED REFERENCES

Bermant, Charles. "Is IBM's Super PC Where It's AT?" *PC Magazine*, October 16, 1984, pp. 51, 54.

Creative Computing. vol. 10, no. 11, November 1984.

Dologite, D.G. *Using Small Business Computers.* Prentice Hall, 1984.

Freiberger, Paul, and Michael Swaine. *Fire in the Valley.* Osborne McGraw-Hill, 1984.

McWilliams, Peter. *The McWilliams II Word Processor Instruction Manual.* Prelude Press, 1983.

McWilliams, Peter. *The Personnal Computer Book.* Prelude Press, 1982.

McWilliams, Peter. *The Personnal Computer In Business Book.* Prelude Press, 1983.

Schmidt, Richard N. and William E. Meyers. *Electronic Business Data Processing.* Holt, Rinehart and Winston, 1963.

Shelly, Gary B. and Thomas J. Cashman. *Introduction to Computers and Data Processing.* Anaheim Publishing Company, 1980.

Shrum, Carlton. *How to Buy a Personal Computer.* Alfred Publishing, 1982.

Watson, Hugh J. and Archie B. Carroll. *Computers for Business: A Managerial Emphasis.* Business Publications Inc., 1980.

Willoughby, William Edward and Nancy Foster Jacobs. *The ABC's of the IBM.* Sybex Books, 1983.

2

Chapter Outline

Chapter Goals

Upon completion of this chapter you will be able to:

Understand the importance of hardware.

Understand the significance of compatibility.

Identify and name the parts of a microcomputer.

List some of the systems currently available.

Explain how each part of the microcomputer fits into the
    overall system.

HARDWARE OF MICROCOMPUTERS

Microcomputers come in different sizes and shapes. They have many parts that are joined together to form a system. Hardware is that part of the microcomputer you can see and feel. It is difficult to determine the function of microcomputer hardware from its outside appearance. Knowledge of the importance, parts, the available microcomputer hardware, typical **configuration,** and **compatibility** with other brands of microcomputers is a step in the process of learning how to evaluate and select the appropriate hardware for a specific business need.

The microcomputer (see Figure 2–1) is a collection of parts that form a system. In this chapter you will learn how the parts of the system work together.

WHY THE BUSINESS PROFESSIONAL MUST LEARN ABOUT MICROCOMPUTER HARDWARE

The professional must learn about hardware in order to select the best combination of capabilities and cost to match business needs. The microcomputer is an answer to business problems. A microcomputer system consists of application software built upon a hardware foundation. The remaining chapters of this book are devoted to software; this chapter studies the hardware foundation.

In order to purchase a system intelligently, the business professional must know the company's needs, the capabilities of a typical system, and its cost. The professional must also know what can be added and how the system can be expanded to satisfy current and future needs.

One decision managers must make is the selection and justification

FIGURE 2–1
Microcomputer in Use

of microcomputer hardware and software. This book is designed to help you learn about microcomputer hardware, operating systems, and available programs. It will be your responsibility as a manager to study your company's needs. The microcomputer salesperson can help you match hardware and software with your business problems.

HARDWARE: THE PARTS OF A COMPUTER

The parts of a microcomputer include:

- In the CPU Box
  Microprocessor (On Mother Board)
  ROM and RAM
  Cards—PC Boards (Expansion)
  DIP Switches
- Input Devices—Keyboard, Voice Recognition Units
- Output Devices—Monitor (CRT, Screen), Printer
- On-Line Storage Devices and Media.

Each manufacturer uses a design philosophy, called design architecture or just architecture. Many designs use the concept of a mother board. A **mother board** is a printed circuit board containing the microprocessor, some computer memory, and selected controller circuits to direct the signals that are received from external connectors, and often the ability to be expanded. Figure 2–2 shows a printed circuit board and Figure 2–3 examines the inside of a microcomputer.

The concept of design architecture may be illustrated by comparing the Apple IIe and the IBM PC. Both of these microcomputers have a number of slots into which are inserted cards with special capabilities. The Apple looks at slot number one for the printer controller card; the IBM PC seeks a printer card in whatever slot it may be. The Apple IIe looks for slots; the IBM PC looks for function.

Another part of microcomputer design architecture determines how the microcomputer is packaged. The microcomputer may be in one container or come in a number of parts. The main unit, that is called the CPU box, contains the microprocessor (CPU), memory (ROM and RAM), expansion cards, and configuration switches (DIP switches). Input, out-

Mother board:
A printed circuit board or card containing the microprocessor, computer memory, and selected controller circuits to direct the signals that are received from external connectors.

FIGURE 2–2
Printed Circuit (PC) Boards

FIGURE 2–3
Inside a Microcomputer

FIGURE 2–4
Diagram of a Microcomputer
System

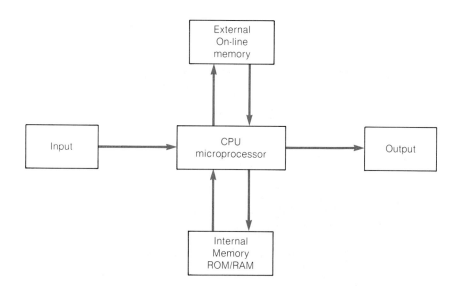

put, and on-line storage devices may or may not be in the CPU box depending on the design architecture. Figure 2-4 shows an overall diagram of a microcomputer system.

In the CPU Box

The CPU box usually contains a microprocessor mounted on a printed circuit board, ROM and RAM, other printed circuit boards, and DIP switches.

Microprocessors (on Mother Board) The microprocessor is commonly found on the mother board inside the CPU box. A microprocessor is a single chip that is the central processing unit of the microcomputer. It contains an arithmetic and logic unit, a control unit, and registers. With the addition of a power supply, memory, and other circuitry, the microprocessor becomes a complete microcomputer. Figure 2–5 illustrates the size of a microprocessor.

Bits are combined to create characters, **bytes,** and for communication, **word size.** Some of the more popular microprocessors, the number of bits used per word size, and the operating systems that are available for them are found in Table 2–1. Microcomputers commonly process 8, 16, and 32 bits at one time. A 16 bit microcomputer may process two eight-bit bytes (characters) at one time. The overall speed of a microcomputer is a function of the number of bits per word, or word size.

To be useful in business applications a microprocessor needs a minimum word size of eight-bits. The word size determines:

- Potential speed
- Maximum RAM that may be used directly
- Sophistication of programs

The microprocessor, combined with an operating system, determines

Bit:
A binary digit. The microcomputer uses a binary number system consisting of 0 and 1. A bit is a 0 or a 1.
Byte:
A sequence of binary digits taken as a unit. Eight binary digits per byte microcomputers are currently the most common. Seven or eight bits are used to create characters.
Word Size:
In microcomputer communication the bits per character is also referred to as word size.

FIGURE 2–5
The Size of the Z80
Microprocessor

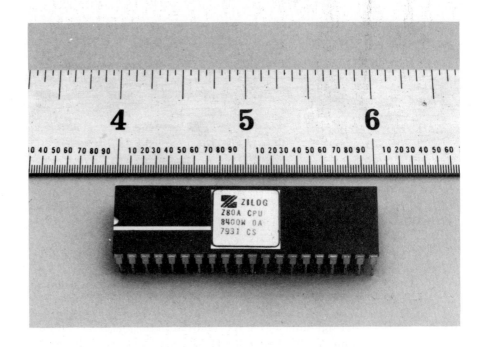

the maximum file size and the programs available to solve business problems. You will learn more about operating systems and how they perform their tasks in the next chapter.

ROM and RAM Microcomputers contain both ROM and RAM internal memory. ROM, read only memory, contains instructions for the micro-

TABLE 2–1
Microprocessors

Microprocessor	Word Size	Operating system
Intel 4004	4 bit	none
Intel 8008	8 bit	none
Intel 8080	8 bit	CP/M
Intel 8085	8 bit	CP/M
Zilog Z80	8 bit	CP/M
		TRS-DOS*
MOS Technology		
6502	8 bit	Apple DOS
Intel 8086	16 bit	MS-DOS
Intel 8088	$8/16$bit	MS-DOS
		PC-DOS
		CP/M 86
Intel 80286	16 bit	MS-DOS
Motorola		
68000	$16/32$bit	UNIX
		TRS-DOS *
		MS-DOS
		CP/M 86

Radio Shack uses the trade name TRS-DOS for the operating system on all their computers except the models that use MS-DOS, no matter what chip is used.

computer. RAM, random access memory, is available for the user to store programs and data.

The amount of ROM needed depends on the manner in that the microcomputer is to be used. In transportables and desktop microcomputers, ROM may be used for getting the system started and for containing special-purpose programs. ROM (See Table 2–2). contains a program called a "boot strap" program, that is used to load the operating system into the RAM of the microcomputer from external devices where it is stored. Loading the operating system from an on-line storage device is often called booting.

TABLE 2–2   Use of ROM

Types of Microcomputer	Start System	Operating System	Word Processing	Spread-sheet	Communi-cation	Custom (*)
Pocket	x	x		x	x	x
Briefcase	x	x	x	x	x	x
Transportable	x					
Desktop	x					

* Application programs supplied on PROMs or EPROMs.

Microcomputers use ROM, PROM (programmable read only memory,) and EPROM (erasable programmable read only memory) to store selected application programs. Briefcase microcomputers use these chips to store word processing, data base, and communications programs. A popular method of supplying insurance sales professionals with programs for pocket and other portable microcomputers is through the use of EPROMs.

The business problems that may be solved depend on the application programs available. The programs available are a function of the amount of RAM and the programming skill of the program's creator. The amount of RAM needed by specific programs will be examined in later chapters.

Measuring RAM and ROM Before proceeding further we need a measure of RAM. Microcomputer memory, RAM and ROM, is measured in K (see Figure 2–3), or kilobytes, units of 1024 bytes. Most eight-bit microcomputers contain 64K, 65,536 bytes (2 raised to the 16th power, or 64 times 1024). The eight bits are called a byte. Some eight-bit microcomputers can use over 64K, but only with the use of special programming procedures. Sixteen-bit computers can use over half a million bytes of memory.

TABLE 2–3 Measuring Memory

Power of	Bytes	Kilobytes (K)
2^0	1	0
2^{10}	1024	1
2^{16}	65536	64

Generally, only pocket microcomputers and starter systems have less than 2K of RAM. Programs using such limited memory may do many tasks in small increments. They use small amounts of data at a time. Despite these limitations, many business applications are found for these machines. Real estate sales professionals use them for calculating mortgage information, while insurance sales professionals use them in lieu of rate books.

Pocket microcomputers often contain RAM that maintains its memory when the machine is turned off. CMOS, complimentary metal oxide semiconductor, is used because it requires little power. Bubble memory, a thin magnetic recording film, is used because it requires no power. This means the microcomputer contains its programs and data when turned off. When the sales professional walks in to give a presentation, perform an analysis, or make a sales presentation, the microcomputer is ready. An on-line storage device is not required for the storage of programs and data using bubble memory.

Microcomputers with 48K to 64K were the business standard for several years. These machines could do word processing, electronic spreadsheets, data base maintenance, graphics, and communication. Each application was generally created as a stand-alone (not integrated) program. Most business applications, such as general ledger programs, were available for these machines.

With the introduction of the IBM PC, available RAM expanded from 64K to 640K. At first the only programs available were expanded versions of the ones used in 64K microcomputers. Soon, integrated programs started to appear. Integrated programs now combine word processing, spreadsheets, data base, graphics, and communication. Programs that allow multi-tasking, operating more than one program at a time, and multi-users, two or more people sharing the same microprocessor, were developed.

Many business professionals need only the programs and other capabilities available in microcomputers with 64K of memory. These individuals are benefiting from the expanded memory capabilities in newer systems by a drop in the price of the 64K machines. In addition, as programmers gain experience, they are able to create programs that fit within the 64K limit and do many of the same things that programs do with the larger amounts of memory. On the other hand, some microcomputers can now use over 3Megabytes, 3 million bytes, of RAM.

When selecting a microcomputer, you must determine the maximum amount of RAM needed by the specific program you plan to use. Some programs will often not be able to take advantage of extra memory in your computer. Generally, electronic spreadsheet, data base, and engineering/scientific graphics programs require the most RAM.

PC-boards:
Printed circuit boards that are used to expand the capabilities of a microcomputers.

Cards, PC-Boards (Expansion) The capabilities of the microcomputer may be expanded with internal cards or boards called printed circuit boards **(pc-boards.)** Some boards or computers may be expanded with chips.

Many microcomputers have slots for adding additional circuits on microcomputer boards (cards) for expanded capabilities. PC-boards are available to add memory, to connect to telephones, for **serial** and **parallel communication** (out of specified ports,) to use voice recognition units, to use bar code readers, to operate laboratory equipment, as well as for other special needs. Some cards are referred to as multifunction cards because they add a number of functions rather than one. Many manufacturers produce microcomputers that accept the same physical cards as the IBM PC. Microcomputers which accept the same physical parts are **physically compatibile.**

The outside of a microcomputer is a neat looking box (see Figure 2–6). Looking at a desktop unit with its top removed you will see a collection of computer chips, printed circuit boards, disk drives, power supply, cooling fan, and some empty slots for additional cards.

Even the smallest microcomputer may be expanded through the purchase of special cartridges and chips.

DIP Switches DIP, Dual Inline Package, refers to a housing commonly used to hold a chip. A **DIP switch** is usually a series of toggle switches mounted in a DIP approximately the same size as a chip.

DIP switches must be set to tell the microcomputer the amount of memory installed, the peripheral devices connected, and the communication procedures used between devices in most microcomputers. Setting the DIP switches, (configuring the parts of the microcomputer system) is usually done by the seller of microcomputers.

Serial communication port:
Connection to communicate, sending one bit after another in series.
Parallel communication port:
Connection to communicate over a number of "parallel" wires at the same time.
Physical compatibility:
The capability to exchange physical parts with other microcomputers.

DIP switch:
A series of toggle switches mounted into a DIP, that are mounted on a pc-board. The switches are used for system configuration.

FIGURE 2–6
The IBM XT

Input Devices

The most common **input device** for business microcomputers is the keyboard. Most keyboards look like typewriters with the addition of a numeric keypad and function keys. There are differences among the keyboards produced by different manufacturers. Some are better used for word processing, while others are better for programming.

The most common keyboard is call QWERTY. It is named for the order in which the letters are arranged in the top row. The arrangement of keys on QWERTY keyboards were designed to slow down the user. The Dvorak keyboard layout is designed to assign the most used letters to the stronger fingers. Both QWERTY and Dvorak keyboards are available for microcomputers.

Microcomputers may be operated with voice recognition devices (see Figure 2–7). Current technology involves two types of voice recognition. The microcomputer can learn to recognize general voice instructions or distinguish individual voices. Individual voice recognition may be used for security and identification. The microcomputer can learn to make selections from a list of choices. It is possible to dictate letters and complete documents.

Devices such as the "bar code reader," "mouse," "joy stick," "koala and pen pad," "optical character readers (OCR)," and "touch sensitive screens" may also be used for data input (See Figure 2–8). Table 2–4 lists how these devices are used.

FIGURE 2–7
Microcomputer with Voice Recognition

(a)

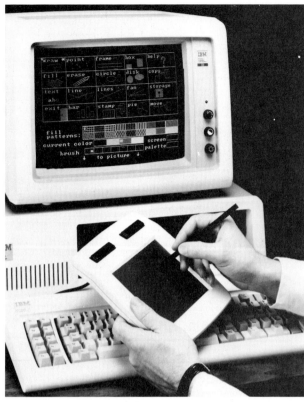

(b)

(c)

(d)

FIGURE 2–8   Input Devices: (a) Mouse, (b) Koala Pad, (c) Bar Code Reader, and (d) Touchscreen

TABLE 2–4
Input Devices

Device	How Used
Bar Code Reader	Device that reads cost and inventory bar codes.
Mouse	Controls screen cursor (pointer) by moving mouseacross a flat surface.
Joy stick	Device used to control video games by moving asmall stick or bar.
Koala pen pad	A surface, pad, is written on and the cursormoves in a similar manner on the monitor.
OCR	Optical character readers for printed charactersand hand writing.
Touch sensitive screens	Selection from a screen list is made by pressing a finger against the screen.
Cash registers	Entry of data into the cash register is saved for future use.

The keyboard, bar code reader, and cash register data entry devices have found the most use in business. For handicapped workers, special effects, and special situations some of the other input devices are used.

Microcomputers can receive input from (and output to) other computers over telephone lines using modems (both input and output devices). Modems convert the signals that come over the telephone lines so the computer can understand them.

Ouput Devices

Output device:

A device connected to the microcomputer through which data and instructions are communicated to the user of other devices.

The primary **output devices** are the monitor and printer.

Monitors The most common microcomputer output device is the monitor, the second most common is the printer. Purchasers of the IBM PC and look-alikes must select from color/graphic or monochrome monitor by installing a card to work with one of these output devices. The monochrome monitor produces a sharp character and is an outstanding selection for word processing. It will not produce graphics unless a special card is added.

The decision to use monochrome or color/graphics is dependent on the programs used in a business. For example, the integrated spreadsheet program Lotus 1–2–3 requires a color graphics card to use its graphics functions. Lotus graphics will not operate on the IBM PC monochrome card.

The small screens on pocket and briefcase computers are often LCD, liquid crystal displays, or electroluminesant (see Figure 2–9). These screens are flat and lend themselves to easy transport and storage.

There are two types of monitors. Monochrome monitors are green, amber, yellow, and black and white. Color monitors are composite (medium resolution) and RGB-red, green, and blue (high resolution.)

Pixels:

The dots on the microcomputer's screen used to create numbers, graphics, and other characters (letters, numbers, and symbols).

There are currently four levels of resolution, or sharpness of image:

■ Low: Monitors that can display 80 characters on a line.
■ Medium: Capability to display 320 by 200 dots **(pixels.)**

FIGURE 2–9
LCD on NEC

- High: Capability to display 640 by 200 pixels.
- Super-High: Capability to display up to 1024 by 1024 pixels.

The increase of screen resolution means a better image quality.

Printers The most common method of getting hard copy from a microcomputer is through a printer. The common types of printers are:

- dot matrix
- letter quality
- laser
- ink jet
- thermal
- plotters

The selection of a printer depends on printer type and your business needs as shown in Tables 2–5 and 2–6.

The dot matrix printer (see Figure 2–10) uses small pins to produce dots on paper to form letters and other characters. The quality of the letters is a function of the number of dots used per letter. The newer and more expensive models produce the highest quality output. Some dot matrix printers produce characters at the rate of 50 to 600 characters per second.

Dot matrix printers can produce small letters, compressed or condensed mode, to increase the number of characters output per line on standard paper. Businesses using data bases and spreadsheets often use

TABLE 2–5 Types of Printers

Type of Printer	Method of Letter Creation	Quality Draft	Quality N.L.Q.*	Quality Letter	Graphics Variable Size Letters	Approximate Characters per Second	Price Range
Dot Matrix	Uses dots to create image	x	x		x	80 to 600	$100 to $2,000
Letter Quality	Typewriter style		x			12 to 55	$300 to $3,000
Laser **	Many dots per char.	x	x	x	x	8 pages per minute ***	over $3,000
Ink-Jet **	Uses ink jet	x	x	x	x	80 plus	$300 to $1,500
Thermal	Uses heat sensitive paper or ribbons	x	x		x	no limits	$50 up
Plotter	Uses pens				x	****	$350 to $10,995

* N.L.Q.—near letter quality

**The laser and ink-jet printers use a large number of dots per character. The more dots used, the nearer the output is to a character produced by a single impact.

***Eight pages per minute is approximately 572 characters per second.

****Plotters use pens to create a character. Their speed may be as slow as two characters per second, depending on the type of character and its size.

TABLE 2–6
Business Use of Printers

Business application	Printer needs
Word Processing-Letters	Letter-quality output.
Spreadsheets	Large number of characters per line and speed.
Data Bases	Large number of characters per line and speed.
Graphics	Dot addressable control and plotters.
Special effects	Proportional printing (such as in this book.)

the increased characters per line such printers provide. Special sideways printing programs are available when a greater number of characters per line is needed.

Special characters are available on many dot matrix printers including Greek and other foreign languages, scientific symbols, and (dot addressable) graphic characters. Some printers have the capability of allowing the user to define their own characters.

Letter quality printers use thimbles, balls, and daisy wheels (see Figures 2–11). The letter formed looks exactly like that produced by a typewriter. These printers are generally slower than dot matrix printers. Speeds vary from 12 to 55 characters per second.

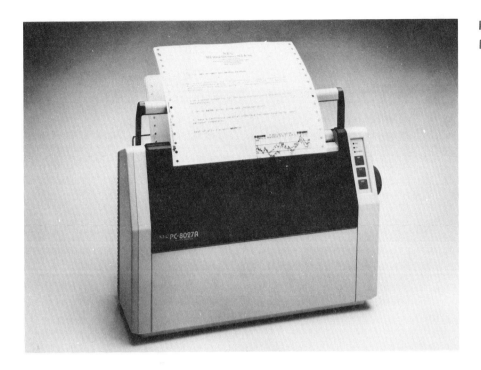

FIGURE 2–10
Dot Matrix Printer

The laser printer (see Figure 2–12) uses technology similar to some copying machines. The slower, low-cost models have maximum output of eight pages per minute. The quality of output is competitive with traditional letter quality printers. There are no limitations to the images that can be produced by a laser printer.

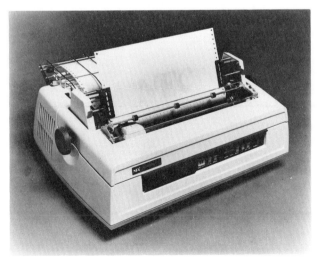

FIGURE 2–11   Daisy Wheel Printer and Daisy Wheel

FIGURE 2–12
Hewlett-Packard LaserJet
Printer

The ink jet printer (see Figure 2–13) produces letters by spraying a jet of ink through small pin holes. It is not limited to letters and can produce many special effects. The speed is in the same range as dot matrix printers.

Thermal printers use a heating element to make a letter or character on either heat-sensitive paper or on regular paper with a heat-sensitive ribbon. The units vary from low-price units designed for home and traveling microcomputers to high quality, high speed, and high priced units.

Plotters use pens to produce their images (see Figure 2–14). Some hold the paper and move the pens, while others hold the printing head

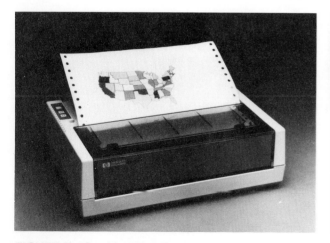

FIGURE 2–13   Hewlett-Packard ThinkJet Printer and Printhead

FIGURE 2–14
Hewlett-Packard Plotter

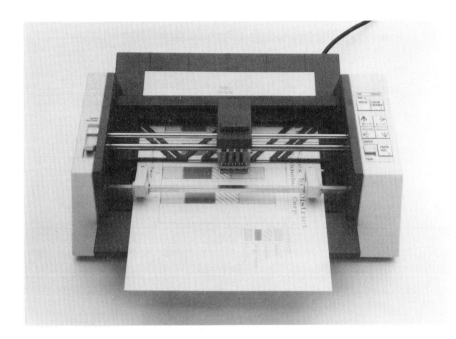

fixed and move the paper. Some use drums while others print on a flat surface. Generally, a plotter is much slower than other output devices. It is primarily used for graphics, CAD, CADD, and special effects.

There are four methods of feeding paper into a printer:

1. Single sheet friction feed
2. Automatic sheet feed
3. Pin feed
4. Tractor feed

Any and all types of paper may be fed in using friction feed (see Figure 2–15). Using pin or tractor feed the paper must have a tractor along the outside edge to guide it.

On-Line Storage Devices

On-line storage means memory that is available to your microcomputer through communication cables. It is not part of the internal RAM or ROM. **On-line storage devices** are considered to be external to the microcomputer, even though they are commonly built into the same case as the microcomputer.

The lowest cost on-line storage device commonly used is a cassette tape recorder. The most popular device is a five and one quarter-inch floppy disk drive. Other devices used on microcomputers include hard disks (which are replacing the floppy disk drive in many business offices,) eight-inch disk drives, quarter-inch (streaming) tapes, and three and one half inch disk drives.

The Apple IIe, Apple look-alikes, IBM PC, IBM look-alikes, and most

On/Off-line:
The operation of computer equipment at the same time as other equipment under the control of the microprocessor (on-line.) Independent operation is called off-line.

On-line storage devices:
Devices available to the microcomputer through communication cables.

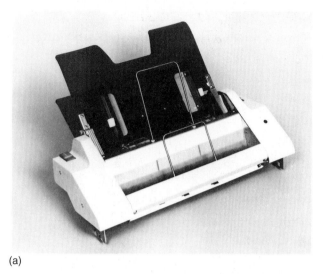
(a)

(b)

FIGURE 2–15   Mechanisms for Feeding Paper (a) Sheet Feeder and (b) Tractor Feed

other microcomputers use cards, called disk controller cards, for controlling on-line storage devices. Each type of data storage device requires its own card.

The type of on-line storage device is a function of the availability, size, and application of the microcomputer. Table 2–6 lists the varieties of on-line storage media and devices, and where you may expect the device to be used. Figure 2–16 shows a briefcase computer that uses a built-in mini-cassette. Figure 2–17 shows some external on-line devices for a briefcase microcomputer.

Five and One-Quarter Inch Disk Drives The most common data and program storage device is the five and one-quarter inch floppy disk drive. A floppy disk drive is an electromechanical device that rotates a diskette and feeds signals into and from the diskette as directed by the controller

Table 2–6   On-Line Storage Media and Devices

Microcomputer Size	Cassette Tape*	Bubble memory inch	3½ inch	5¼ inch	8 inch	Fixed/Removable Hard Disks
Pocket Microcomputers	X					
Briefcase/Lap Microcomputers	X	X	X	X		
Transportables			X	X	X	X
Desktop	**		X	X	X	X *** ****

*Both regular and mini-cassette tape recorders are used.

^^Starter units, which are desktops when expanded, often use cassette storage in their minimum configuration. Some use the CMOS low power system for storage.

***Other media and devices that are available but not widely used are the Bernouli box, laser disks, ¼ inch streaming tape, RAM cartridges.

****Cassette-type tapes are also used for backup of hard disks.

FIGURE 2–16
Epson with Built-in
Microcassette

circuits. The controller circuits are managed by a microcomputer through its operating system.

Eight-Inch Disk Drives The Radio Shack Models II, 12, and 6000 micro-computers, among others, use eight-inch disk drives (see Figure 2–18).

FIGURE 2–17
On-Line Devices for the
NEC-8201

FIGURE 2–18
**Radio Shack Model 12
Eight-Inch Disk Drive**

On-line storage media:
Material used to store microcomputer files.

The trend in the use of **on-line storage media** is towards small devices. The dominance of the five and one-quarter inch disk drive over the eight-inch drive seems to be primarily due to size and technology.

Three and One-Half Inch Disk Drives The Macintosh and some lap microcomputers are being equipped with three and one-half inch drives (see Figure 2–19). Data storage devices are yet to be standardized. A microcomputer using three and one-half inch disk drives cannot read the information on a five and one-quarter inch diskette. Likewise, a three and one-half inch diskette cannot be read in a five and one-quarter inch drive.

For smaller microcomputers the smaller drives fit into the limited space available.

Hard Disk Drive Hard disk drives are rigid storage devices that come as cartridge, disk pack, or are fixed and not removable. Some hard disks can be installed within a microcomputer in the same space as a five and one-quarter inch disk drive. Figure 2–20 shows an IBM XT with an internal hard drive.

On-Line Storage Media

Many different types of media are used to record computer files.

The disk or diskette is a plastic circle with a coating of magnetic material that rotates within the outer sleeve. You must be careful not to

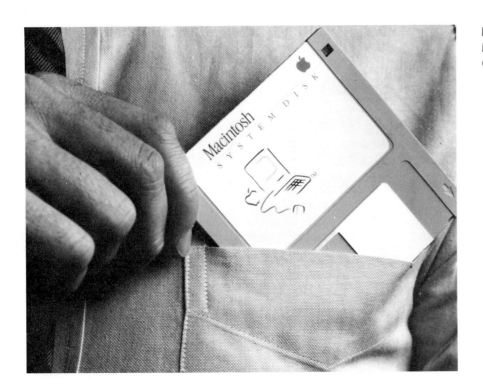

FIGURE 2–19
Macintosh Three and
One-Half Inch Diskette

FIGURE 2–20
Internal Hard Drive IBM XT

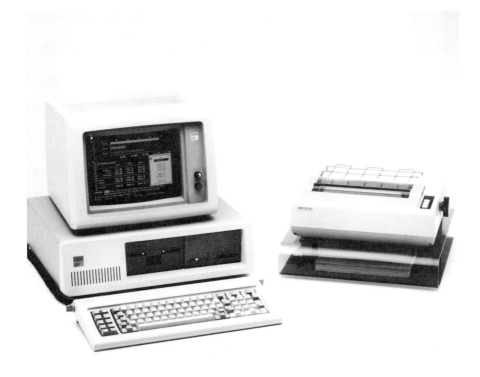

Tracks:
A magnetic circle on a disk or diskette for storing data.
Sector:
A division of a track on a disk.

touch the magnetic surface. The oil from your fingers will damage the surface. Figure 2–21 is a sketch of a diskette with its parts identified. Figure 2–22 shows the **track** and **sector** divisions of a diskette.

On the upper right side is a square cutout. This is the write-protect notch. On eight-inch disks it must be covered for reading and writing, while on the five and one-quarter inch diskette it must be uncovered for reading and writing. The eight-inch disk is uncovered for read only and the five and one-quarter is covered. The index hole on disk and diskette is used by some microcomputers to locate the data on the media. The rotation hole is in the middle of the diskette and is used by the disk drive to rotate the media.

The three and one-half inch diskette is similar internally to the larger diskettes, and has a hard plastic shell that opens automatically when inserted into the disk drive. It does not require a paper case or sleeve, but must be treated with care.

Handling rules for disks and diskettes include:

1. Do not allow the disk-diskette to come near magnetic fields such as those generated by television sets and electric motors.
2. Do not remove the disk-diskette from the microcomputer when it is operating. (A red light indicates when a disk drive is moving.)
3. Do not force fit the disk-diskette into the drive.
4. Do not write on the disk-diskette with a hard device. It is best to write on the label before placing it on the diskette.

FIGURE 2–21
Diskette

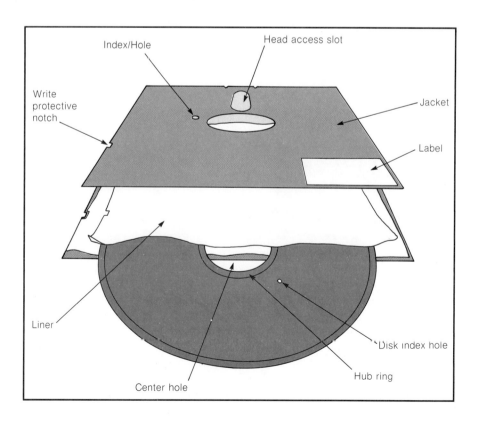

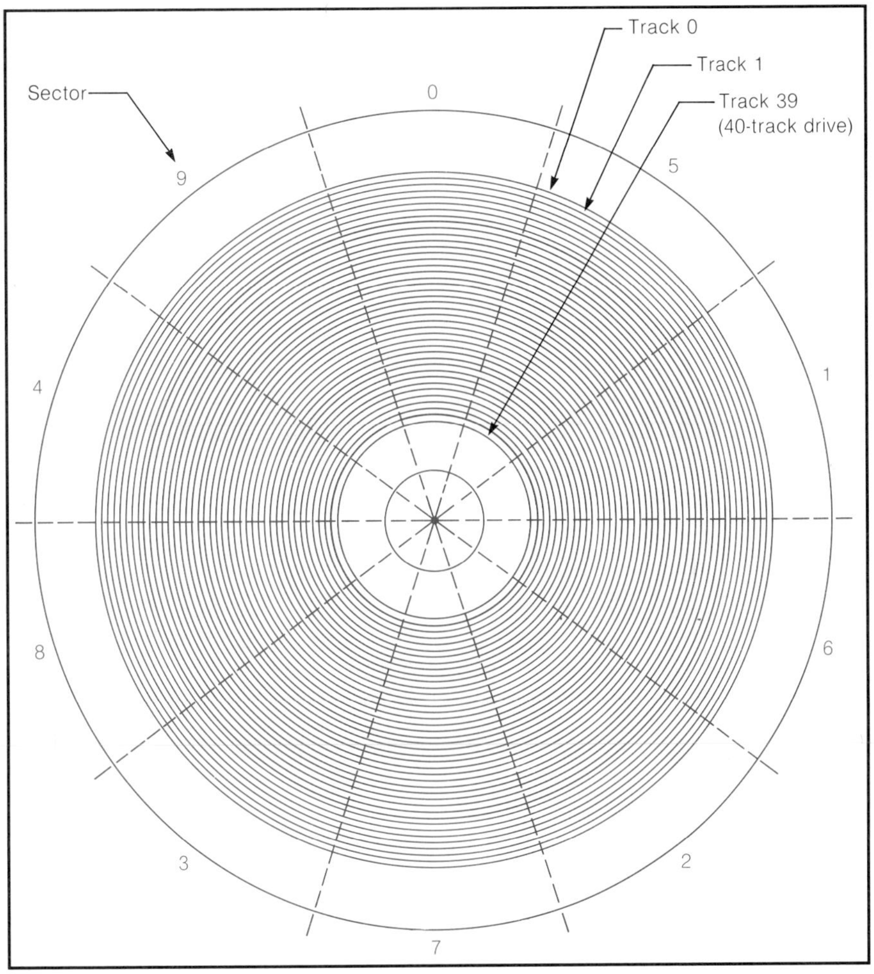

FIGURE 2–22
The Tracks and Sectors of a Diskette

5. Do not touch the magnetic part of the disk-diskette.
6. Do not expose the disk-diskette to the direct heat of the sun by storing it on the dashboard of your car or in a similar manner.
7. Do not expose the disk-diskette to extreme cold.
8. Do keep the disk-diskette in its protective envelope except when in use.
9. Do handle the disk-diskette by its edges.

When placing a diskette in a disk drive, the diskette is held by the edge with the write-protect notch to the left and the label facing up. It is gently placed in the disk drive and the door is closed.

When a microcomputer is started it will look for the operating system in a particular disk drive, called the default drive. When the disk drives lie side by side, the default drive on American-manufactured microcomputers is located on the left. When drives sit on top of each other, you must learn the disk drive designations, since they vary among manufacturers.

The size of a disk or diskette is not the only factor that determines the amount of data that may be stored. Disks and diskettes may be single-sided/single-density (SSSD), single-sided/double-density (SSDS), double-sided/double-density (DSDD), and quad density (QD). Single-sided means that only one side of the diskette is used to store information. The density rating indicates the closeness in which data is stored and determines the capacity of the storage media. For diskettes with storage densities greater than double density, the number of tracks is used as a measure of the potential capacity of the diskette. Diskettes store from 50,000 to over a billion characters (see Table 2–7).

The type of disks and diskettes to purchase should match your system specifications. If you are using a microcomputer such as the IBM AT with quad density 1.2Megabyte diskettes, this type of diskette must be used.

Even when you handle disks and diskettes carefully they will fail. A copy of all program and data diskettes should be made and stored in a separate location for insurance.

USER WINDOW

The accountant placed his new MS-DOS transportable microcomputer on his desk. He opened the instruction book and read the instructions: "Remove the master diskette from its envelope and insert in drive A."

He located the "master diskette" and removed it from the booklet where it was stored. He then carefully pried off the "envelope" and removed the plastic disk. It did not fit into the disk drive.

REVIEW OF SELECTED SYSTEMS

There is a wide selection of microcomputers available in each size class: pockets, briefcase and lap, transportables, and desktops. The numbers

TABLE 2–7   Commonly Used On-Line Storage Media and Devices Approximate Capacities

	3 ½ inch	5 ½ inch	8 inch	Fixed/ Removable Hard Disks
Single-sided/ Single-density		50K to 90K	92K	
Single-sided/ Double-density	400	160K to 200K		
Double-sided/ Double-density	400K to 800K	300K to 400K	500K	
Quad density		750K to 3Megabyte	1.2Megabyte	5Megabyte to 1Gigabyte *

* A Gigabyte is 1,000,000,000 bytes

and capabilities of microcomputers in all size classes are great. We have selected typical microcomputers in each class for illustration (see Tables 2–8 to 2–11).

MICROCOMPUTER COMPATABILITY

When a business requires more than a single microcomputer it is important that they be able to function as a system. **Operational compatibility**—the capability of microcomputers to work together as a system—is one important aspect that must be considered in a professional environment where more than a single microcomputer is used. Physical compatibility involves the capability to exchange physical parts, such as the pc-boards used to add capabilities.

The single microcomputer office does not need to be concerned with compatibility except when expansion is anticipated or data is being transferred from an outside source. When the business professional must work with others who are using microcomputers, the need for compatibility begins. When a second or third microcomputer is added, the problem of compatibility becomes critical. The number of offices with multiple microcomputers is increasing rapidly.

The problem of compatibility exists between different brands and even within the same brand of microcomputers produced at different times. The capabilities of microcomputers have grown. A five-year-old

Operational compatibility: The capability of microcomputers to work together as a system.

TABLE 2–8 Pocket (Handheld) Microcomputers

Manufacturer	Casio Computer Corp.	Sharp Electronics Corp.	Tandy Corp.
The CPU Box			
Model	FX-700P	PC-1250A	PC-4
Size	6.5x2.75x.375	5.3125x2.75x.375	6.5x2.75x.375
Weight	9 oz.	4 oz.	4 oz.
ROM	13K	24K	16K
Software	BASIC	BASIC	BASIC
RAM	2K	3.5K	0.5K
Power	Battery	Battery	Battery
Expansion			
Cassette Interface	X	X	X
Printer		X	X
RAM			Expandable to 1K
Input devices			
Keyboard	X	X	X
Output devices			
Display LCD lines	1	1	1
Characters	12	24	12
On-line Storage	Cassette	Cassette	Cassette
Price	$80	$110	$70

TABLE 2–9   Briefcase and Lap Microcomputers

Manufacturer	Epson America Inc.	NEC Home Electronics Inc.	Tandy Corp.
The CPU Box			
Model	HX-20	PC-8201A	Model 200
Size	11.67x8.5x1.75	11.875x8.5x2	2.1875x11.75x8.5
Weight	4 lbs.	3.75 lbs.	4.5 lbs.
Microprocessor	2 6301	80C85	80C85
ROM	32K	32K	72K
Software	BASIC	BASIC	BASIC
	Word Processing	Word Processing	Word Processing
			Communications
RAM	16K	16K	24K
Power	Battery	Battery/AC	Battery/AC
Expansion			
Cassette Interface	X	X	X
RAM	To 32K	To 64K	To 72K
External RAM		X	
Input devices	Keyboard	Keyboard	Keyboard
	Bar Code	Bar Code	Bar Code
Output devices			
Display LCD lines	4	8	16
Characters	20	40	40
Printer			
Built-in	X		
External	X (Serial)	X (Parallel)	X (Parallel)
Serial Commun.	X	X	X
Modem			X
On-line Storage			
Microcassette	X		
Cassette	X	X	X
Floppy disk		X extra	X extra
Price	$795	$795	$995

Table 2–10   Transportable Microcomputers

Manufacturer	Compaq Computer Corp.	Kaypro Corp.	Panasonic Inc.
Operating System	MS-DOS	CP/M	MS-DOS
The CPU Box			
Model	Portable Computer	Kaypro II	Senior Partner
Size	20x16x8.5	18x15.5x8	18.5x13.1875 x8.25
Weight	28 lbs.	26 lbs.	28.75 lbs.
Microprocessor	8088	Z80	8088
ROM	32K	2K	16K
RAM	128K	64K	128K
Power	AC	AC	AC
Expansion			
RAM	To 640K		To 640K

Table 2–10   (continued)

Manufacturer	Compaq Computer Corp.	Kaypro Corp.	Panasonic Inc.
Input devices	Keyboard Bar Code, etc.	Keyboard Bar Code, etc.	Keyboard Bar Code, etc.
Output devices Display Monitor	9-inch green	9-inch green	9-inch green
Printer			
Parallel	X	X	X built-in
Serial	X	X	X
Serial Commun.	X	X	X
On-line Storage			
Floppy disks	X (360K)	X (191K)	X (360K)
Hard disk	extra	extra	extra
Price	$2,500	$1,600	$2,200(1 drive)

Table 2–11   Desktop Microcomputers

Manufacturer	Apple Computer Corp.	International Business Machines	Tandy Corp.
Operating System	Apple-DOS PRO-DOS, CP/M*	PC-DOS	TRS-DOS and XENIX (Version UNIX)
The CPU Box			
Model	Apple IIe	IBM PC	TANDY 6000
Size	1.25x1.5x.375	1.67x1.25x.5	large
Disk drives			
external	X		X
Microprocessor	6502	8088	68000
ROM	8K	40K	not available
RAM	128K	256K	512K
Power	AC	AC	AC
Expansion			
RAM		To 640K	
Serial Comm.	X	X	X
Parallel Printers	X	X	X
Input devices	Keyboard Bar Code,	Keyboard Bar Code,	Keyboard, etc.
Output devices			
Display Monitor	external	external	
Printer			
Parallel	X	X	X
Serial	X	X	X
Serial Commun.	X	X	X

(continued on following page)

Table 2–11   (continued)

Manufacturer	Apple Computer Corp.	International Business Machines	Tandy Corp.
On-line Storage			
Floppy disks	X (140K)	X (360K)	
Eight inch disks			X (1.25Meg)
Hard disk	extra	extra	X (15Meg)
Price **	$1,995	$3,020	$4,499 (two disks)

*CP/M add on extra for Apple IIe.
**Prices for basic unit and operating system only.

microcomputer may be expected to have some features that are not compatible with newer models of the same brand. For example, the IBM PC cannot read or write on the IBM AT 1.2Megabyte diskettes.

The problem of operational compatibility is one problem that has not been completely solved. Microcomputers produced by different manufacturers, or different models produced by the same manufacturer, are often not compatible.

Operational compatibility has several aspects:

1. Being able to use the same organization for recording data on a diskette.
2. Being able to write data on the same diskette.
3. Being able to read common data files from diskettes.
4. Being able to use common data files.
5. Being able to use common programs created in BASIC or similar languages.
6. Being able to use common machine language programs.

The first four aspects are the most important in business situations. A business organization must have a common set of data, a common memory. Without a common memory, an organization is only a series of parts, often working at cross purposes. The capability to use the same program on more than a single microcomputer is often not as important as the exchange of data files.

Data files may be transferred using communication methods such as those discussed in chapter 8, but this method of transfer is usually not as fast as direct disk reading and writing.

In many cases you may purchase, at extra cost, programs and special hardware that make it possible to overcome the limitations of your microcomputer and read diskettes from a foreign microcomputer. The cost of disk-reading systems varies from $30 to $300. When an organization has been using microcomputers for a number of years, such extra cost add-ons are useful when making the newly purchased microcomputer part of the existing system. Although these add-ons will solve some of the compatibility problems, it is best to avoid them in the first place.

You have learned the importance of hardware. It is the foundation upon that the microcomputer system is built. The parts of the microcomputer have been identified as well as the ways in which they work together to form a system. Some of the systems currently available in the market-place have been reviewed. The importance of compatibility when using different microcomputers has been reviewed.

The key points of this chapter are:

1. Hardware is that part of the microcomputer you can see and feel.
2. The professional must learn about microcomputers in order to select the best combination of capabilities and cost to match the needs of a company.
3. The parts of a microcomputer include:
   In the CPU box
      Microprocessor
      ROM and RAM
      Cards—PC boards (Expansion)
   Input devices
   Ouput devices
   On-line storage devices (media.)
4. The CPU box usually contains a microprocessor mounted on a printed circuit board, ROM and RAM, other printed circuit boards, and dip switches.
5. The keyboard is the most used microcomputer input device. Others include voice recognition devices, pads, a mouse, bar code readers, and joy sticks.
6. The primary output devices are the monitor and printer.
7. External storage devices are on-line, available to the microcomputer through communication cables.
8. There is a wide selection of microcomputers available in each size class: pockets, briefcase and lap, transportables, and desktops.
9. When a business requires more than a single microcomputer it is important that they be able to work together.

Compatibility
Configuration
DIP switch
Input devices
Microprocessor
Mother board
On-line storage devices

On-line storage media
On/Off-line
Operational compatibility
Output devices
PC-boards
Physical compatibility
RAM
ROM

1. Why is it important to know about microcomputer hardware?

2. What is compatibility? What does configuration have to do with compatibility?

3. What is the relationship of hardware and software?

4. What are the hardware parts of a microcomputer system?

5. What is the architecture of a microcomputer? Compare the design architecture of the Apple IIe and IBM PC.

6. What is a microprocessor?

7. What are RAM and ROM? Why are they important to the business user?

8. How is the amount of memory in a microcomputer measured?

9. What are PC-boards and how can a business user take advantage of them?

10. What is an input device? What is the most commonly used input device?

11. What is an output device? What are the most common output devices found on microcomputers?

12. What is resolution? What are the four levels of screen resolution?

13. Identify the types of printers available.

14. What is on-line storage? What is an on-line storage device?

15. What is the most common data and program storage device on a microcomputer?

16. What is on-line storage media?

17. Identify the parts of a microcomputer five and one-quarter inch diskette.

18. What is the square notch on the right side of a disk-diskette and how is it used?

19. Review the rules for the correct handling of disks-diskettes.

20. What are the six levels of operational compatibility?

1. From your local newspaper find some advertisements for microcomputers. Identify the microcomputers being sold and prepare a short discussion of the nature of these microcomputers.

2. Obtain a copy of a microcomputer magazine from your library, local computer store, or bookstore. Select any article relating to microcomputer hardware and prepare to discuss the information contained in the article.

3. Examine several copies of the Wall Street Journal or national news magazines. Identify some articles about microcomputer hardware and prepare a short discussion.

4. Identify the radio and television advertisements for microcomputer hardware currently being run. What type of hardware or store is being advertised?

5. Identify the type of hardware sold through:
   a. Local retail stores
   b. Discount and department stores
   c. Mail-order outlets
   d. Office supply outlets.

6. Look up the hardware outlets listed in the yellow pages of your telephone book. What equipment might you expect to be able to purchase locally?

Dologite, D. G. *Using Small Business Computers.* Prentice-Hall, 1984.

Freedman, Alan. *The Computer Glossary.* Prentice-Hall, 1983.

Kalb, Ken. *The Kaypro—An Application Guide.* Creative Computing, 1983.

Lewis, Gerard. *Macintosh: The Appliance of the Future with Disk.* Banbury Books, 1984.

Shelly, G. and T. Cashman. *Introduction to Computers and Data Processing.* Anaheim Publishing Company, 1980.

Sippi, C. and R. Sippi. *Computer Dictionary.* Howard W. Sams & Co., Inc., 1982.

Veit, Stanley S. *Using Micro-Computers in Business—A Guide for the Perplexed.* Second Edition. Hayden Book Company, 1981, 1983.

Weber Systems Inc.—Staff. *Apple IIe User's Handbook.* Ballantine Books, 1983.

Weber Systems Inc.—Staff. *IBM PC & XT Users Handbook.* Ballantine Books, 1983.

Zimmerman, Steven M., Leo M. Conrad, and Larry Goldstein. *Osborne User's Guide.* Brady Publishing Company, 1983.

Lewis, Gerard. *Macintosh: The Appliance of the Future with Disk.* Banbury Books, 1984.

Shelly, G. and T. Cashman. *Introduction to Computers and Data Processing.* Anaheim Publishing Company, 1980.

Sippi, C. and R. Sippi. *Computer Dictionary.* Howard W. Sams & Co., Inc., 1982.

Veit, Stanley S. *Using Micro-Computers in Business—A Guide for the Perplexed.* Second Edition. Hayden Book Company, 1981, 1983.

Weber Systems Inc.—Staff. *Apple IIe User's Handbook.* Ballantine Books, 1983.

Weber Systems Inc.—Staff. *IBM PC & XT Users Handbook.* Ballantine Books, 1983.

Zimmerman, Steven M., Leo M. Conrad, and Larry Goldstein. *Osborne User's Guide.* Brady Publishing Company, 1983.

Chapter Outline

Chapter Goals

Upon completion of this chapter you will be able to:

Understand the importance of the operating system to the business professional.

Define the tasks of an operating system.

Identify and examine the features of the more popular operating systems.

OPERATING SYSTEMS

An operating system is the program that controls the printer, monitor, one or two disk drives, and a hard disk drive, if connected, and central processing unit so they all work together. The user must be able to control all the microcomputer parts to obtain useful results.

An operating system consists of:

1. Functions: program-routines built into the operating system and always available.
2. Utilities: programs available on the diskette with the operating system.

Many **functions** and utilities involve saving, recalling **(loading)**, moving, changing, copying, and keeping track of **files.** Files usually contain data in the form of text and numbers or instructions in the form of programs.

Routines may be either functions or utilities depending on the operating system. Examples of routines are:

1. Preparing a diskette to receive data or programs.
2. Copying a diskette.
3. Saving a data or program file.
4. Bringing a data or program file into RAM.
5. Removing data or program files from the directory.

Microcomputers may be classified into "family" groups according to the operating system that is used. There are six popular operating systems, or microcomputer **families:**

1. Apple DOS—Used by Apple II series.
2. Apple Macintosh disk operating system.
3. CP/M—Used by many "independent" manufacturers.
4. MS/PC-DOS—Used by IBM in their IBM PC, PC-XT, and PC-AT. MS-DOS is similar to PC-DOS and is used by many "independent" manufacturers.
5. TRS-DOS—Used on many different microcomputers by Radio Shack.
6. UNIX—The Bell Laboratory developed system with advanced features.

WHY THE BUSINESS PROFESSIONAL MUST KNOW ABOUT OPERATING SYSTEMS

The business professional uses the operating system to control the microcomputer when solving business problems. Some of the output the user of a microcomputer might produce are letters, financial reports, evaluations, market surveys, invoices, and checks. Business users are not interested in how the program and data files used to create the business documents are saved, but they must know what to do and what not to do to ensure that errors are not made that may damage these files. Usually, applications programs **interface** with the operating system, but sometimes the business professional must do so directly.

Functions (operating system):
Routines built into the operating system. These routines provide the user with the capability to perform often needed tasks. Functions are loaded into RAM with the operating system and remain there.
Load:
To transfer a file from an on-line storge media into the RAM of a computer so it may be used.
File:
A collection of related material. May be data or programs or both.
Routine:
A part of a program that performs specific tasks.
Families:
Groups of microcomputers that use the same or similar microprocessor and the same or similar operating system. These groups have similar capabilities.

Interface:
A common boundary between independent systems; in the field of microcomputers the connection between two parts of the system; the programs and hardware that make it possible for two parts of the microcomputer system or two computers to work together.

The business professional must know about the operating system because:

1. Knowledge is required to accomplish some tasks.
2. Knowledge solves problems when they occur.
3. Knowledge saves time.

Knowledge Required

The business professional must know how to make **backup** copies of programs and data files. Having backup copies of programs and data eliminates the potentially devastating effects of storage media failures.

The creation and maintenance of a business data set costs dollars for hardware, software, time, and effort. These dollars may be wasted if the data are lost due to the lack of backup copies and poor operating practices. Once a business becomes experienced in using a data set, it is difficult to do without it even for a short period of time.

Backup:
A copy of a disk, diskette, or file.

Solves Problems

Problems occur even with the best designed system and programs. When these problems occur, knowledge may turn a disaster into a simple inconvenience.

It is not uncommon for operating systems to be upgraded. With MS/PC-DOS version 2.0 came the capability to increase the amount of storage on a diskette from 320K to 360K. When systems older than 2.0 are used to read the high capacity diskette, a lot of junk appears on the screen, but no damage is done to the diskette. If the older system is used to change or write something on the new diskette, program and data files could be damaged. Knowing that an error has occurred and what not to do may prevent the loss of valuable business programs and data.

Saves Time

There are a number of ways to perform a task. Knowledge of the operating system makes it easier to select the best method.

In CP/M and MS/PC-DOS a text file may be examined by using a word processor, or by typing the word TYPE followed by the file specification and <CR> when in the disk-operating system. The second method is much faster if the objective is to simply find out what is stored in a particular file.

<CR>:
Press the return or enter key.

TASKS OF OPERATING SYSTEMS

The operating system controls and coordinates the parts of a microcomputer system so they work together as a system. Operating system tasks are performed using built-in functions and add-on utilities. The operating system functions, utilities, and hardware define the limits of a microcomputer system's capabilities. For example, you cannot obtain printed output unless you have an operating system with the capability and the hardware to do the job.

Built-in functions are loaded into RAM when the system is loaded and are always available. Utilities are programs recorded on a diskette. The user must tell the computer to load utilities into RAM when they are needed. That diskette must be available when they are used.

A set of **conventions** (operating rules) makes it easier to use functions and utilities. There are conventions for communication between all the parts of the microcomputer system.

Conventions:
The standard and accepted abbreviations, symbols, and their meanings for users of microcomputers.

Functions

The functions built into the operating system provide capabilities that the business professional will need often. Routines commonly included as functions are:

1. System Operating Functions
   a. Booting the system (loading system from diskette to RAM).
   b. Storage and retrieval of files on disk or diskette.
   c. Examining the directory of files.
2. Controlling Communication Functions
   a. Controlling screens, printers, and communication ports.
   b. Controlling the date and time.
3. Housekeeping Functions
   a. Transferring files between diskettes.
   b. Transferring systems between diskettes.
   c. Keeping track of what is on a disk or diskette.
   d. Erasing files from diskettes.
   e. Renaming files.
4. Additional Functions
   a. Windowing.
   b. Multi-tasking.
   c. Multi-using.

System Operating Functions—*Booting the System* The first thing an operating system must do is to get the system started. There are two methods of starting your microcomputer. One is with the machine turned off, called a cold boot. The second is with the machine turned on, called a warm boot.

There is a small program recorded in the ROM of your microcomputer that starts the process of reading the operating system code from diskette or hard disk. This is called loading the operating system or boot strapping.

The boot strap routine is usually small, just large enough to read into RAM a set of instructions used to load the remaining operating system code from diskette or hard disk into RAM. The Apple and MS/PC-DOS microcomputers start with a cold boot, while CP/M and TRS-DOS microcomputers are first turned on and then the diskette is inserted before starting the booting process.

Most microcomputer operating systems will look for a program or data file on the disk drive that is the currently **logged drive.** When a system is started the **default drive** that becomes the active drive is the lower numbered or lettered drive. Table 3–1 lists the default drive by operating system.

The cold boot steps are:

1. Place a diskette with an operating system in the default drive.
2. Turn the microcomputer on.

When the machine starts, the diskette is read and the operating system is loaded. This is called a cold boot. Many CP/M and TRS-DOS users are warned not to use this cold booting method.

Logged drive:
The disk drive from which data and programs are read.
Default drive:
The disk drive from which data and programs are read unless the microcomputer is instructed otherwise. The default drive is the logged drive if not additional instructions are given.

System	Default Drive (Originally Logged Drive)
Apple DOS	Slot #6 * Drive # 1
Apple Macintosh	Internal drive
CP/M	A
MS/PC-DOS	A
TRS-DOS	System must be in drive 0. Does not used logged drives procedures.

* The Apple may have the disk controller card in different slots. The operating system will look at the first slot with a disk controller card as the default drive.

**TABLE 3–1
Default/Logged Drives**

A warm boot may be used by most microcomputers. It starts with the microcomputer running, a diskette in the default drive with an operating system, and a reset instruction. Table 3–2 lists the reset instructions for selected systems.

System	Reset Procedures
Apple DOS	Press control, open apple, and reset keys together.
Apple Macintosh DOS	Reset key on side.
CP/M	Press reset key (location variable.)
MS/PC-DOS	Press control, alt., and del. keys together.
TRS-DOS	Press reset key on side or top of keyboard.

**TABLE 3–2
Reset Methods**

After giving the reset command, the boot strap program will take over in the same manner as a cold boot.

The operating system may be loaded directly from some hard disks. Usually, the microcomputer first looks for a diskette in the default drive, and if one is not found, it then changes the default drive to the hard drive and continues with the process of loading the system into RAM. Some hard disk drive systems do not boot from the hard disk drive, but require that you load the operating system from the default drive or a pre-boot program (which transfers control to the hard disk drive.)

Some TRSDOS and MS/PC-DOS versions require that you enter the date and time at the beginning of an operating session. In some cases you will be able to press <CR> and not actually enter the date. If a version requires that you enter certain information, it will not let you continue until you do.

Storage and Retrieval of Files on Diskettes After the system is booted, the task of organizing, indexing, and locating data and program files on data storage devices is one of the most important operating system functions. Table 3–3 is a review of the procedure for storage and Table 3–4 for retrieval of data and programs on cassette tape (to illustrate what must be done) and diskette (to illustrate what the operating system does). The diskette system is assumed to have two disk drives, the first one labeled A and the second B.

Your knowledge of how to save a file on a cassette tape recorder should help you understand what a microcomputer must do when saving a file on diskette. The task that must be done is the same when saving a file on both a cassette tape recorder and a disk drive. (The cassette tape recorder is assumed to have a counter.)

TABLE 3–3
Steps Required When Recording Files

Cassette Tape	Diskette
The recording of microcomputer programs or data on a cassette tape requires the user to perform the following housekeeping chores:	The disk operating system performs the task of keeping track of the programs and data stored on the diskette:
1. Prepare a cassette tape by cleaning it with a bulk cassette eraser or start with a new tape	**1.** Prepare a diskette for program and data by placing a diskette with the operating system on it in drive A and a new diskette in drive B. The instruction to FORMAT the diskette in drive B is entered.
2. Prepare the program or data to be saved.	**2.** Prepare the program or data to be saved.
3. Load a new cassette tape into the recorder. (Tapes may be erased and re-used.)	**3.** Tell the operating system to save the program or data.
4. Set the counter and locate where on the tape the beginning of the program or data file will be located.	
5. Keep a careful record of where the recording starts.	
6. Connect the recorder to the microcomputer.	
7. Place the recorder in play/record mode.	
8. Tell the microcomputer operating system to record the file.	
9. Keep a careful record of where the recording ends.	

When the microcomputer records the material, it starts by placing a beginning of file code marker, and then records the information followed by an end of file code marker, often called EOF. You must carefully record where on your tape you have saved material, in order to prevent the overwriting of valuable information.

The diskette **FORMAT** instruction prepares a directory for the diskette. The disk operating system records the name and location of each file on the disk in the directory.

Once the material is stored on tape or diskette you may shut off your microcomputer. The program or data may be reloaded into the RAM of your microcomputer as shown in Table 3–4.

FORMAT:
Instructions used to tell the microcomputer to prepare a diskette or disk for use. Magnetic marks are made on the media to identify tracks and sectors where data is to be stored.

TABLE 3–4
Steps Required When
Recalling Files

Cassette Tape	Diskette
1. Start the microcomputer with a warm or cold boot. 2. Rewind the tape. 3. Connect the tape recorder to the microcomputer. 4. Place it in the run mode. 5. Tell the microcomputer- operating system what to load. (Programs and data files are stored on tape.)	1. Start the microcomputer warm or cold boot. 2. Put disk in drive B. 3. Tell the disk operating system to load the file.

The microcomputer operating system searches the tape until the beginning of file marker is found. It then reads the information stored on the tape into RAM until the EOF marker is encountered. The program or data can now be used. The process may be repeated as many times as you wish in a manner similar to replaying one of your music tapes.

The microcomputer disk operating system checks the disk's directory to find the file. The file is then loaded. The control that the operating system has over the recording and retrieval process is minimal with external cassette tapes, a little greater with internal minicassette tape recorders, and complete with diskettes, disks, and hard disk systems. One reason why cassette and other types of tape storage have not been as popular as disk and hard disk storage is that data must be stored and accessed on tape sequentially. When a file is needed on a tape the computer must often start at the beginning of a tape and search for the file's beginning. On a disk the computer finds a directory track and then goes directly to where the file is stored.

There are a number of different methods for organizing files on a diskette or hard disk. The most popular method for diskettes has been just a series of individual files. For hard disks a **hierarchical file** structure (see Figure 3–1) is popular.

Examining the Directory Disk operating systems perform the function of keeping a list of the programs, data, and other files stored on a media. Directory is a common name for this file. Examining a directory is simple (see Figure 3–2). In CP/M, MS/PC-DOS, and TRS-DOS you simply type DIR<CR> to get the directory of the diskette in the logged drive.

To get the directory of any other drive, the instruction is usually DIR n:<CR> in CP/M and MS/PC-DOS, where n stands for the letter of the

Hierarchical Files:
A file structure consisting of a top down organization. Files are organized in what is often referred to as a tree structure. Some operating systems allow sophisticated security to be established for hierarchical files.

FIGURE 3–1
Hierarchical Files

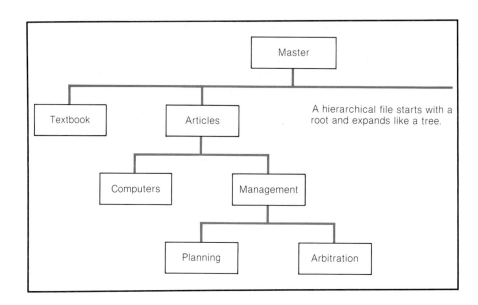

A hierarchical file starts with a root and expands like a tree.

drive (A, B, C, etc.) or the name of the subdirectory. In TRS-DOS the instruction for non-default diskette directory is DIR :i<CR>, where i is the drive number 0, 1, 2, or 3.

Under Apple DOS 3.3 the directory instruction is CATALOG<CR> for the default drive, and CATALOG,D2<CR> for the second drive. Us-

FIGURE 3–2 Examining the Directory of a Diskette Using MS/PC-DOS.

```
A>DIR<CR>

 Volume in drive A has no label
 Directory of A:\

CHAP    12   43392   3-29-85   9:52a
CHAP    10   29440   4-13-85  11:46a
CHAP    11   23424   4-16-85   9:17a
    3 File(s)  265216 bytes free


A>
```

The instruction may be given in uppercase or lowercase. The microcomputer tells you what files are on the diskette, the size of each file, the date and time the file was started, and the amount of bytes still free to use on the diskette.

ing PRO-DOS you will be given a menu of system utilities from which to select.

Most operating systems allow you to give instructions to your operating system using either upper or lowercase letters. There are some exceptions. Some CP/M instructions and utilities cannot find a file saved using lowercase. UNIX uses lowercase letters for systems instructions. Apple DOS 3.3 requires the use of uppercase only.

For hard disks with large volumes of files, a tree directory structure has been developed. UNIX was the first operating system to use this type of directory. This type of directory is used under MS/PC-DOS 2.0, UNIX, and Apple's PRO-DOS among others. The number of branches is limited in some operating systems. The branches are called subdirectories. The set of subdirectories from the main directory to the one of interest is called a path.

Controlling Communications Functions The microcomputer communicates with printers, monitors, plotters, and communication devices through ports. Some of the more common ports found on microcomputers are:

1. **Centronics connection,** parallel printer port.
2. RS-232C serial communication and printer port.
3. Disk drive port.
4. Keyboard port.
5. Monochrome monitor (one color) port.
6. RGB (Red-Green-Blue, color) monitor port.
7. RS 422 serial port.
8. IEEE-488 parallel port for laboratory equipment.

Centronics connection:
The name of the standard parallel connector. Centronics was the first printer company to make this connection popular.

One job of the operating system is to control the communication between the CPU and the ports (see Figure 3–3). Before this control can be executed the hardware and software must be configured to operate with the operating system being used. As a user you need not concern yourself with the communication process. For example, when you type on the keyboard, the operating system is controlling the communication from the keyboard to the other parts of the system. Your concern is simply to type the characters correctly on the keyboard.

In MS/PC-DOS and some versions of TRS-DOS the time and date may be entered at the beginning of a session and used by all programs that require such information. Some microcomputer systems have printed circuit boards with clocks and batteries that provide this information automatically.

Housekeeping Functions No matter how careful you are in setting up a microcomputer system, it will require adjustments over time. A new business application will occur that requires a different or improved collection of programs. MS/PC-DOS housekeeping functions such as COPY, and the utility such as DISKCOPY, make it easier to move files to reorganize for the new needs.

FIGURE 3–3
Outlet Ports on Microcomputer

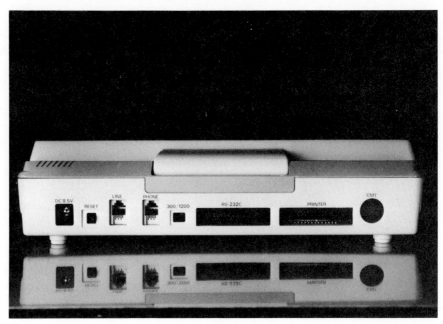

It is also often convenient to erase files that are no longer wanted and to rename files to fit a new pattern. The MS/PC-DOS routine that performs this task is ERASE. During moving, erasing, and renaming, the operating system will keep track of what files are available and where on the diskette they are stored.

Additional Operating System Functions Additional features some operating systems offer include windowing (see Figure 3–4), multi-tasking, and multi-using. Windowing allows you to split the screen into two or more "windows." You may view different combinations of files, parts of files, and different activities. The capability to look at two word processing documents and to transfer text between them may speed the creation of new business documents.

Multi-tasking is the capability of a microcomputer to do more than one task at a time. A business professional can, for example, maintain communications with another computer while creating a document. Information from the second computer may be transferred into the document periodically.

Multi-using gives the microcomputer **timesharing** capabilities for more than one **terminal** to share the same microprocessor. Individuals using these terminals share the microcomputer's microprocessor, data and program files, and peripherals.

Microcomputers may be connected in a LAN, local area network, to share files and peripherals. Networks are important to the business office where a number of individuals must use the same files or the number of peripherals such as printers are limited.

Timesharing:
More than one terminal may be connected to and operated at one time on the same microcomputer.

Terminal:
A computer work station, input/ output device. It may consist of a keyboard and a monitor or be a microcomputer.

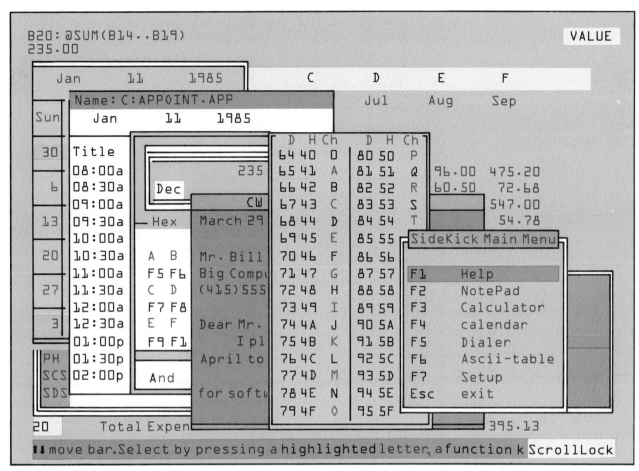

```
B20: @SUM(B14..B19)                                          VALUE
235.00
```

FIGURE 3-4 Operating System Windows with Sidekick

Utilities

Utilities are programs that add to the capabilities of an operating system; they are stored on the disk, not in RAM. Utilities include:

1. Housekeeping Utilities
   a. Preparing diskettes for use (FORMAT).
   b. Making backup copies of programs or data.
2. Additional Utilities
   a. Copying screens, text, and graphics.
   b. Sorting lists.
   c. Determining that printer port is used.
   d. Determining the configuration of the communication performed.

Housekeeping Utilities—FORMAT One utility that must be used each time a new data diskette is created is FORMAT. This utility comes in a variety of names in different operating systems. Formatting is the process by which magnetic markers are placed on a diskette to identify where data are to be stored. These locations are divided into tracks and sectors. One track is identified as the directory track, where the list and location of all files are maintained. The amount of data which can be stored on a diskette is a function of the manner in that it is formatted (organized).

USER WINDOW

The professor set up his new microcomputer on his desk. He checked the instruction book carefully and then selected the word processing program from the collection of programs he had purchased with his computer. He placed a data diskette in the second disk drive.

After typing a short letter he instructed the microcomputer to save it on the diskette in his second disk drive. The program terminated with an error.

Following the instructions in the manual, he repeated the process over and over again, with the same results.

A student walked in who owned a microcomputer. After a short discussion the student asked him, "Did you FORMAT the data diskette?"

As soon as the question was asked the professor knew his problem was that he had not formatted the diskettes.

A little knowledge about the operating system conventions help make the microcomputer work for you.

There are file copy routines, copy routines, and hard disk backup routines available in most operating systems. The file copy routine copies individual files to a formatted diskette. The diskette copy routine copies an entire disk to a second disk. The hard disk backup routine copies the files from a hard disk to one or more floppy diskettes. In MS/PC-DOS the individual file copy routine is a built-in function; the disk copy routine, diskcopy, and the hard disk backup routines are utilities.

When a program is purchased or created, the first task should be to make a copy in case the original is damaged. Some programs are sold **copy protected** with limits on the number of copies that may be made to prevent illegal copying. The producers of these programs often provide a backup service to owners who register their purchases with the sellers.

After a program or data diskette has been copied, we recommend that one copy be stored at a different location.

Copy protected (programs): Programs sold with a limit placed on the number of copies a user may produce.

USER WINDOW

Bill was almost finished with his term report. There was a rainstorm developing outside but he did not notice. He heard thunder. Bill quickly saved the file and made a backup.

Soon there was a complete loss of power. The file in the machine was lost. After the storm the backup copy was used to complete the report.

It is best to shut down when a storm approaches. If you cannot stop, make extra backups and keep the second copy out of the microcomputer.

Making a Backup Diskettes and hard disks fail. Backup copies of diskettes are needed to prevent loss of data and program files. The process of making backup copies varies from system to system. Most failures seem to occur when you do not have a backup. When an individual first purchases a microcomputer, the instructions are to make a backup of the operating system diskette, store the master, and use the backup as the working diskette. The documentation for this task is often poor, misleading, or missing. The user often has no microcomputer knowledge. Sometimes experience and knowledge gained on one system works to the user's disadvantage due to the manner in which the task is performed. In Table 3–5 is a listing of the names of the various functions and utilities used in different operating systems to make diskette backups.

TABLE 3–5   Names of Backup Function or Utility Routines

Apple-DOS	Apple-PRO-DOS	CP/M	MS/PC-DOS	TRS-DOS
COPYA	part of utilities menu	COPY* COPYDISK**	DISKCOPY	BACKUP

*Osborne 1 using CP/M
**Epson QX-10 using CP/M

The backup routine can be started after the system has been loaded and the date and time questions answered as required. You should get in the habit of always placing the master in a specific drive and the new diskette in the other. We recommend that you copy from 1 to 2 on the Apple (internal to external drive using the Apple IIc), 0 to 1 in TRS-DOS, and A to B on CP/M and MS/PC-DOS microcomputers.

Specific routines may be part of the operating system or they may be independent programs. The location varies between systems and versions of systems. Most backup routines are separate utilities. It is usually necessary to have the system diskette in the microcomputer when the utility is called. To illustrate the different methods used in various operating systems to perform various routines the backup routine has been detailed for the Apple DOS, MS/PC-DOS, and TRS-DOS.

Making a Backup on the Apple The Apple microcomputer operating under DOS 3.3 starts the backup process when RUN COPYA<CR> is typed. You must use uppercase only in the Apple. The first screen in the backup process shown in Figure 3–5.

The Apple is designed with eight slots. Each slot is numbered. Slot 6 is the default (expected) location of the disk controller card. Each disk

```
APPLE DISK DUPLICATION PROGRAM

ORIGINAL SLOT:      DEFAULT = 6
```

FIGURE 3–5
Apple Backup

controller card can handle two drives, 1 and 2. You must know how the Apple you are using is set up. To complete the backup process you must follow the instructions on the screen.

Making a Backup Using MS/PC-DOS The DISKCOPY A: B:<CR> instruction in MS/PC-DOS results in the instruction shown in Figure 3–6.

```
Insert source diskette in drive A:
Insert target diskette in drive B:
Strike any key when ready
```

Following these instructions carefully results in a copy of the diskette in drive A being produced on the diskette in drive B.

Making a Backup Using TRS-DOS When using TRS-DOS in the Radio Shack Model III typing the word BACKUP<CR> starts the backup process. Figure 3–7 illustrate the starting screen.

FIGURE 3–7
TRS-DOS Backup

```
TRSDOS Model III Backup Utility Ver 1.3

SOURCE Drive Number?
```

The source drive may be identified as 0. The next question requires you to identify the destination drive, which may be 0 or 1. In this operating system each diskette must be assigned a password. You must know the password of the source disk to complete the backup process.

Additional Utilities Almost any program may be added as a utility in a given operating system. A utility added to MS/PC-DOS is SORT. This utility sorts lists rapidly. It may be used by business professionals to alphabetize the directory of files on a diskette.

Normally the IBM PC uses a parallel printer. If a serial printer is used, the MODE utility is available to tell the microcomputer about the change in printers. This same utility is also used to tell the microcomputer what communication settings to use to communicate with this serial printer.

Communication Conventions

There are four instances in which conventions are used to communicate:

1. From microcomputer to business professional.
2. From business professional to microcomputer.
3. Between microcomputers.
4. From microcomputer to peripherals.

Communication requires conventions for the two partners to understand each other. As a professional user you must learn what is expected by the microcomputer when certain messages appear on the screen.

From Microcomputer to Business Professional Among the communication conventions from the microcomputer to the business user are:

1. <CR> or an arrow that starts down and then turns left: Means press the carriage return or enter key.
2. Usually ∧n means to press the control or Ctrl key while simultaneously pressing the other key (n). C is the break instruction in some operating systems.
3. Esc means to press the escape key or to send the code number 27 to a device.
4. Filename refers to the name of a data or program file. Filespec refers to the disk drive where the file is located, a colon, the path (if any), the filename, a decimal point, and an extender. A path is needed on hard disks that are divided into sub-directories. See Figure 3–8.
5. .BAK as the extender on a filename means the file is a backup file.
6. .COM as the extender on a filename means the file is a command file. It is usually run by typing its name and pressing <CR>.
7. .BAS as the extender on a filename means the file is a BASIC program file.

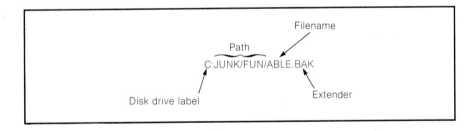

**FIGURE 3–8
Sample Filespec**

From Business Professional to Microcomputer Included in the communication conventions from the business professional to the microcomputer are:

1. The filename must fit the limitations of the operating system. Some accept blanks, most do not. Some do not limit characters such as, others do.
2. Most systems start on the default or logged disk drive. Drives are identified as A, B, C, ... or 0, 1, 2, ... or Slot 6-drive 1, Slot 6-drive 2. Each operating system has a convention.
3. When entering values into the microcomputer most programs do not allow the use of commas in numbers. The number 1,000 must be entered 1000<CR>.
4. When using word processors a carriage return is needed at the end

of a paragraph. If you enter one on each line the program usually will not work as expected.

5. To make the program expand beyond the end of file. There is a special code at the end of each file, called an end of file marker (EOF). In a word processing file it is usually necessary to press the enter key. The down arrow will not work to expand a word processing file.

Between Microcomputers There are a number of communication conventions used by microcomputers to communicate with each other. The American Standard Code for Information Interchange, **ASCII,** is often part of the convention. In ASCII, numbers are used to represent a set of fixed characters. For example, capital Z is represented by the number 90, while the lowercase z is represented by 122. As far as the microcomputer is concerned, it records the numbers 90 and 122 as **binary numbers,** not uppercase and lowercase.

Microcomputers save program and data files in special binary code (machine language) and in ASCII. Most **binary files** are specific to a microprocessor and an operating system. ASCII files may be transferred between microcomputers.

From Microcomputer to Peripherals The communication of data from microcomputer to printer, printer plotters, and most other peripherals uses the same ASCII code that is used for communication between microcomputers. This is why a printer may be operated by many different microcomputers.

MICROCOMPUTER FAMILIES

The combination of microprocessor and operating system forms the basis for microcomputer families. The six popular operating systems or microcomputer families, are:

1. Apple DOS and PRO-DOS
2. Apple Macintosh DOS
3. CP/M
4. MS/PC-DOS
5. TRS-DOS
6. UNIX.

Operating systems are created for a specific microprocessor. They are a series of programs usually written in the basic **instruction set** of the microprocessor.

Each family is built on a different microprocessor, hardware system, and operating system. The general rule is that families are compatible. Families can:

1. Use the same machine language programs.
2. Use the same high level language programs.
3. Use the same data files.

ASCII:
American Standard Code for Information Interchange. ASCII is a seven-bit binary code. Numbers from 00 to 127 can be produced with a seven bit binary number. The decimal number 90 is 1011010. Each number in ASCII stands for a character or control instruction.

Binary number:
A number consisting of 0 and 1. Each 0 or 1 is a bit. The decimal numbers 0 to 126 require 7 bits. To add the decimal numbers 127 to 255 requires the 8th bit.

Binary file:
Programs stored in machine language form. A binary file may be directly executed by the microcomputer.

Instruction set:
Instructions built into the computer. The instruction set is contained in the microprocessor.

TABLE 3–6
Use of ASCII Files

Type of File	Percentage of Programs That Produce ASCII files
Word processing files	90%
Electronic spreadsheets	90%
Data base	70%
Graphics (data files)	60%
picture files	10%
Communication	100%
Special application programs	80%

The MS/PC-DOS family can read, write, and format the same diskettes.

In general, the only method of transfer between families is by use of ASCII files. The data files that may be saved in ASCII and our estimates of the percentage that can be saved in this manner are shown in Table 3–6.

Table 3–7 identifies six popular microcomputer families and the microprocessor upon which they are built.

TABLE 3–7   Microprocessor and Operating Systems

	Apple/DOS	Macintosh	CP/M	MS/PC-DOS	TRS-DOS*	UNIX **
6502	X					
8088				X		X
68000		X			X	X
Z80			X		X	

*Tandy Radio Shack uses TRS-DOS for operating systems built on a number of different microprocessors.

**UNIX is the exception. This operating system is written in the C programming language, and will run on most systems when the C language is available.

The methods of transferring files between families include:

1. Communication over cables and telephone lines.
2. Use of special programs to read different diskette formats.
3. The purchase of special printed circuit boards, pc-boards, that give a microcomputer in one family the capabilities of some other family.

The addition of special pc-boards is the only current method of using machine language programs from one family in another family. High-level programs, such as BASIC programs, may sometimes be transferred by converting to ASCII and then corrected to work in the second family.

There are many versions of each operating system. An operating system is like a language; it is alive and constantly growing and improving. As the capabilities of hardware improve, operating system programs are usually rewritten to take advantage of these enhancements. If an operating system stops improving, it will soon fall by the wayside since newer and better systems will take its place. New operating systems generally maintain the capability to do what the older systems do, i.e., they are downward compatible. The older system generally cannot have the newer capabilities added, as the systems are not upward compatible.

Apple DOS and PRO-DOS

The Apple family started with the Apple I and has progressed to the Apple II, II+, IIe, and IIc. All use the 6502 microprocessor family, including the Apple IIc, which is a portable and uses the 65C02 chip. The Apple operating system has developed through a number of versions. The most current versions are Apple DOS 3.3 and PRO-DOS, that operate on the Apple II+, IIe, and IIc. This long history has resulted in a large collection of programs available for Apple microcomputers.

Menu:
A list of microcomputer actions displayed on the screen from which the user selects the one wanted.

Apple PRO-DOS is easier for the beginner to use because it is **menu** driven and the user does not have to remember how to perform specific functions. The PRO-DOS design and its hierarchical file structure are ideal for hard disk drives.

Many of the Apple disk operating instructions use unique words. For example, CATALOG<CR> or CAT<CR> calls up the directory of an Apple disk. DIR<CR> is used by most other systems for the same or similar instruction.

Apple Macintosh DOS

The Apple Macintosh uses the Motorola 68000 microprocessor and has its own operating system. The Motorola 68000 is a 32-bit microprocessor with 16-bit I/O **buses.** The operating system of the Macintosh is visual. It is built around the use of a mouse that moves the cursor for menu selection. The system set a new standard in graphics capabilities that is being copied by special program developers for other systems.

Bus:
Pathway or channel for data and instructions between hardware devices.

The power of the Macintosh operating system is also one of its limitations. The operating system forces all program developers to use the visual approach rather than allowing the developer to create options for the user.

The Macintosh uses three and one-half inch disk drives. Without the addition of special hardware and software, diskettes from other microcomputers cannot be read. Programs and data files are best transferred using communication procedures or as part of a network.

CP/M—Control Program/Microcomputer

CP/M is the defacto standard operating system for eight-bit microcomputers based on the 8080, 8085, and Z80 microprocessors. There are versions of CP/M for sixteen-bit microcomputers such as CP/M-86, Concurrent CP/M, and MPM-86.

The eight-bit version of CP/M was designed with a few built-in functions and many separate utilities. This allows for a greater amount of RAM for application programs and data because the operating system needs only a small amount of RAM. You must learn the name of each utility and call it up directly from the disk's menu. The separate utilities include:

- ASM : Used to create a machine language file from assembly language code.
- DDT : Used to **debug** an assembly language program.
- ED : Used to edit a file.
- LOAD : Converts **Hex** files to COM files.
- MOVECPM: Used to relocate the system to make room for special programs.
- PIP : Peripheral Interchange Program used to transfer a file from one diskette to a second.
- STAT: Used to check the status (how much memory is used for each file, the types of files, and how much memory is available for additional use) of disks and system.
- SYSGEN: System Generator used to generate a CP/M operating system on a new diskette.

Debug:
To remove errors from a program.

Hex:
Hexadecimal. A Hex file is a file stored using numbers based on 16 digits.

The utilities most business users must learn about, such as STAT, PIP, and SYSGEN, are needed in many different business applications. Some of the advantages of CP/M for the experienced user are:

1. It is found on many microcomputers.
2. It is easy to switch from one CP/M machine to another.
3. Overlays using menus are available for the new user.
4. There are many business special application programs available to work under CP/M.

Microsoft Disk Operating System (MS/PC-DOS)

Microsoft, an independent software company, developed PC DOS, the operating system of the IBM PC, under contract with IBM. Microsoft also produces and markets MS-DOS, an operating system similar to PC-DOS, for independent manufacturers.

Some of the advantages of MS/PC-DOS are:

1. Standard disk format making data file transfer easy.
2. Large number of programs available.
3. Growing number of users meaning a continuous growth of program availability.
4. It is easy to switch from one MS/PC-DOS machine to another.
5. Overlays using menus are available for the new user.

Independent manufacturers produce machines that are either close to the IBM PC for compatibility or have better speed, resolution, and other features. In putting a business system together involving several microcomputers, you must balance the compatibility factor with the increase in capabilities of these independently produced microcomputers.

The dominance of IBM in the microcomputer market has resulted in the MS/PC-DOS operating system becoming the de facto standard for

16-bit systems. The original version was PC-DOS 1.0, designed for the IBM PC with single-sided 160K disk drives. Each additional version of MS/PC-DOS was developed to add capabilities. The most important reason for PC-DOS 1.1 was to handle 320K double sided disk drives. PC-DOS 2.0 was developed to handle 360K double sided disk drives and hard disks. PC-DOS 2.1 was developed to handle the extra peripherals of the IBM PC Jr. PC-DOS 3.0 and 3.1 were developed to handle the additional capabilities of the IBM PC/AT such as multi-using, mult-tasking, and high capacity disk drives.

Tandy Radio Shack [TRS-DOS]

Tandy/Radio Shack markets an array of microcomputers using a variety of microprocessors. With the exception of its TRS-80 Model 1000, 1200, and 2000 using MS-DOS, and its Model 6000 using Xenix (Microsoft adaptation of UNIX), all its microcomputers use the name TRS-DOS for the operating system.

The microcomputer models upon which "TRS-DOS" is used include:

Microprocessor	Model
Z80	4 (Also uses CP/M)
Z80/68000	12
Z80/68000	6000 (Also uses XENIX)
6809	Color Computer
80C85	100
80C85	200

Diskette storage capacity of Tandy's computers starts at 50,000 and goes to over 1 million bytes. The capability varies by operating system release and model of microcomputer. It is often difficult to move data and programs between different models.

UNIX

Bell Laboratories developed UNIX in 1970 in assembly language and then redeveloped it in the C language. UNIX will work on most microcomputers that have the C language available. When a new microcomputer is developed, UNIX can be added easily when the C language becomes available.

In 1973, UNIX was distributed to many universities, nonprofit organizations, and government entities for use of larger computers. Many programming utilities and features were developed for UNIX by these groups. These utilities and features include:

1. Hierarchical file system for the control of files.
2. Multi-tasking.
3. Windowing.
4. Multi-using.

5. Enhanced communication capabilities.

6. Good programming environment.

UNIX is expected to continue to be a leader in innovative ideas and concepts. It led the way in the development of many features now found in other operating systems.

SUMMARY

You have learned why knowledge of the operating system is important to the business professional. You have learned about the tasks of the operating system. You have learned to identify some of the more popular operating systems, and you have seen how some of the capabilities are used. You have learned that:

1. An operating system is the program that controls the parts of the microcomputer system so they all work together.

2. The business professional uses the operating system to control the microcomputer when solving business problems.

3. The operating system controls and coordinates the parts of a microcomputer system so they work together as a system.

4. The functions built into the operating system provide capabilities that the business professional will need often.

5. Utilities are programs that add to the capabilities of an operating system.

6. Some of the communication conventions are:
   a. From microcomputer to business professional.
   b. From business professional to microcomputer.
   c. Between microcomputers.
   d. From microcomputer to peripherals.

7. The combination of microprocessor and operating system forms the basis for microcomputer families.

KEY TERMS

Backup	Functions
Default drive	Logged drive
Families	Operating System (OS and DOS)
File	Routine
FORMAT	Utilities

REVIEW QUESTIONS

1. What is the prime function of an operating system and what does it consist of?

2. What is the difference between functions, routines, and utilities?

3. What is a file? What is stored in a file?

4. Identify and explain five routines commonly available in operating systems.

5. Name the six popular operating system families. What are the characteristics of a microcomputer family?

6. Why must the business professional know about operating systems?

7. What routines are commonly included as operating system functions?

8. What are the two methods of starting a microcomputer?

9. How does knowledge of what an individual does when saving a file on a cassette recorder help you understand what a microcomputer does when recording files on diskettes?

10. What is a hierarchical file? Why is the organization of this type of file compared to a tree?

11. What is the instruction to examine the directory of the diskette in the default or logged disk drive?

12. What communications are controlled by the operating system?

13. What is done to a diskette when it is formatted by the operating system?

14. Why should backup copies of diskettes be made?

15. What is the backup utility called on the Apple, CP/M, MS/PC-DOS, and TRS-DOS systems?

16. Name the four instances in which conventions are required in microcomputer communications.

17. Identify some of the communication conventions you must know as a business user when communicating with a microcomputer and its operating system.

18. What is a code? What is ASCII? What is the difference between lowercase letters and uppercase letters in ASCII?

19. In what ways might you generally expect compatibility within a family?

20. What are the three methods of transferring files between microcomputer families?

21. What is the de facto standard operating system for eight-bit microcomputers?

22. What are some of the advantages of CP/M for the experienced user?

23. What are some of the advantages of MS/PC-DOS?

24. When did universities get involved with UNIX, and what was their contribution?

25. Identify some of the special features developed for UNIX.

1. Get a microcomputer magazine out of the library or from your local bookstore with an article on disk operating systems. Prepare a short discussion of the material in the article.

2. Survey organizations (business, academic offices, government) and identify the type of microcomputer and the operating system in use. Why do you think the hardware and operating system was selected?

3. Interview a faculty member or other microcomputer user who is an advocate of a particular operating system and summarize his/her views.

4. From a recent issue of a microcomputer magazine, identify current developments in operating systems and their meanings for the business user.

5. From material in the chapter and your library, review the operating systems currently in use and their features. Prepare a forecast of future developments in operating systems.

1. This set of assignments is to get you started.
   a. Make a backup (DISKCOPY) of the diskette.
   b. Examine the directory of the diskette and if possible, type a copy of the directory.
   c. Identify the routines performed by three of the utilities or programs listed in the directory.

2. Use the FORMAT command to prepare a diskette for use.

3. Use your operating system to copy a disk file from one diskette to another.

4. Use the TYPE instruction in MS/PC-DOS and CP/M to examine the contents of individual files. Which files are ASCII, which are not?

5. The following is a list of MS/PC-DOS utilities. Use them or their substitutes in the operating system available:
   a. SORT
   b. CHKDSK
   c. MODE
   d. TREE

Explain the tasks performed by each of these routines.

SELECTED
REFERENCES

Caggiano, Joseph. *The Easy Guide to Your Macintosh*. Sybex Books, 1984.

Chertok, Barbara Lee. *IBM PC Owner's Manual*. Prentice-Hall, 1983.

DeVoney, Chris. *MS-DOS User's Guide*. Que Corporation, 1983.

DeVoney, Chris. *PC DOS User's Guide*. Que Corporation, 1983.

King, Richard Allen. *The IBM PC DOS Handbook*. Sybex Books, 1984.

McGilton, Henry, and Rachel Morgan. *Introducing the UNIX System*. A Byte Book, McGraw-Hill Book Company, 1983.

Miller, David. *Apple ProDOS Data Files*. Prentice-Hall Books, 1984.

Murtha, Stephen, and Mitchell Waite. *CP/M Primer*. Howard W. Sams & Co., Inc., 1980.

Operating Manuals for Apple, CP/M (Osborne 1 and Espon QX-10), MS-DOS and PC-DOS, TRS-DOS, and UNIX V.

Sippi, Charles, and Roger Sippi. *Computer Dictionary*. Howard W. Sams & Co., Inc., 1982.

Thomas, Ph.D., Rebecca. and Jean Yates. *A User Guide to the UNIX System*. Osborne/McGraw-Hill, 1982.

Zimmerman, Steven M., Leo M. Conrad, and Larry J. Goldstein. *Osborne User's Guide*. Robert J. Brady Co., 1983.

Chapter Outline

Chapter Goals

Upon completion of this chapter you will be able to:

Understand why word processing is valuable to the business professional.

Define the tasks that may be performed with a microcomputer word processing program.

Identify some commercial word processing programs.

Understand why word processing programs are easy to use.

WORD PROCESSING

Doug Houston Real Estate

Doug Houston Real Estate is a two person real estate office consisting of one broker and one agent. The agency's business is primarily concerned with the sale of commercial investment property, including hotels, motels, apartments, and large tracts of land for development.

When evaluating the feasibility of starting the business the two associates identified their principal activities:

1. Contacting potential sellers and "listing" properties.
2. Developing "packages" describing the financial picture (market and income analysis), physical location, and values of similar properties.
3. Contacting potential buyers and presenting the properties for consideration.
4. Closing the sale. Aiding in handling the closing details.
5. Organizing and managing investment groups for the purchase and operation of investment properties.
6. Operating and managing investment properties.

They expected that most of the associates's time would be spent communicating with buyers and sellers. This communication would take the form of phone calls and letters.

They determined that a microcomputer could aid in producing letters, customer data collection, analysis, and electronic mail.

Word processing:
The creation, storage and retrieval, and printing of text files.

Text file:
A computer file that contains words and characters. Such files are commonly created during word processing.

Text:
Characters found on paper, on the screen, or stored in a microcomputer text file. Text may be a letter or a manuscript length book.

The microcomputer may be used as a word processor. **Word processing programs** can create/edit, save, recall, and print word processing **text files.** The business user can start a document, save it, and then return to complete it at some future time.

Word processing is the creation of quality documents for professional or other purposes. Electronic word processing is the creation of documents on a microcomputer, using a word processing program. Basic word processing program features include:

1. Creating the **text** file.
2. Editing the text file.
3. Saving and recalling the text file.
4. Printing the text file.

Additional features found in some word processors include:

1. Special printing effects.
   a. Boldfacing.
   b. Additional fonts such as italics.
   c. Proportional spacing
2. Document assembly from files with pre-written text.
3. Print spoolers.
4. Windows.

Commonly found add-on utility programs include:

1. Spelling checkers.
2. Merge print for mass mailing.

3. Table of contents generators.
4. Index generators.
5. Footnote programs.
6. Style checkers.

WORD PROCESSING HARDWARE

Word processing requires a microcomputer, a word processing program, and a printer. The minimum hardware requirements include:

1. Enough RAM to support the word processing program.
2. Input device such as a keyboard.
3. A monitor upon which to edit.
4. A printer that can produce output of the desired quality.
5. A storage device such as disk drives or memory, which retains text when the microcomputer is turned off.

RAM Needs

The amount of RAM needed for a particular word processing program depends on how the program is written and upon the operating system of the microcomputer. You will find some word processors operating under CP/M in 64K, which requires 128K in MS-DOS due to additional features.

Input Device—Keyboard

All microcomputers have some type of input device. The one most often used for word processing is the keyboard. Other devices, such as optical character readers and voice recognition devices are available.

Monitor

The two types of monitors are: monochrome monitors green, amber, yellow, or black and white; color monitors-composite or RGB (red, green, and blue).

Some monitors produce higher quality characters than others. Some monitors designed for graphics will not produce as sharp a letter as a monitor designed for text. Color monitors often produce a poorer quality letter than black-white, amber, and green screen monitors. Generally, you get what you pay for in monitors. High-resolution color monitors are available at additional cost.

For word processing, the standard monitor produces 80 characters across, and either 24 or 25 lines down. A full page of text is 66 lines in length. Some microcomputer monitors are capable of handling 66 lines, allowing the user to see the entire page at once.

Most word processors work with all combinations of color or monochrome monitors, but in a different manner. Many word processors display underlining and boldface type correctly on one or the other configuration, some display the output correctly on both. If you want to take advantage of all the features of a word processor, you must make sure you have the correct configuration.

Printers

A word processing microcomputer must be able to control a printer. This is done through ports. Printers are available for both parallel and serial ports.

MICROS IN ACTION

Doug Houston Real Estate found that they needed two printers: a high speed dot matrix printer for drafts and graphics and a letter quality printer to produce letters that matched the output of a typewriter.

They found that they needed a draft of almost every letter created. The time needed to produce this draft was kept to a minimum by a 200-character-per-second dot matrix printer. They used a cloth ribbon that had a long life and could be used many times.

Once the letter had been completed, they used a slow-speed, low-cost letter quality printer that operated at 18 characters per second. A single-strike carbon ribbon was used to achieve a high-quality letter.

All types of printers may be used for word processing. The most commonly used printers include letter quality printers and dot matrix (see Figure 4–1). The letter quality printer produces a document in the same manner as a typewriter, and is limited only by the daisy wheel, ball, or thimble **fonts** available. Printers that produce characters from dots or in a similar manner come with many features that make it possible to produce special effects (see Figure 4–2):

Font:
A style of letter or character such as Italic, Courier, or Prestige.

1. Enhanced (large) print.
2. Compressed or condensed print.
3. Special fonts (italic, scientific, Greek).
4. Underlining.
5. Bold and near letter quality letters.
6. Subscript and superscript.
7. Graphics.

FIGURE 4–1 Dot Matrix versus Letter Quality Letters

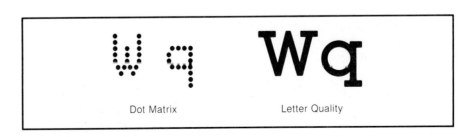

Dot Matrix   Letter Quality

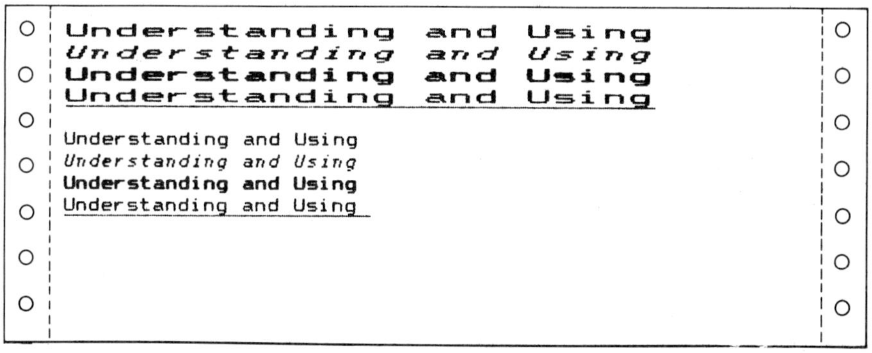

```
┌─────────────────────────────────────────────┐
│ ○   Understanding  and  Using           ○    │
│ ○   Understanding  and  Using           ○    │
│ ○   Understanding  and  Using           ○    │
│     Understanding  and  Using                │
│ ○                                       ○    │
│     Understanding and Using                  │
│ ○   Understanding and Using             ○    │
│     Understanding and Using                  │
│ ○   Understanding and Using             ○    │
│                                              │
│ ○                                       ○    │
│                                              │
│ ○                                       ○    │
└─────────────────────────────────────────────┘
```

FIGURE 4–2 Dot Matrix Output—Special Effects

To obtain all the features available in a printer it must be matched (configured) with the word processor so that the proper codes are sent between the microcomputer and printer. Some word processors have special menu-driven routines that make configuration easy.

Storage Devices

Word processing requires a method of saving text. Any of the devices discussed in chapter 2 may be used. The most common configuration is a two disk drive system or one disk drive and a hard disk.

WHY THE BUSINESS PROFESSIONAL SHOULD KNOW ABOUT WORD PROCESSING

Word processors are valuable tools for the business user. Professionals who do their own typing and those who use secretaries can profit from word processing programs. Those who use the word processor themselves receive direct benefits.

The amount of time needed to produce an individual letter becomes important as the number of letters created becomes large. Some business professionals spend over half their time producing letters. Microcomputer word processing reduces the amount of time between creation and production of a printed document.

A completed document with an error, an excessive amount of correction fluid, or any other mark of poor quality makes a negative impression on a business contact. Word processing helps produce quality documents by allowing screen editing for easy correction of errors and by creating hard copies quickly without introducing new errors that might need correction fluid.

┌───┐
│ ███ USER WINDOW ███   │
│   │
│   Have you ever done this?   │
│   After working on the term paper for two weeks, the final │
│   typed copy is read and two misspelled words are found. The │
│   decision is made to "live with it" because the time and   │
│   effort required to make the corrections are just not worth │
│   it.   │
└───┘

Many business professionals have some typing training but are not expert typists. Professionals with marginal typing skills may take over the entire typing and letter creation process and produce quality documents exactly the way they are wanted.

MICROS IN ACTION

Both the broker and agent in the Doug Houston Real Estate office had marginal typing skills. To take advantage of these skills a microcomputer with a word processing program was purchased. An outside trainer was hired and both broker and agent learned to use the equipment and program. They found they could produce quality letters, proposals, contracts, and other documents.

Microcomputer word processing programs commonly cost between $39 and $700. Most microcomputers are equipped to handle word processing with no additional costs for hardware other than a printer. A printer capable of producing the type of output wanted is often the only additional expense other than the word processing program.

For the professional who has typing assistance, the word processor makes things easier, faster, and improves the document quality. The use of microcomputer word processing changes the skills needed by the secretary typist from speed and accuracy on the keyboard to knowledge in the use of the microcomputer and its programs. The secretary may increase his or her output in the same manner as the professional who directly uses the microcomputer and its word processor.

A document needs to be proofread once, and then only the changes need be proofed as they are made. Errors may be introduced during editing, but this is rare. No new errors are introduced with the printing of the revised document. The time to prepare the first copy of a document may not be significantly reduced with word processing, but if a second or third draft is needed, the word processor can turn them out with ease.

The advantage of microcomputer word processing over a typewriter depends on:

1. The microcomputer system.
2. The specific typewriter.
3. The skill of the user of alternate equipment.

The advantage to the user of the IBM PC type microcomputer with a word processing program over an electric typewriter include:

1. The availability of screen editing.
   a. The ability to overwrite, insert, and delete.
   b. The ability to reformat and control the margins without retyping.
   c. The ability to make global changes and search for strings.
   d. The ability to make block moves of text.
   e. The ability to send the printer special instructions.

2. The ability to save and recall for later edit.
3. The ability to produce a hard copy with a few key strokes.
4. The ability to use the add-on utility programs.

When similar letters are being prepared, the word processor makes the job easier:

1. The original letter is copied under a new filename.
2. The word processor is used to edit the new letter for the next addressee.
3. With a few keystrokes, the word processor is instructed to print the letter on the printer.

On a typewriter each letter would have to be completely retyped.

WORD PROCESSING FEATURES

The features of word processing programs make text creation easy. Word processing program features may be classified into five groups:

1. General features.
2. Text creating and editing features.
3. Saving and recalling the text file features.
4. Printing the text file features.

General Features

There are some general features found in most word processing programs. They include:

1. Menu driven versus function keys.
2. Conventions.
3. Type of file backup.
4. Types of printer control.
5. Disk or RAM based.

Menu Versus Function Keys Most word processors on MS/PC-DOS microcomputers use the **function keys** to send special instructions from the user to the microcomputer. On the IBM PC the function keys are located on the left side of the keyboard. In CP/M, the control key in combination with keyboard numbers on the top or side of the microcomputer is often used as a function key. In WordStar, the "begin underline" instruction may be sent by pressing Ctrl P (P) and then Ctrl S (S). On the IBM PC in WordStar the underline instruction is sent by pressing function key F5. A function key may be used to move to the beginning of a text file, mark the ends of a **block,** mark the beginning and ending of underlining and bold facing, and to perform other special tasks saving keystrokes.

Generally, function keys are used in combination with the on-screen

Function key:
Keys found on the left side of the IBM PC keyboard, or the top of some look-alikes that send custom instructions to the microcomputer. In some programs the user may define the instructions sent by the function keys.

Block:
A collection of characters with beginning and ending markers that must be entered by the user.

menu. A menu is a selection of different actions that may be taken. For example, in pfs:WRITE, you will see the menu shown in Figure 4–3 on the screen.

This menu allows you to choose whether you want to begin to edit your document, to define the formats used to produce the page, to print the current file, to read a text file from disk or save or remove, to clear the text from the memory of your computer, or to exit the system.

In pfs:WRITE, function keys F1 and F10 have several uses. Pressing F1 at any time will result in a "HELP" appearing on the screen. Help menus and aids are available in many programs. They are screen explanations that may be called up by the user when needed to aid in learning or remembering how some task is performed. Careful reading of screen instructions and use of the help menus often make using programs easier.

Conventions Word processing programs, as a group, have a number of conventions that are usually followed. Three common ones are:

1. <CR> should not be used at the end of each line.
2. The control key "∧" is used in combination with other keys to perform special functions.
3. The Esc key is used for special printer instructions.

Do Not Press <CR> Each Line You should not press the carriage return at the end of each line due to word warp. **Word wrap** occurs in most word processing programs automatically when the text reaches the end of a line. The last word is moved to the next line when there is no more

Word wrap:
The moving of the last word in a line to the next line when there is no room between margins.

FIGURE 4–3 Word Processing Menu

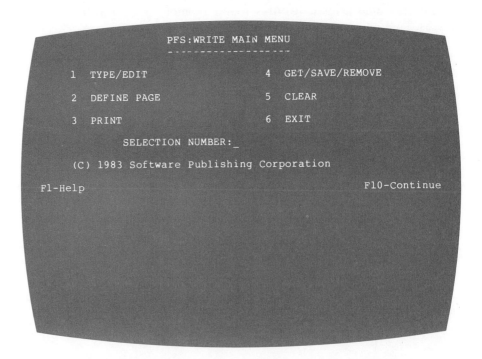

```
                    PFS:WRITE MAIN MENU
                    - - - - - - - - - - - - - - - - - -


         1   TYPE/EDIT              4   GET/SAVE/REMOVE

         2   DEFINE PAGE            5   CLEAR

         3   PRINT                  6   EXIT

                 SELECTION NUMBER:_

         (C) 1983 Software Publishing Corporation

     F1-Help                                        F10-Continue
```

room on that line, according to the margins you have specified. You may overrule the automatic word wrap by entering a <CR> at the end of a line.

The Control Key Microcomputer keyboards have a limited number of keys. Each key sends a number to the computer. These numbers instruct the microcomputer to perform specific functions. Some special functions require numbers that can be produced only with a combination of the control key and some other key being pressed at the same time. For example, the number 26 is produced by pressing ^Z. It is used to signify the end of file in some systems. Most programs insulate the user from such details by entering such end of file markers automatically.

The Esc Key The Esc key creates the number 27. Often, combinations of numbers such as 27,21 are sent to printers to give them special instructions. The 27,21 combination, when sent to a Radio Shack Daisy Wheel II printer, tells it to line feed as needed by an IBM PC type microcomputer. The 27,21 codes must be sent to the printer each time it is turned on. These codes may be sent by a special program and by many word processing programs. These numbers are referred to as codes.

Type of File Backup Some word processors add the extender .BAK to the old copy of the text file for backup purposes, while the current working text file is saved under the original name.

We recommend that you use the disk utilities to make a copy of your diskette periodically. A copy on two physically separate diskettes is better than two copies on the same diskette.

Types of Printer Control Word processors may be classified into two types. The first type is on screen formatting and is often referred to as:

"What you see is what you get."

Word processors of this type allow you to create text on the monitor that is then copied "exactly" to the printer. There are no word processors that do this job completely, although some come very close. Word processing programs of this type include:

- pfs:WRITE
- Microsoft Word
- WordStar

The match between what you see on the monitor and what is produced on a printer is not perfect, because the capabilities are not matched. Printers can handle superscripts and subscripts, compressed and expanded print. At present, monitors cannot handle all these capabilities.

Originally, word processors could boldface or underline on the printer but not on the monitor. Many of the newer word processors can perform these tasks on the screen. Some word processors are near to the goal of producing on the screen what is printed on the printer. As the number of pixels (dots) available on the monitor increases, the goal comes closer. The monitor and printer capabilities must be matched.

The second type of word processor is off screen formatting called:

"Embedded printer commands."

Word processors of this type include:

- Electric Pencil
- Volkswriter.

These programs make it easy for you to type text into the word processor in an efficient manner. Printer instructions are embedded into the text. For example, a special character such as a dot, semicolon, or ">" is placed in the first position on a line. Following the special character is an instruction, such as "LS = 2". This means to switch to double spacing when the text is printed.

As in many real-life situations, most word processors do not necessarily fit into one or the other classification but both on and off screen formatting.

Disk or RAM Based

Word processing programs may be designed to be:

1. Program and text all in RAM.
2. Program in RAM, text recalled from disk as needed.
3. Parts of program stored on disk recalled as needed, text in RAM.
4. Parts of program stored on disk recalled as needed, text recalled from disk as needed.

Generally, the greater the parts of the program and text in RAM, the greater the speed of the program. The capacity of RAM based programs is limited by the amount of RAM, while the capacity of disk based programs/text is limited by the amount of on-line storage. The difference in performance of word processing program design has been reduced as speed, RAM capacity, and on-line storage capacity of microcomputers have increased.

Text Creating and Editing Features

The text creating and editing features are what make the word processor valuable to the business user. These features include:

1. The capability to overwrite, insert, and delete.
2. The capability to reformat and control the margins without retyping.
3. The capability to make global changes and search for strings.
4. The capability to make block moves of text.
5. Rulers.
6. Headers and footers.
7. Page numbering and page breaks.
8. Soft hyphen.

Text editors are programs that allow you to enter text (create) easily. Thereafter, characters, words, or complete paragraphs may be inserted or deleted anywhere in the text file. You can make changes with ease, and you can see the changes as they are made on the monitor.

The microcomputer monitor is an ideal place to accomplish the editing task. Most word processors allow for full-screen editing. This means you may move the **cursor** to any location on the monitor and make whatever changes, additions, or corrections needed. You may **scroll** through a document (text file), looking at it over and over again.

One advantage of electronic editing is that, once you have entered the text, you do not need to type the material a second or third time. You enter the text once, and save it as a text file on a computer storage media.

The Capability to Overwrite, Insert, and Delete A word processor may be in the overwrite or insert modes. Some word processors control the shape or size of the cursor, to let you know which mode they are in, while others will display the words INSERT ON.

Overwrite means the word you are entering replaces the text that was formerly at the location of the cursor. **Insert** means that when a word is typed into existing text, the text following it is moved to the right to make room.

Figure 4–4 shows a word processing screen in overwrite mode, with the cursor located at the beginning of the word "displayed". The words "OVERWRITE ON" in the upper right part of the screen often do not appear. The absence of any words means the overwrite mode is on.

Starting with Figure 4–4 the words "We are now overwriting" are typed. Figure 4–5 indicates the results.

Many IBM PC word processors use the "Ins" key, found in the lower part of the numeric keypad, to switch between insert and overwrite mode. It is next to the "Del" key, which is used to **delete** unwanted letters by many word processors. In some word processors, pressing the

Text editor:
Software that makes creating, changing, storing, and retrieving of text in a file possible.

Cursor:
A symbol on the monitor that indicates where text will be typed. The cursor is often a line (_) or a box. It may be steady or blinking.

Scroll:
Text is moved up or down to display text that cannot be shown on the monitor at one time.

Overwrite:
When a character is typed, it replaces the character formerly at the location of the cursor.

Insert:
When a word is typed into existing text, the text that follows it moves over to make room.

Delete:
An instruction to remove a character, block, or file. When characters are removed, the text closes up.

FIGURE 4–4 Diskette
Misspelled

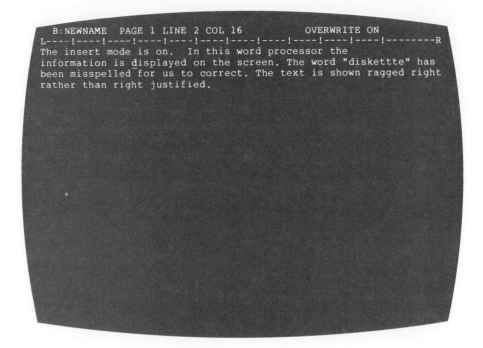

```
B:NEWNAME   PAGE 1 LINE 2 COL 16              OVERWRITE ON
L----!----!----!----!----!----!----!----!----!----!--------R
The insert mode is on.  In this word processor the
information is displayed on the screen. The word "diskettte" has
been misspelled for us to correct. The text is shown ragged right
rather than right justified.
```

Del key will delete the character to the left of the cursor, rather than the one at the place where the cursor is located. The use of special keys such as Ins and Del are program specific.

FIGURE 4–5 Overwriting
in Word Processing

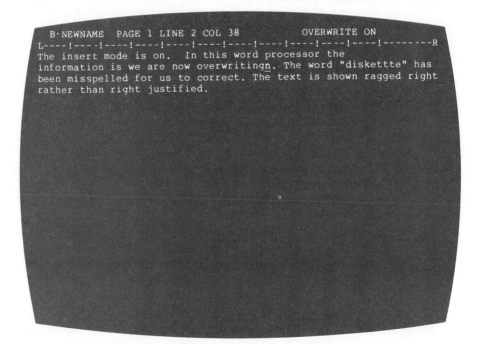

```
B·NEWNAME   PAGE 1 LINE 2 COL 38              OVERWRITE ON
L----!----.!----!----!----!----!----!----!----!----!--------R
The insert mode is on.  In this word processor the
information is we are now overwritingn.. The word "diskettte" has
been misspelled for us to correct. The text is shown ragged right
rather than right justified.
```

Changing from the overwrite mode to the insert mode results in Figure 4–6.

If the words "WE ARE NOW INSERTING" are typed, the screen will change to Figure 4–7.

The plus + sign in line two of Figure 4–7 indicates that the line flows off the screen because of the newly inserted material. The text is not lost; reformatting puts the text back on the screen between existing margins. Some word processors do this while others will push all the material down as shown in Figure 4–8.

Figure 4–9 shows a word processing screen with some text, with the cursor located in the upper-left position and the insert mode on.

One way to correct the misspelling in Figure 4–9 is with the use of the Del key. Figure 4–10 shows the cursor located under one of the letters "t" that must be removed.

After the delete instruction is given the screen changes to that shown in Figure 4–11.

Word processors operating in microcomputers without special keys, such as Del and Ins, use the control key with combinations of other keys to perform the same tasks. The availability of special keys makes the use of word processing programs a little easier.

The Capability to Reformat and Control the Margins without Retyping
The word processor is capable of controlling margins with the press of a button. It can then line up the text on both margins, if desired. When text is lined up evenly on the right margin it is called right justification.

In the "what you see is what you get" type word processor, the text on the monitor occasionally must be reformatted. Most word processing

FIGURE 4–6   The Insert Mode is Turned On

FIGURE 4–7 The Act of Inserting

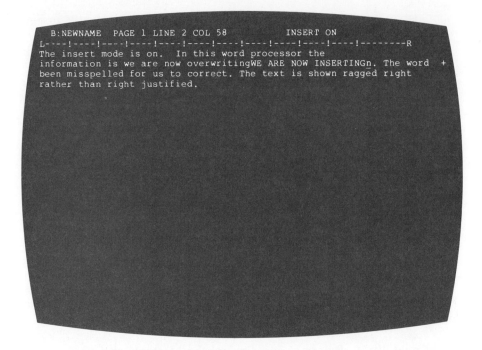

```
  B:NEWNAME   PAGE 1 LINE 2 COL 58          INSERT ON
L----!----!----!----!----!----!----!----!----!----!--------R
The insert mode is on.  In this word processor the
information is we are now overwritingWE ARE NOW INSERTINGn. The word  +
been misspelled for us to correct. The text is shown ragged right
rather than right justified.
```

programs do this automatically. One, WordStar, requires you to instruct the microcomputer when such reformatting is wanted. This type of reformatting is not required in the embedded printer command type word processor, such as Electric Pencil.

FIGURE 4–8 The Results of Inserting

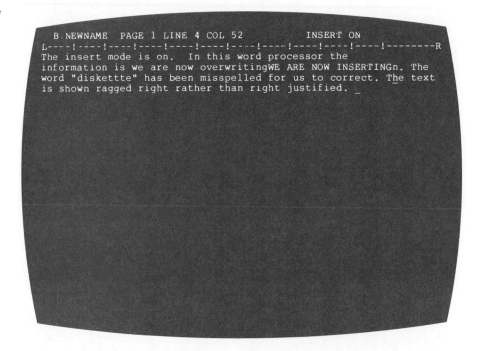

```
  B:NEWNAME   PAGE 1 LINE 4 COL 52          INSERT ON
L----!----!----!----!----!----!----!----!----!----!--------R
The insert mode is on.  In this word processor the
information is we are now overwritingWE ARE NOW INSERTINGn. The
word "diskettte" has been misspelled for us to correct. The text
is shown ragged right rather than right justified. _
```

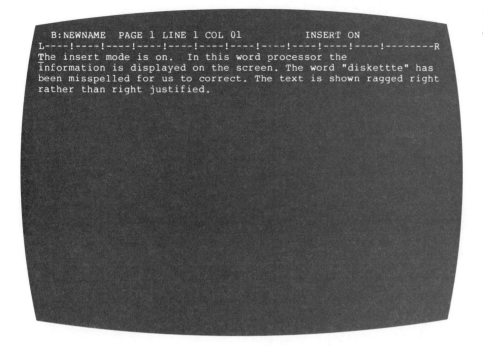

FIGURE 4–9 Starting Over
Again without Changes

```
   B:NEWNAME   PAGE 1 LINE 1 COL 01            INSERT ON
L----!----!----!----!----!----!----!----!----!----!----!--------R
The insert mode is on.  In this word processor the
information is displayed on the screen. The word "diskettte" has
been misspelled for us to correct. The text is shown ragged right
rather than right justified.
```

Figure 4–12 shows the text before any changes were made. The text is not right justified.

After the justify-right instruction is given the screen changes to that shown in Figure 4–13.

FIGURE 4–10   Correcting
Spelling

```
   B:NEWNAME   PAGE 1 LINE 2 COL 57            INSERT ON
L----!----!----!----!----!----!----!----!----!----!----!--------R
The insert mode is on.  In this word processor the
information is displayed on the screen. The word "diskettte" has
been misspelled for us to correct. The text is shown ragged right
rather than right justified.
```

FIGURE 4–11   Delete Key
Corrects Spelling

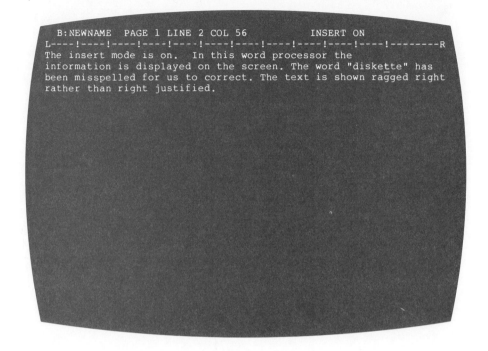

```
    B:NEWNAME   PAGE 1 LINE 2 COL 56           INSERT ON
    L----!----!----!----!----!----!----!----!----!----!----!--------R
    The insert mode is on.  In this word processor the
    information is displayed on the screen. The word "diskette" has
    been misspelled for us to correct. The text is shown ragged right
    rather than right justified.
```

The margins may be adjusted with a few simple keystrokes and then the microcomputer can be instructed to reformat as shown in Figure 4–14.

Line spacing may be adjusted with another simple command and the text again reformatted as shown in Figure 4–15.

The Capability to Make Global Changes and Search for Strings One term commonly used in word processing is "strings." A **string** is simply a character or group of characters. All word processors have the capability to search for a string and/or to replace one string with another.

String searches and replacements are made in different ways. For example, some word processors, when told to find the string "the", will include the string "The" (that is, they will find all words spelled t-h-e regardless of whether the "t" is uppercase or lowercase). Others will ask you if uppercase and lowercase should be ignored before performing the search. Some word processors are capable of an exact match only.

The Capability to Make Block Moves of Text A block is a section of text identified with beginning and ending markers that must be entered by the user. The marker at the beginning may be the same as at the end, or different. Once identified, the block may be copied, moved, or erased. **Copy** means another image of the block is created at a new location. **Move** means the original copy is erased, and the block appears at another location. **Erase** means the block is removed from the file. A number of word processors can insert a block of text saved under a filename on a diskette, or find a block of text in the middle of one file and move it to another.

String:
A character or characters. Strings may be one or more characters in length.

Copy:
To duplicate an image of a block at a new location.
Move:
To relocate a block.
Erase:
To remove a block.

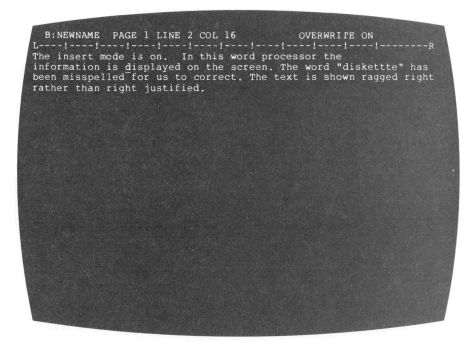

FIGURE 4–12 Starting Over with Diskette Misspelled

Figure 4–16 shows the screen before beginning the block operation.

A block is marked by identifying its beginning and end as shown in Figure 4–17.

After moving the cursor beyond the end of the text and giving the

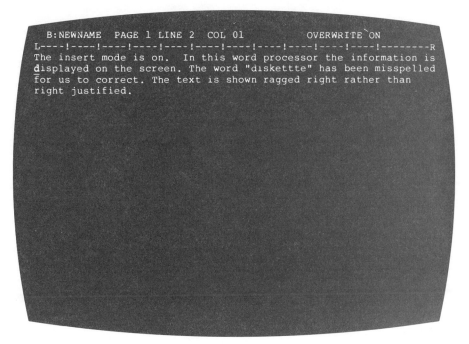

FIGURE 4–13 Right Justified (The Text is Now in Error)

FIGURE 4–14 Margin
Adjustment

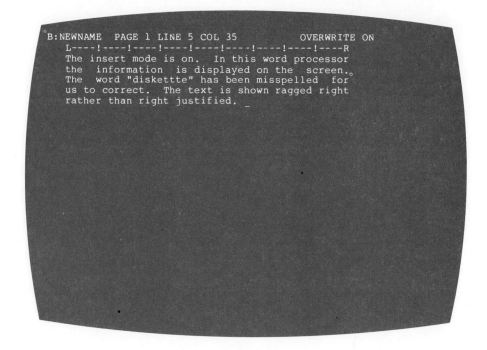

```
B:NEWNAME   PAGE 1 LINE 5 COL 35            OVERWRITE ON
  L----!----!----!----!----!----!----!----!----!---R
  The insert mode is on.  In this word processor
  the  information  is displayed on the  screen.
  The  word "diskettte" has been misspelled  for
  us to correct.  The text is shown ragged right
  rather than right justified.  _
```

copy instruction, Figure 4–18 results. If the move instruction is given, Figure 4–19 results. If the erase instruction is given, Figure 4–20 results.

Some word processors will leave the text formatted as shown while others will fill in and reformat. Most move the block markers to the new

FIGURE 4–15 Double
Spacing

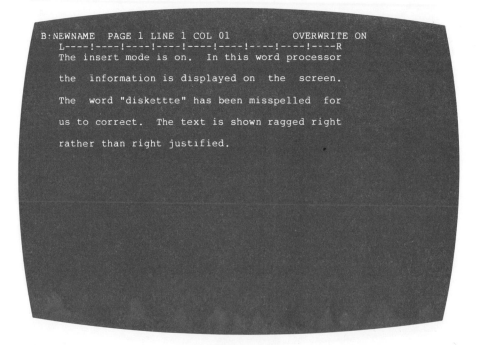

```
B:NEWNAME   PAGE 1 LINE 1 COL 01            OVERWRITE ON
  L----!----!----!----!----!----!----!----!----!---R
  The insert mode is on.  In this word processor

  the  information is displayed on  the  screen.

  The  word "diskettte" has been misspelled  for

  us to correct.  The text is shown ragged right

  rather than right justified.
```

location along with the block. Sometimes you will need to "unmark" text before proceeding.

Rulers Each word processor displays its screen differently. Along the top or bottom of the screen you will generally find a ruler that helps the user locate the cursor and tab locations. Word processing users should check the screen layout.

Headers and Footers The addition of page headers and footers can be important when you are assigned the task of producing a document in a specific format. In the past, most publishers and universities had specific methods for handling headers and footers. The trend is for them to be more flexible. However, you may still find yourself faced with the problem of a specific location and format requirement for footnotes and page titles.

Page Numbering and Page Breaks The default mode of many word processors is to print the page number, while others will not do so unless instructed. Some locate the page number on the top of the page while others put it on the bottom.

A word processor that automatically locates the page number in the manner wanted may be the best selection. If your office needs are for letters and other such documents, you should select a word processor that defaults to no page number.

Generally, only word processors that format on the screen will be able to display page breaks during the editing process. If page breaks and other on-screen formatting are important, the selection of an on-screen word processor is best.

Soft Hyphen and Spaces The placement of proper hyphenation has not generally been solved. Some word processors will aid you in the placement of (hard) hyphens during the editing process. Others allow you to place a (soft) hyphen in a word or words to be used, if that word appears at the end of the line.

You may sometimes wish to control the location of two or more words so they are on the same line. The placement of a hard space be-

FIGURE 4–16   Starting
Again

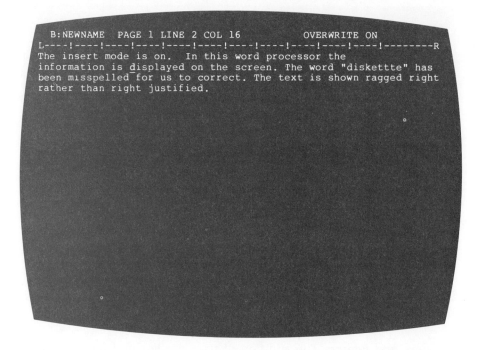

```
     B:NEWNAME   PAGE 1 LINE 2 COL 16            OVERWRITE ON
L----!----!----!----!----!----!----!----!----!----!----!--------R
The insert mode is on.  In this word processor the
information is displayed on the screen. The word "diskettte" has
been misspelled for us to correct. The text is shown ragged right
rather than right justified.
```

tween the words in some word processors forces the program to handle
the string as a single word during format. The two words will always
appear on the same line. A soft space allows the word processor to separate the words on two lines if required by the format process.

FIGURE 4–17   Marking the
Block

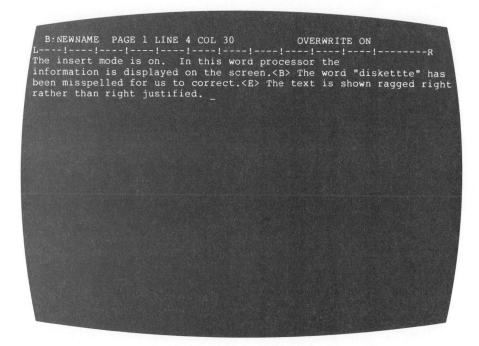

```
     B:NEWNAME   PAGE 1 LINE 4 COL 30            OVERWRITE ON
L----!----!----!----!----!----!----!----!----!----!----!--------R
The insert mode is on.  In this word processor the
information is displayed on the screen.<B> The word "diskettte" has
been misspelled for us to correct.<E> The text is shown ragged right
rather than right justified. _
```

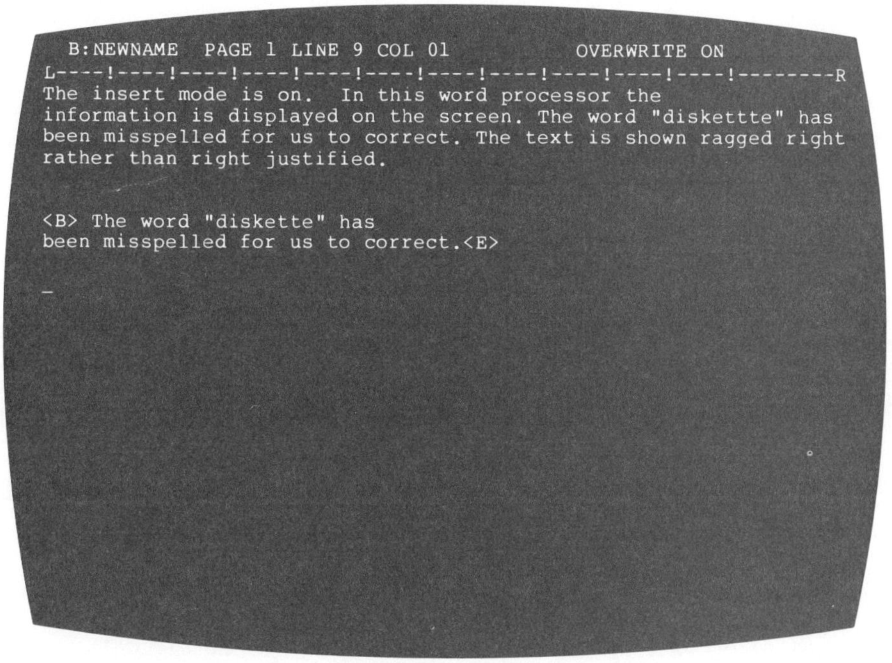

FIGURE 4–18   Copying a
Block

```
   B:NEWNAME   PAGE 1 LINE 9 COL 01            OVERWRITE ON
L----!----!----!----!----!----!----!----!----!----!----!-------R
The insert mode is on.  In this word processor the
information is displayed on the screen. The word "diskettte" has
been misspelled for us to correct. The text is shown ragged right
rather than right justified.


<B> The word "diskette" has
been misspelled for us to correct.<E>

_
```

Saving and Recalling Text File Features

Text must be saved on disk and then recalled for future editing. All word
processing programs save text files. Some save the text as ASCII files,

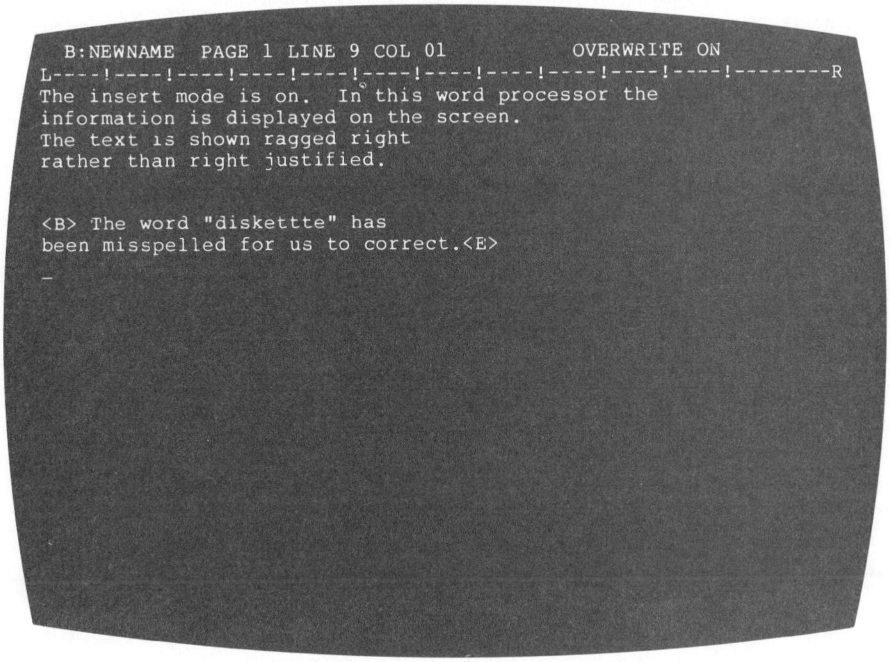

FIGURE 4–19   Moving a
Block

```
   B:NEWNAME   PAGE 1 LINE 9 COL 01            OVERWRITE ON
L----!----!----!----!----!----!----!----!----!----!----!-------R
The insert mode is on.  In this word processor the
information is displayed on the screen.
The text is shown ragged right
rather than right justified.


<B> The word "diskettte" has
been misspelled for us to correct.<E>

_
```

FIGURE 4–20   Erasing a
Block

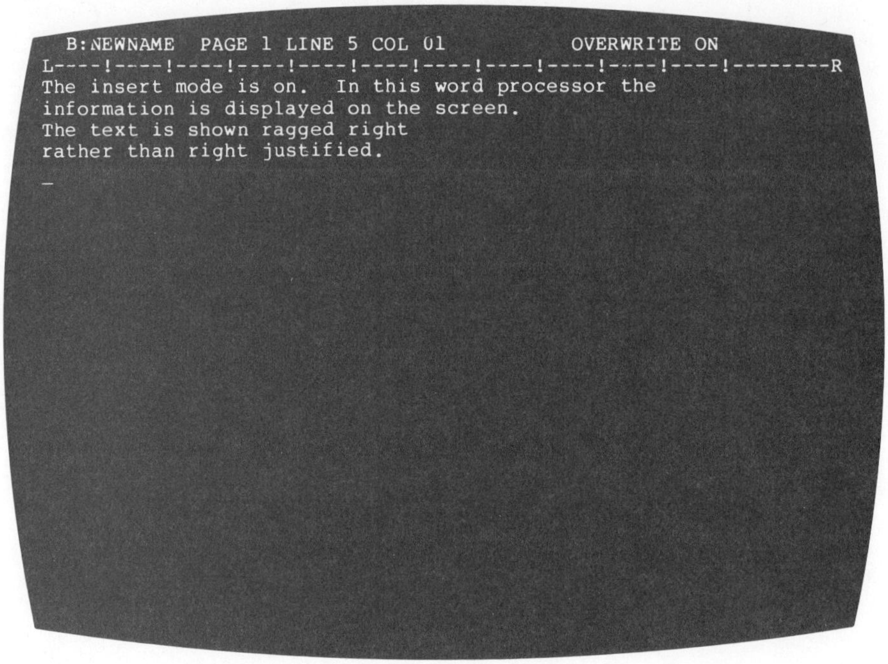

```
    B:NEWNAME   PAGE 1 LINE 5 COL 01              OVERWRITE  ON
L----!----!----!----!----!----!----!----!----!----!----!--------R
The insert mode is on.  In this word processor the
information is displayed on the screen.
The text is shown ragged right
rather than right justified.

_
```

some as near ASCII files, and some in special code. A near ASCII file is a file that uses the ASCII codes, has some additional control codes, and may be edited to an ASCII file without excessive effort.

Word processors that may produce ASCII files include Electric Pencil, Volkswriter, and WordStar (in its non-document mode). WordStar document files are near ASCII because they include hidden characters that are not consistent with the ASCII standard.

A standard, such as ASCII, is required when you transfer files between word processing programs. The standard is also used for transferring information between microcomputers, spreadsheet programs, and database programs. The ASCII file printed on disk by other programs may be moved into many word processing programs for additional editing and report preparation. Many word processing programs come with utilities to ease file transfer.

When transferring files between programs that use ASCII files, problems should be minimal. Embedded instructions may have to be removed either before or after transfer. For creating ASCII files in programs using near ASCII files, you may need to purchase special programs.

Printing the Text File Features

The final step in a word processing program is the production of a hard copy. Printer controllers are programs or routines that are part of the word processor; they take the file created by the text editor and produce hard copy using a printer. Usually the print routine is called from a menu, by function keys, using a combination of several keys, or directly from the disk operating system by calling a printer program.

You may find a printed draft is unnecessary. We recommend that you edit on the monitor, and then use a printed draft for additional error corrections. Examination of the screen helps find some errors, while examination of a printed document helps find others.

ADDITIONAL FEATURES OF WORD PROCESSORS

Word Processors have special features of value in particular business situations. Some word processors come as complete or almost complete packages while others that are limited may have their capabilities expanded by the addition of special utilities. Some of the additional features you may expect in many word processors are:

1. Special printing effects.
   a. Bolding.
   b. Additional fonts such as italics.
   c. Proportional spacing.
2. Document assembly from files with pre-written text.
3. Print spoolers.
4. Windows.

Special Printing Effects

Many printers are capable of producing special effects, such as large print, compressed print, graphics, bold, font changes, subscript, superscript, **proportional spacing,** and enhanced. A few word processing programs include the capability of sending special codes to the printer that produce these effects. These codes are communicated by the word processing program using numbers. The word processor must either be configured to handle a particular printer or be capable of sending any number directly to the printer.

Proportional spacing:
Allows for difference in letter size to make the document look like typeset material.

Document Assembly

When the same words are used over and over again, as in a legal office, document assembly capabilities of word processors make the task easier and more efficient.

There are five ways to assemble a document:

1. Insert or merge text on the screen.
2. Create a file from that other text files are called during the printing process.
3. Append at the end of files other text files to be called during printing.
4. Use a menu driven program to assemble a document.
5. Use the capability in DOS to add one file to another.

Many applications including advertising, law, academic proposals, medical reports, contracts, and more require a word processor with this capability.

Print Spoolers

Programs are available that set aside part of RAM or create a special file on the disk to be used to hold text that is on its way to the printer. The text is fed into the reserved area faster than it would be into a printer. As soon as all the text is in the reserved area the microcomputer is free to perform other tasks.

Print spoolers are often referred to as print buffers when they are external to the microcomputer. Printers may be purchased with built-in RAM to act as print spoolers. The print spooler is an example of multitasking; the microcomputer can do two things at the same time.

Windows

A feature that is most useful when performing word processing is splitting the screen into "windows," (see Figure 4–21). Each word processor with windows uses them a little differently. In general, each window may display a part of the same document or entirely different documents. Text may be transferred between windows. Windows are most useful when creating a custom document from a series of other documents.

COMMONLY FOUND ADD-ON UTILITIES

You may often buy add-on programs to perform routines that are not available in a particular word processor. Some commonly found add-on programs are:

1. Spelling checkers.
2. Merge print for mass mailing.
3. Table of contents generators.
4. Index generators.
5. Footnote programs.
6. Style checkers.

Spelling Programs

Spelling programs help produce documents without errors. These programs use several different methods for checking spelling. One method is a table look up type, where words are compared to a pre-recorded dictionary. Generally, spelling programs will work on any ASCII file, including programs saved as near ASCII files.

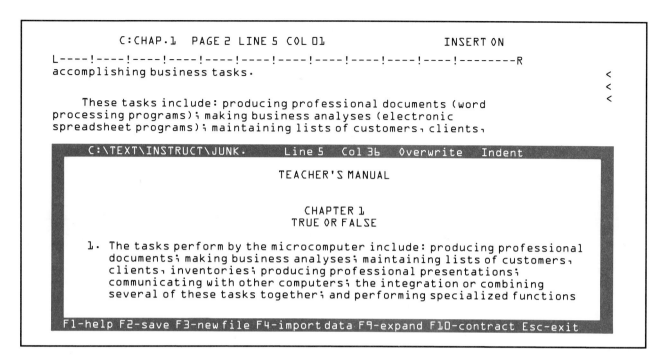

```
        C:CHAP.1   PAGE 2 LINE 5 COL 01                    INSERT ON
L----!----!----!----!----!----!----!----!----!----!----!--------R
accomplishing business tasks.                                        <
                                                                     <
    These tasks include: producing professional documents (word      <
processing programs); making business analyses (electronic
spreadsheet programs); maintaining lists of customers, clients,
┌─────────────────────────────────────────────────────────────────┐
│ C:\TEXT\INSTRUCT\JUNK.       Line 5   Col 36   Overwrite   Indent │
│                         TEACHER'S MANUAL                          │
│                                                                   │
│                            CHAPTER 1                              │
│                          TRUE OR FALSE                            │
│                                                                   │
│  1. The tasks perform by the microcomputer include: producing professional │
│     documents; making business analyses; maintaining lists of customers,   │
│     clients, inventories; producing professional presentations;            │
│     communicating with other computers; the integration or combining       │
│     several of these tasks together; and performing specialized functions  │
│                                                                   │
│ F1-help F2-save F3-new file F4-import data F9-expand F10-contract Esc-exit │
└─────────────────────────────────────────────────────────────────┘
```

FIGURE 4–21   *Word Processing Windows*

MICROS IN ACTION

The broker was a poor speller. Each time he produced a document he had to get help in checking his spelling. A spelling program was purchased. It was loaded into the microcomputer and tried out on a letter that had been created by the agent. The broker found three spelling errors.

The spelling program helped improve the quality of documents, and was more than worth its purchase price.

Spelling programs will identify words that are not in their dictionary. The word may not be in the dictionary because:

1. It is a proper name.
2. The word is not included in the dictionary.
3. The word is misspelled.

Some spelling programs will help you find the correct spelling for a word by displaying similar words on the screen. Some programs point out the problem and let you solve it. If you spell the word "computer" as "commuter", this error will not be identified. Commuter is a word. The spelling program can find misspelled words, not misused words.

Merge Print for Mass Mailing

An example of a merge printing program for mass mailing is MailMerge, an add-on to the word processing program WordStar. It allows the preparation of mail list data files that may be used to produce multiple letters addressed to different individuals. MailMerge aids in the preparation of envelopes, document assembly, and the continuous printing of multiple files. Mailing list programs provide names and addresses for business applications. Some mailing programs personalize mass mailings.

Table of Contents, Index Generators, Footnote Programs

Completing a large manuscript involves many details. The creation of a table of contents, the searching and identification of terms for an index, and the proper location of footnotes are just a few of these details. There are a number of programs that facilitate these tasks. Each works a little differently and have different levels of user involvement. Most programs are designed to operate with a specific word processing program or with word processors that produce ASCII files.

Style Checkers

Style (grammar) programs will check a document for common typographical errors, writing style, and sentence level. Common errors, such as writing the word "can not" as two words rather than one, will be found by grammar programs, but not by spelling programs. Words such as "very" will be identified by grammar programs as being unnecessary. Wordy phrases such as "in the case of" will be found by a grammar program. Double words such as "the the" will be found. This error is common in word processing.

These style programs make great teaching aids. They will point out questions and problems without becoming annoying. Most of the current versions cannot correct errors, but just alert the writer to possible stylistic errors.

COMPARING WORD PROCESSORS

The features of word processing programs are compared in Table 4–1. These comparisons relate to the stated versions only and are based on available data before publication.

TABLE 4–1 Comparison of Word Processing Features

Hardware Features	pfs: Write	Multi-mate	Volks-writer	Microsoft Word	WordStar
Configuration					
Min. RAM	128K	256K	64K	128K	64K
Min. Number Drives	1	1	1	1	1
Monochrome*	x		x	x	x
Color-		x			
General Features					
Copy Protected	Yes	No	No	Yes	No
Easy Printer Configuration	No	Yes	Yes	Yes	Yes in later versions
Menu Drive		x	x		x
Function Keys	x	x	x	x	x
Windows	No	No	No	Yes	No
Document Assembly	File	Yes	File	Sequential Only	No
Spell Check	Extra	Built In	Extra	Extra	Extra
Help Screens	Yes	Yes	Yes	Yes	Yes
Editing Features					
Right Justified	Yes	To Printer	To Printer	Yes	Yes
Block Moves	Yes	Yes	Yes	Yes	Yes
Reformat	Auto/manual	Auto	Auto	Auto	Manual
What You See	x			x	x
Embedded		x	x		
Save/Recall Features					
Backup of Text Files	User Control	User Control	User Control	Automatic	Automatic
ASCII Files	No**	No**	Near	Near	Near
Printing Features					
Graphics *** On Printer	No	Yes	Yes	Yes	Limited
Proportional Spacing ***	No	Yes	Yes	Yes	Yes
Built-in Spooler	No	Yes	No	No	No

*All systems work with both monochrome and high-resolution cards. The x indicates which way it works best.
**Have routines that make it possible to read and write ASCII files.
***Printer controls—works only if the printer has the capabilities called for.

SUMMARY

This chapter has demonstrated the importance of word processing to the business professional. It has defined the tasks of word processing and identified some of the commercial programs. You should also understand why word processing is so easy to use. The important concepts covered include:

1. The microcomputer may be used as a word processor.
2. Word processing saves time, increases document quality, reduces the typing skill level needed, reduces the amount of coordination needed between individuals, and does not require a large investment.
3. Word processing requires a microcomputer, a word processing program, a printer that can produce text of the quality needed by the application, and usually two disk drives.
4. Electronic word processing programs have general, text creating/editing, saving and recalling, and printing features.
5. The general features of a word processor include the trade off between menu-driven program and function keys, the conventions used, the type of file backup procedures, and the type of printer control designed into the system.
6. Text editing involves overwriting, inserting, and deleting, formatting and margin control, and the movement of strings and blocks.
7. Text must be saved on a disk and then recalled for future editing.
8. No program can do everything you need. Each has some feature that is of special value in a particular business situation.
9. You may often buy add-on programs to perform routines that are not available in a particular word processor.

KEY TERMS

Block
Copy
Cursor
Delete
Erase
Function key
Insert

Move
Overwrite
String
Text editor
Word processing
Word wrap

REVIEW QUESTIONS

1. What is word processing?

2. What is text? What is a text file?

3. What are the basic features of a word processing program?

4. Identify some of the commonly found add-on utility word processing programs.

5. Identify the minimum hardware needs for word processing.

6. What are some of the special printer effects useful in word processing?

7. How does the word processing program help produce quality documents?

8. How does word processing help the professional with marginal typing skills?

9. What are the advantages of electronic word processing over using a standard typewriter?

10. Identify some of the general features of word processing programs a user should be concerned with.

11. Identify three common word processing conventions.

12. What are two general types of word processing programs?

13. What is a text editor? What is the importance of such a program?

14. What is full-screen editing?

15. Identify the exact meaning of overwrite, insert, and delete.

16. What is right justification?

17. What is a string?

18. What is a block? What does it mean to copy, move, and erase a block?

19. Why is a standard ASCII file needed in word processing?

20. What is a print spooler?

21. What do style programs do?

DISCUSSION AND
APPLICATION
QUESTIONS

1. Find a magazine advertisement for a word processor. How much does one cost? What kind of features are being advertised?

2. Survey an office that uses electronic word processing. What kind of word processor is being used? Why was this one selected for this office? Was it a good choice?

3. Use the yellow pages of your telephone book to identify where word processing programs and equipment may be purchased.

4. Identify alternate equipment and techniques to word processing. Where are they available locally?

5. After being introduced to the use of word processing in your laboratory, use magazine and other sources to study electronic typewriters. How do the two compare?

6. If the school's mainframe computer has a word processing program, find out about it. How does it compare to the one available on your microcomputer?

7. Examine the school's bulletin board for advertisements for typing and word processing services. What do they cost? What is being offered?

8. Examine your local newpaper and the telephone yellow pages for word processing services. What is available?

LABORATORY ASSIGNMENTS

1. Identify the word processor(s) available in your laboratory. What type of word processor is it?

2. Type the following text into your word processor:

```
                                    Current date

Mr. William Anderson
Acquisition Manager
The Large Motel Chain
1122 Office Building West
New Town, New York 11111

Dear Bill:

    As per our conversation of April 12th, I have prepared
a proposal on the sale of our motel.  Included in the
proposal are the motel's income and cost figures for the
past two years.  Our asking price for the motel is $10
million, which includes a 2% commission for the real estate
brokers.

Sincerely,


Your Name
Manager
```

Print the same letter to three additional individuals at different addresses.

3. Use the letter from the preceding assignment and make a copy of it. Change it to a memo and send it to three additional individuals as follows.

```
                              Current date

From: Your Name

To: Mr. William Anderson
    Acquisition Manager
    The Large Motel Chain
    1122 Office Building West
    New Town, New York 11111

Subject: Sale of Motel

As  per our conversation of April 12th,  I have  prepared  a
proposal on the sale of our motel.  Included in the proposal
are the the motel's income and cost figures for the past two
years.  Our asking price for the motel is $10 million, which
includes a 2% commission for the real estate brokers.
```

4. Prepare a letter notifying the members of a club that a meeting is being scheduled. Use the edit capability of your word processor to change the name of the club member, and send individual letters to all members.

5. Change the letter in the preceding assignment to a memo and repeat the assignment.

6. Make a copy of the text file of the letter from assignment number 2, and load the letter into the word processor of your microcomputer.
- a. Use the search capability of your word processor to examine every occurrence of the word "motel".
- b. Change all "motel" to "restaurant" using the global change capability of your word processor. Print a copy of the new letter.
- c. Change "restaurant" back to "motel".
- d. Use the block move capability of your word processor to reorder the sentences from 1–2–3 to 3–2–1. Print a copy.

7. Use the TYPE command of your disk operating system to examine one of your word processing text files. Is it an ASCII file? It is a near ASCII file?

8. In your word processor type James Magary's words:

"Computers can figure out all kinds of problems, except the things in the world that just don't add up."

Use the block copy capability to copy the sentence ten times. Save the first copy and with a partner and see how many ways you can rewrite the statement. Print a copy of the results.

9. If a spelling program is available, use it on a document you have prepared, and report on its performance.

10. Identify other types of word processing support programs available. Try them and report on their value.

SELECTED REFERENCES

The Benchmark, The Word Processor Version 3.0. Metasoft Corporation, 1980.

Dologite, D.G. *Using Small Business Computers.* Prentice-Hall, 1984.

Hogan, Thom, and Mike Iamimico. *Osborne 1 User's Reference Guide.* Osborne Computer Corporation, 1981.

Start-Pac, Quick Self Instruction System for WordStar, CP/M Programming, and SuperCalc. Osborne Computer Corporation.

Veit, Stanley S. *Using Micro-computers in Business,* 2nd edition. Hayden Book Company, 1983.

WordStar Installation Manual. MicroPro International Corporation, 1983.

WordStar General Information Manual. MicroPro International Corporation, 1983.

WordStar Reference Manual. MicroPro International Corporation, 1983.

Zimmerman, Steven M., Leo M. Conrad, and Larry J. Goldstein. *Osborne User's Guide.* Brady Publishing Company, 1983.

5

Chapter Outline

Chapter Goals:

Upon completion of this chapter you will be able to:

Understand the importance of electronic spreadsheets to the business professional.

Define the tasks of electronic spreadsheets.

Identify the more popular electronic spreadsheets.

Use some of the functions of an electronic spreadsheet.

ELECTRONIC SPREADSHEETS

A1: 'Hotel Analysis Model   READY

	A	B	C	D	E	F
1	Hotel Analysis Model					
2		Category	2			
3		Region	E			
4			'80 Act	'81 Act	'82 Pro	'83 Pro
5						
6	Avg night rental		$61.38	$65.06	$68.31	$78.56
7	Occupancy rate		79.21%	75.23%	74.29%	73.35%
8	Revenues		$9,927,488	$9,890,117	$10,381,964	$11,789,462
9						
10	Expenses					
11		Salaries	$2,242,332	$2,233,891	$2,324,500	$2,651,510
12		Maintenance	$3,474,621	$3,461,541	$3,633,687	$4,126,312
13		Supplies	$1,342,196	$1,337,144	$1,403,642	$1,593,935
14		Utilities	$519,704	$517,748	$543,496	$617,178
15		Other	$1,699,586	$1,693,188	$674,828	$2,298,945
16	Profit (Loss)		$649,049	$646,606	$1,801,812	$501,582
17						
18		1982	1983	1984	1985	
19	Inflation	5%	15%	9%	10%	
20						

CALC

Spreadsheet:
A method for organizing, calculating, and presenting financial, statistical, and other business data for managerial decision-making.

The **spreadsheet** is a business tool. It has been used to solve business problems since the invention of paper and pencil. A spreadsheet is a method for organizing, calculating, and presenting financial, statistical, and other business data that you would use as the basis for your managerial decision-making.

The spreadsheet has been used by business people and other planners since the invention of paper and pencil. Examples of applications for spreadsheets include budget control and forecasting, accounting ledgers and working papers, production planning, investment, cash flow, and annual operating data. Most business, financial, and statistical problems that may be solved with pencil and paper are spreadsheet type problems.

This chapter introduces you to the capabilities of spreadsheets. As you learn more about business in your other courses, you will come to appreciate the value of spreadsheets.

As a student of business you will find electronic spreadsheet programs among the most valuable programs available for the microcomputer. The electronic spreadsheet has become a best seller mainly because it allows you to: solve business problems on the microcomputer without the help of professional programmers; perform calculations at high speed and without errors; format reports; and print reports automatically.

There are a number of spreadsheet programs available for microcomputers. The first spreadsheet program was VisiCalc, that was followed by SuperCalc, Multiplan, and others.

BASIC HARDWARE NEEDS

Electronic spreadsheets require standard microcomputer hardware, but may need extra RAM.

The microcomputer hardware needs for electronic spreadsheets include:

1. RAM
2. Input Devices—Keyboards
3. Monitor
4. Printer
5. On-Line Storage

RAM

Electronic spreadsheets vary in their requirements for RAM. However, the capacity in terms of the number of columns and rows, and the capabilities of the spreadsheet, is directly related to the amount of RAM. Spreadsheets are available for CP/M microcomputers with a total of only 64K of RAM. These spreadsheets can handle many problems. However, when spreadsheets are integrated with other features or become large in size, the amount of RAM required may grow to 192K and more. MS/PC-DOS or other microcomputers with the capability to handle large amounts of RAM must be considered when you use large spreadsheets.

Input Devices—Keyboards

Data may be entered into electronic spreadsheet programs using any of the many devices available on microcomputers. The keyboard is the most common.

Monitor

There are few special needs for monitors when using electronic spreadsheets. Monitors with 80 columns and 24 or 25 lines are sufficient for most spreadsheet needs. Special monitors capable of producing a greater number of columns or rows are nice to have, but are not required.

Printer

The number of spreadsheet columns produced on a printer is a function of its size. Table 5–1 identifies the number of nine character spreadsheet columns different sized printers may produce. The maximum capacity of printers is lower than the smallest spreadsheet program. To obtain a complete copy of a spreadsheet, it is often necessary to print it in parts and tape the parts together.

TABLE 5–1
Printer Size Versus
Spreadsheet Columns

Printer Size	Number Characters	Number of Nine Character Spreadsheet Columns
Normal Carriage		
Regular Size Print	80	8
Compressed Print	132	14
Wide Carriage		
Regular Size Print	132	14
Compressed Print	220	24*

*Some printers can print as many as 255 characters, resulting in 28 columns of nine characters each.

Programs are available for selected dot matrix printers that allow you to print down the page, rather than across the page. This capability may help produce a complete report without taping in some situations.

On-Line Storage

Spreadsheets require a minimum of a single disk drive to a maximum of a disk drive and a hard disk. The amount of spreadsheet storage needed, in combination with the other work performed by the microcomputer, determines on-line storage requirements.

WHY THE BUSINESS PROFESSIONAL SHOULD KNOW ABOUT ELECTRONIC SPREADSHEETS

Electronic spreadsheets save time, increase calculation accuracy, and make it possible for managers to perform powerful evaluations. You may use numerical data (manually or on a computer) to determine solutions for many types of business problems. One way of developing this data in an organized and orderly fashion is to use the spreadsheet. The accounting ledger (see Figure 5–1) is an example of a common manual type of spreadsheet.

Electronic spreadsheets:

1. Save calculation time and increase accuracy
2. Make "what if" calculations possible
3. Produce a final report
4. Save and recall spreadsheets for reuse
5. Do not require a big investment
6. Solve business problems

Save Calculation Time and Increase Accuracy

Calculations take time. Add a column of numbers. Then add them a second time. Often, the results are not the same. Even with the use of a calculator with a tape there are problems in getting the numbers correct.

Electronic spreadsheets have been modelled after manual ones. They both have **labels, numbers,** and **formulas.** Figure 5–2 shows a spreadsheet for adding up a column of numbers that represent incomes from different sources. The spreadsheet is divided into **columns** A, B, and C and **rows** 1, 2, ... 6. A location in the spreadsheet is called a **cell.** Cell A1 contains the word "Income".

The spreadsheet in Figure 5–2 has labels "Income", "-----", and "======". It has a single formula: "SUM(A2:A4)". This formula form is found on many different spreadsheet programs. It means to add up the values in cells A2, A3, and A4, and then to place the result in cell A6. In some spreadsheet programs "@SUM(A2:A4)" or "@SUM(A2...A4)" may be the formula format required.

In an electronic spreadsheet you enter the labels, the formulas, and then the numbers; and the program takes over. When a value is changed, the system automatically performs the calculations needed.

Labels:
Words identifying columns, rows, or overall titles.
Numbers:
Mathematical values.
Formula:
Rules defining the relationship (outcome) between numbers used in the spreadsheet.
Column:
Vertical division of screen and spreadsheet.
Row:
Horizontal division of screen and spreadsheet.
Cells:
Column (vertical division) and row (horizontal division) intersect on screen and spreadsheet.

USER WINDOW

The microcomputer sales manager set up his outside sales force on his electronic spreadsheet. He calculated his sales, commissions, costs, and profit position in hours rather than in days.

Make "What If" Calculations Possible

The capability of the electronic spreadsheet to perform automatic recalculation means you may make many changes and see the results of these changes immediately throughout the entire spreadsheet. When performing an analysis this type of change is often referred to as a **"What If"** change or a "sensitivity analysis." Questions such as "what if the sales were 50% of the estimate," or "what if sales were 200% of the estimate," may be answered. The sensitivity of the results to particular estimates may be determined.

What If?:
The investigation of economic and business consequences assuming that changes in business decisions are to be made, and the conditions under which the decisions are made.

MICROS IN ACTION

Scott Paper Company made an evaluation on the profitability of investing in a new piece of production equipment. The sales forecast was uncertain due to unstable market conditions. The evaluation was run using 50%, 100%, and 150% of the best sales estimates.

The risk and profitablity of each level of sales were evaluated.

Manual calculations that take hours, days, or even weeks are performed in seconds by an electronic spreadsheet. Generally, the larger the spreadsheet, the more time saving the electronic spreadsheet becomes.

FIGURE 5–1   An Accounting Ledger

Interim Statement of Operation
For the Six Months Ended February 28, 1985

		1	2 Home Office	3 Pascagoula	4 Goutier	5 ALCO	6 Chickasaw
1	Revenues		0	139796	16503	0	57920
2	Operating Expenses						
3	Advertising		11357				
4	Automotive		1371				
5	Bank Charges		144	188			104
6	Contributions		100				
7	Depriciation			16559	5095	2396	14315
8	Dues & Subscriptions		279				
9	Entertainment		1832				
10	Insurance		815	653			
11	Intrest		978				
12	Janitorial		70				
13	Maintenance & Repairs		360	1005	820	215	2379
14	Miscellaneous		1184	10			
15	Office		11404	562	127		301
16	Postage		108				
17	Professional Fees		8665				
18	Rent		1630	3750	2720	867	1540
19	Salaries- Officers		60923				
20	Salaries- Other		14240	15673	4436		9798

Produce a Final Report

When working with manual calculations, the last step is to have the results organized and typed or otherwise prepared for use by other managers. This step is often difficult to get "right," due to the magnitude of the task of copying many numbers without error. The electronic spreadsheet is capable of printing a hard copy of an analysis in seconds. The microcomputer produces a nicely typed copy ready for managerial analysis and use without errors. Electronic spreadsheets, like all other micro-

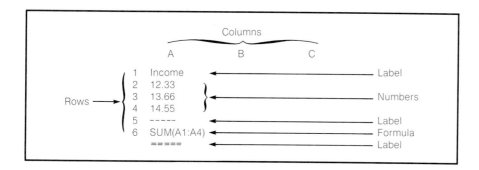

FIGURE 5–2
A Simple Spreadsheet

computer programs, may produce bad results due to incorrect data and formulas. "GIGO" means garbage in garbage out.

Save and Recall Spreadsheets for Reuse

Businesses must perform balance sheet and similar calculations over and over again. Each week or each month the same spreadsheet must be produced. The electronic spreadsheet may be saved on disk or hard disk and then recalled, the date changed, the new values entered, a report generated, and the spreadsheet is saved once more for re-use the next period. The labels and formulas once entered do not have to be entered a second time. The more an electronic spreadsheet is used, the greater the benefits derived from it.

Do Not Require a Big Investment

An electronic spreadsheet must be purchased. Its cost varies from $50 to $1,000. Unless you have a need for unusually large spreadsheets, there are no special microcomputer hardware purchases required.

Solve Business Problems

Spreadsheet programs may be used in most areas of business. Some applications are listed in Table 5–2.

TABLE 5–2
Applications of Electronic
Spreadsheets

Professional Area	Applications
Accounting	General ledgers, trial balances, checkbook balancing, data collection reports, amortization schedules, depreciation schedules.
Banking	Ratio analysis, cash budget, capital budgeting-net present value, internal rate of return, profitability index, optimization analysis, loan analysis.

(continued on following page)

TABLE 5–2
(continued)

Professional Area	Applications
Finance and Economics	Ratio analysis, cash budget, capital budgeting-net present value, internal rate of return, profitability index, optimization analysis, amortization schedules, depreciation schedules.
Marketing (Transportation and Logistics)	Analysis of marketing surveys, marketing projections, inventory control analysis, location evaluation, marketing mix analysis, distribution analysis.
Personnel Administration	Personnel needs analysis, personnel use analysis, insurance needs, job analysis and evaluation.
Quantitative Management	Optimization applications, inventory analysis and control, production control, Performance Evaluation and Review (PERT).
Retail Merchandising	Pricing, inventory control, marketing mix, turnover analysis.
Statistics	Analysis of variance, regression analysis, calculations of averages and standard deviations.
Training	Training records, tests records, performance analysis.

ELECTRONIC SPREADSHEET FEATURES

Electronic spreadsheet programs have some general, configuration, interfacing, and add on features. The features of electronic spreadsheets may be classified as:

1. General
     Calculation
     Editing
          Recalling cells
          Inserting/deleting columns and rows
          Additional editing features
     Storing and recalling
     Printing
2. Windows
3. Interfacing
4. Integrated spreadsheet programs.

General

Electronic spreadsheet programs solve business problems using labels, numbers, and formulas. They divide the computer screen into a series of columns and rows. Capital letters A, B, etc. are used by many electronic spreadsheets to identify columns, and appear across the top of the screen. A row runs across the screen and is usually labeled by number down the left side of the screen.

Cells are identified by their column-row or row-column position, such as G4, meaning column G and row 4. A cell is commonly nine characters wide and one line high. You may control the width of individual columns on many spreadsheets. The maximum number of columns and rows is determined by the specific program used. The original version of VisiCalc had 64 columns and 254 rows, most current programs have greater capacities.

A cell may contain a label, a number, or a mathematical formula. A label is a word placed in a spreadsheet cell to identify output. Labels may be used as overall titles, or as column or row headings. Some spreadsheet programs allow you to specify a label-cell as a title which may be automatically printed on all hard copies, even those not including the title cell.

A cursor which may be a line, or reverse video (the background of the cell is light and the letters dark) is used to indicate which cell is active or current. Labels, numbers, or formulas may be entered only into the active cell.

MICROS IN ACTION

One Scott Paper Company accountant set up an electronic spreadsheet form using labels and mathematical formulas. A clerk without mathematical training was given the form to fill in with the correct information. After the form was completed, the accountant checked the input and found only one number had to be changed. The amount of professional time and cost was reduced by allowing most of the calculations to be performed by the clerk.

The methods used to move around spreadsheets vary depending on the program. In Lotus 1–2–3 the options include:

1. Press function key F5 to call a go-to option. You enter the cell you wish the cursor to move to, such as B7, and the program moves the cursor as instructed.

2. Use of PgUp, PgDn, Home, and End keys on numeric keypad. Home key returns the cursor to cell A1. The End key and the down arrow key pressed sequentially moves the cursor to the last entry in the spreadsheet.

3. Tab to move the cursor to the right. From column A the cursor is moved to column I, from column I to column Q. Shift Tab moves the cursor to the left in a similar manner.

4. Pressing the Scroll Lock key results in the cursor remaining in a fixed position and the spreadsheet moving around it. Pressing Scroll Lock a second time returns the cursor to the original method of moving.

Function keys are used in a customized manner in each spreadsheet program. Table 5–3 details how they are used in Lotus 1–2–3.

The three character extender on the filename is used by many spreadsheet programs to identify the type of file stored on the disk. Table 5–4 identifies the use of extenders in Lotus 1–2–3.

There are many features included in each spreadsheet program. You

TABLE 5–3
Lotus 1–2–3 Function Keys

Function Keys	Application
F1:Help	Display Help screens-press [Esc] to return to ready mode
F2:Edit	Switch to/from Edit Mode for current entry
F3:Name	(Point Mode only) Display menu of range names
F4:Abs	(Point Mode only) Make/Unmake cell address "absolute"
F5:Goto	Move cell pointer to a particular cell
F6:Window	(Split-screen only) Move cell pointer to other window
F7:Query	Repeat most recent Data Query operation
F8:Table	Repeat most recent Data Table operation
F9:Calc	Ready Mode: Recalculate worksheet Value and Edit Modes: Convert formula to its current value
F10:Graph	Draw graph according to most recent graphing specification

Range (spreadsheet):
The identification of the cells in a spreadsheet by the specification of the cell in the upper left position and the cell in the lower right position.

Protected cell:
A cell that has been protected from change by the spreadsheet designer.

may control the format of individual cells, a **range** of cells, or the entire spreadsheet. The range A5...C7 identifies the cells A5, A6, A7, B5, B6, B7, C5, C6, and C7. You may "protect", create a **protected cell,** the entry of new data into specific cells. It is good practice to "protect" the cells with labels when a standard form is created. The range commands of Lotus 1–2–3 are listed in Table 5–5 to illustrate some of these capabilities.

Numbers (values) may be presented in general, fixed, scientific, currency, and comma format. In some spreadsheets they may be printed as * for simple bar type chart purposes. General format includes in the output as many places to the right of the decimal point as needed (33.4454); fixed format defines the number of values to the right of the decimal point (two to the right results in 33.45); scientific represents the number as required and includes a counter (3.34453E + 1) for locating the decimal point; currency includes a dollar sign and two values to the right of the decimal point ($33.45); and the comma format includes a comma in the correct location (3,433.45).

It is often useful to copy or move a range of cells into another location on the spreadsheet. In many spreadsheet programs this instruction is called replication. In Lotus 1–2–3 the instructions are /Copy, to copy entries to a new location(s), and /Move, to move entries to a new location.

Calculation A number is a value you place in a cell to be used in your calculations, such as the cost of an item, the volume sold, etc.

A mathematical formula is a defined relationship that you place in a cell to calculate the desired results. The formula will appear in the a

TABLE 5–4
File Extenders in Lotus 1-2-3

Extenders	Application
.WKS	Worksheet file
.PRN	Print (text) file
.PIC	Graph (picture) file

TABLE 5–5
/Range Commands of
Lotus 1-2-3

Commands	Application
Format	Number/Formula display
Label-Prefix	Alignment of labels
Erase	Erase cell entries
Name	Maintain set of names for ranges
Justify	Adjust width of label "paragraph"
Protect	Disallow changes to cells (if Protection Enabled)
Unprotect	Allow changes to cells
Input	Restrict pointer to unprotected cells

section of the screen on the top or bottom, but not in the body of the spreadsheet. In the body of the spreadsheet you will see the results of the formula.

All mathematical operations—addition (+), subtraction (−), multiplication (*), division (/), and raising to a power (^) may be performed by electronic spreadsheet programs. In addition, most programs provide special mathematical capabilities, such as adding all values in a column or row, most trigonometric functions, and others. The @ financial functions of Lotus 1–2–3 are shown in Table 5–6.

TABLE 5–6
@ Financial Functions of
Lotus 1-2-3

Financial Functions	Application
@IRR(guess,range)	Internal rate of return
@NPV(x,range)	Net present value
FV(pmt,int,term)	Future value
PV(pmt,int,term)	Present value
PMT(prn,int,term)	Payment

In addition to the mathematical function, spreadsheets may contain logical and special functions such as conditional "If" statements among others. Table 5–7 is a list of the logical functions found in Lotus 1–2–3.

The logical function allows you to direct the actions of the spreadsheet program with the values entered. For example, the @IF(cond,x,y)

TABLE 5–7
Lotus 1-2-3 Logical and
Special Functions

Logical Functions	Application	
@FALSE	0	(FALSE)
@TRUE	1	(TRUE)
@IF(cond,x,y)	x	if cond is TRUE (non-zero)
	y	if cond is FALSE (zero)
@ISNA(x)	1	(TRUE) if x = NA
@ISERR(x)	1	(TRUE) if x = ERR

When determining the truth value of a formula, 1-2-3 considers any non-zero value to be TRUE. Only 0 itself is FALSE.

(continued on following page)

TABLE 5–7
(continued)

Special Functions	Application
@NA	NA (not available)
@ERR	ERR (error)
@CHOOSE(x,v0,v1,...,vN)	Select value
@HLOOKUP(x,range,offset)	Table lookup index row
@VLOOKUP(x,range,offset)	Table lookup index column

Precedence (math):
The order in which mathematical operations are executed. The standard order is parentheses, power, multiplication, division, addition, and subtraction.

Mathematical operator:
Symbol that indicates a mathematical process such as addition (+), subtraction (−), multiplication (*), division (/), and raising to a power (ˆ).

function calculates the formula entered into the conditional position, and, if the number is non-zero, executes the instruction in the x position. If the number is zero, the instruction in the y position is executed.

Electronic spreadsheet programs may or may not use all the mathematical **precedence** rules. Precedence is the order in which **mathematical operators** are executed. It requires all operators (+ , − ,/,*,ˆ) inside parentheses to be performed first, followed by power calculations, multiplication and division, and finally by addition and subtraction. Operations at a common level of precedence are performed from left to right.

The formula: $A = 5 + 2 * 4$, yields the result 28 when executed from left to right. It yields the result 13 when the order of precedence is considered. The $2 * 4$ operation should be executed first and then the value 5 added to that result.

In order of precedence, the operators used on most spreadsheet programs are:

Operation	Operator used by computer
Parentheses	( )
Power	ˆ (Use the up-arrow on Model I
Multiplication	* and Model III TRS-80 for ˆ)
Division	/
Addition	+
Subtraction	−

Absolute reference (spreadsheet):
The indication of where specific data is found in a fixed column/row location.

Relative reference (spreadsheet):
The indication of where specific data are found in terms of a fixed number of columns and rows from the cell where the data are needed.

Some spreadsheets include logical operations in their precedence rules. The arithmetic and logical operators of Lotus 1–2–3 and their precedence are shown in Table 5–8.

A formula may refer to a cell using either an "absolute" or "relative" reference. The options are important when blocks of calculations are moved or copied from one location in the spreadsheet to another.

An **absolute reference** refers to a fixed cell. When cells are moved or copied absolute references do not change. For example, if the interest rate is located in cell B12, all formulas in the spreadsheet should be using B12 no matter where these formulas are, or where they are moved.

A **relative reference** is one that refers to a cell a fixed distance (in terms of columns and rows) from the cell where the formula is located. When cells are moved or copied the relative references are changed to

Operators	Application	Precedence #
ˆ	Exponentiation	7
+	Postive	6
−	Negative	6
*	Multiplication	5
/	Division	4
+	Addition	4
−	Subtraction	4
=	Equals	3
<	Less than	3
<=	Less than or equal	3
>	Greater than	3
>=	Greater than or equal	3
<>	Not equal	3
#NOT#	Logical not	2
#AND#	Logical and	1
#OR#	Logical or	1

Operators with larger precedence numbers are performed first, unless overidden by parentheses. Operators with equal precedence are performed left-to-right.

**TABLE 5–8
Arithmetic and Logical Operators of Lotus 1-2-3**

maintain their relative position. For example, if the formula in cell C22 uses the information in cell A21, use a cell two columns left and one row up. A cell reference may have one parameter fixed and the other relative. In Lotus 1–2–3, a relative cell is assumed unless a dollar sign is placed in the formula (see Table 5–9). In some spreadsheets, the nature of a cell is defined during the move or copy operation.

Some spreadsheets calculate by rows while others calculate by columns. Some allow the user to determine the order of calculation. Most of the time the different order of calculation result in a slightly different round-off only. In some situations where you have a circular set of calculations, such as shown in Figure 5–3, the different order of calculation may yield totally different results. The general rules are; don't use circular references unless absolutely necessary, and always check your results to be sure the spreadsheet formulas are performing the way you want them to.

Example In Figure 5–4, a letter is used to identify a column and a number to identify the row in column-row order. This figure illustrates what

Type of Cell	Cell Indication
Relative cell	B5
Absolute column, relative row	$B5
Relative row, absolute column	B$5
Absolute cell	B5

**TABLE 5–9
Types of Cells in Formulas—Lotus 1-2-3**

a microcomputer screen might look like with cell C2 identified by asterisks and the characters C2.

The primary method of data input into an electronic spreadsheet program is from the keyboard. To place a label in position C2 of the electronic spreadsheet, move the cursor to that location. When the cursor is located in the correct cell, you need to tell the program that you are going to enter a label. Spreadsheet programs vary in how you do this. Some programs require the quote [″]; other programs assume labels are being entered unless you tell it otherwise by entering a mathematical operator, such as a plus sign.

The following steps are performed to enter a label:

1. Locate the cursor at the desired cell.
2. Type the instruction telling the computer that a label is being entered.
3. Type the label and press enter.

Manual spreadsheets are the beginning point for an electronic spreadsheet. The first step is to enter the title. The cursor in an electronic spreadsheet is located in cell A1 as shown in Figure 5–5.

The title "Commission Report" is typed as shown in Figure 5–6.

The title and date are separated in an electronic spreadsheet because the same model is usable for different months by changing the input data. The next step is to move the cursor to cell D1 as shown in Figure 5–7.

The date "January 1999" is typed. The cursor is moved to cell A4, where the salesperson's name, "Pia Martin", is typed and the cursor is moved to cell A6, and the label "Type Sales" is typed. See Figure 5–8.

Cells are usually limited to nine characters in width. You may change the number of characters per column. A character overflow occurs when you type more characters in a cell than allowed. Labels may

FIGURE 5–3
Circular Calculations

```
          Column
Row
          A           B           C
1         12
2
3         +A6  -------->     +A1*A3
4         /\                    |
5         |                     \/
6         +C6  <----------     +C3
7
8
```

+A6 in cell A3 means the value in this cell equals the value in the cell position column A, row 6. +A1*A3 in cell C3 means the value in this cell is the value found in cell A1 times the value found in cell A3. etc.

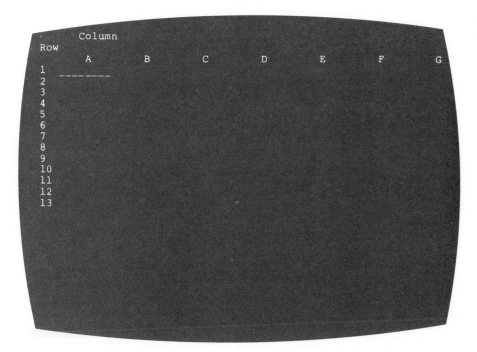

FIGURE 5–4   The Layout
of a Spreadsheet

Row	Column						
	A	B	C	D	E	F	G...
1							
2			***C2***				
3							
4							
5							
⋮							

overflow or be truncated, depending on the spreadsheet program used. Truncation means the characters that do not fit in the cell are dropped off and not shown. They are in the computer memory, but may or may not appear on the screen. In our figures the labels are shown overflowing

FIGURE 5–5   Locating the
Cursor in Cell A1

Row	Column						
	A	B	C	D	E	F	G
1	_____						
2							
3							
4							
5							
6							
7							
8							
9							
10							
11							
12							
13							

FIGURE 5–6
Entering a Label

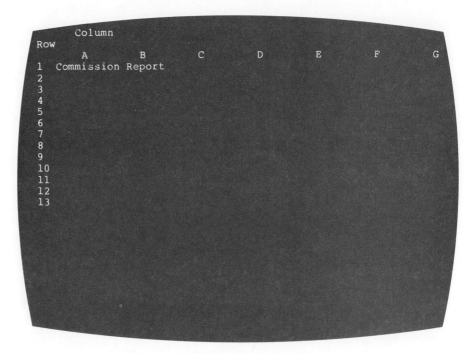

The spreadsheet used assumes labels overflow to next cell when they are too large to fit into a column.

the nine character limitation of an individual column. In spreadsheets that allow overflowing, the text greater than nine characters appears in the next cell, to the right if empty.

FIGURE 5–7
Move Cursor to Cell D1

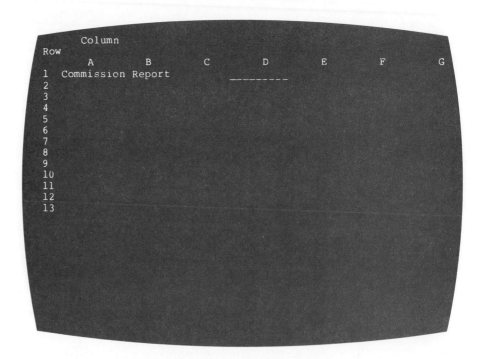

FIGURE 5–8
Enter Names

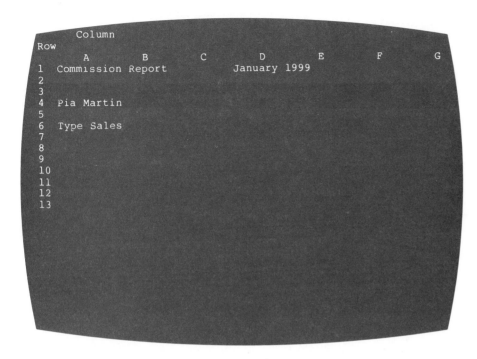

```
        Column
Row
        A           B           C           D           E           F           G
1    Commission Report                  January 1999
2
3
4    Pia Martin
5
6    Type Sales
7
8
9
10
11
12
13
```

Generally, if a label overflows a cell and the spreadsheet allows such overflow, you may type more than the limitation. If the cell in which the overflow occurs is used, the overflowing label is truncated. You should experiment with whatever spreadsheet program you have available to determine how it handles such situations.

The Rate and Sales labels for the column headings in row 6 have been reduced to less than the nine character limit to make them look good, as shown in Figure 5–9.

The row labels, "Computers", "Software", and "Furniture" are added in rows 7, 8, and 9. The spreadsheet as shown in Figure 5–10 is ready for you to enter numbers and formulas.

The next step in the development of the spreadsheet is to place the value of the percent commission in cells C7, C8, and C9. The Sales are placed in cells D7, D8, and D9. The commission dollar amount will be calculated in cells E7, E8, and E9.

Enter the numbers. Use the arrow keys to locate the cursor. The commisssion rate for computers is 8%. The spreadsheet is shown with all the numbers entered in Figure 5–11.

The numbers are located on the right side of the cell while the labels are located on the left. Numbers usually default to being right **justified** while labels default to being left justified.

The spreadsheet formula for calculating commission is Commission = Sales * percent commission * 0.01. The asterisks are used for multiplication. The reason for multiplication by 0.01 is to change the percent commission to a decimal.

For sales of computers, C7 * D7 * 0.01 must be entered in cell E7. Cell C7 contains the percent commission, and cell D7 contains the

Justified (Lined up):
Left justified means lined up evenly on the left, while right justified means lined up on the right.

FIGURE 5–9
Column Headings Added

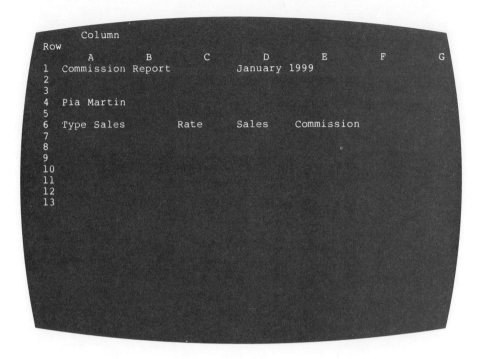

amount of sales. The percent commission was entered as a whole number in location C7.

FIGURE 5–10
Ready for the Numbers
and Formula

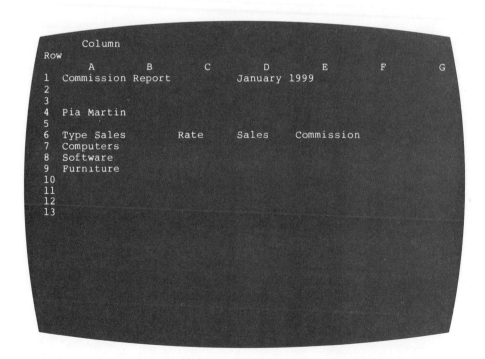

FIGURE 5–11
Entering the Numbers

```
      Column
Row
            A           B           C           D           E           F           G
    1   Commission Report                  January 1999
    2
    3
    4   Pia Martin
    5
    6   Type Sales               Rate        Sales       Commission
    7   Computers                  8          23000
    8   Software                  10          1200
    9   Furniture                 12          5466
   10
   11
   12
   13
```

To enter a formula the steps are:

1. Tell the computer a formula is being entered with a mathematical operator if needed.
2. Type the formula and press <CR>.

Figure 5–12 shows the results of the spreadsheet using the formula you have just entered.

Showing in cell E7 is the number 1840, not the formula. The formula is invisible; only the result of the calculation is shown. Adding the formula for Software, C8*D8*.01, to cell E8, and the formula for Furniture, C9*D9*.01, to cell E9, results in the display shown in Figure 5–13.

No formulas appear in the cells. The results of the calculations are shown. Note that the format of the output is not consistent.

To complete the electronic spreadsheet, enter a line using 9 minus signs as a label in cell E10, and 9 equal signs as a label in E12. Most electronic spreadsheet programs require that you tell them you are using a mathematical operator as a label.

You must enter one more formula in cell E11 (see Figure 5–14). Two alternate forms are possible: +E7+E8+E9 or @SUM(E7..E9). The second form is similar for different spreadsheets. The @SUM(cell start...cell end) form means to add the values in all cells from the starting cell to the ending cell inclusive. For adding large columns of numbers, the @SUM method is more efficient.

Editing You now have an electronic spreadsheet. It may be used as is by replacing the date and the sales numbers for different months. If the

FIGURE 5–12
Formulas Added

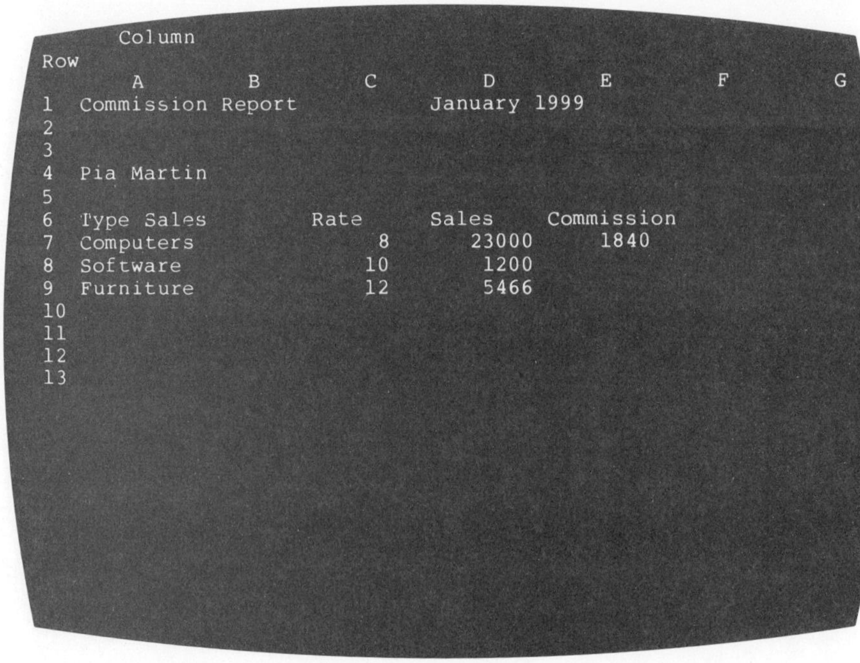

```
        Column
Row
        A         B         C          D          E         F          G
1   Commission Report              January 1999
2
3
4   Pia Martin
5
6   Type Sales           Rate       Sales      Commission
7   Computers             8         23000        1840
8   Software             10          1200
9   Furniture            12          5466
10
11
12
13
```

commission rates change, they may also be replaced. Managers and sales people alike can now play "What If" games.

FIGURE 5–13
Formula Results

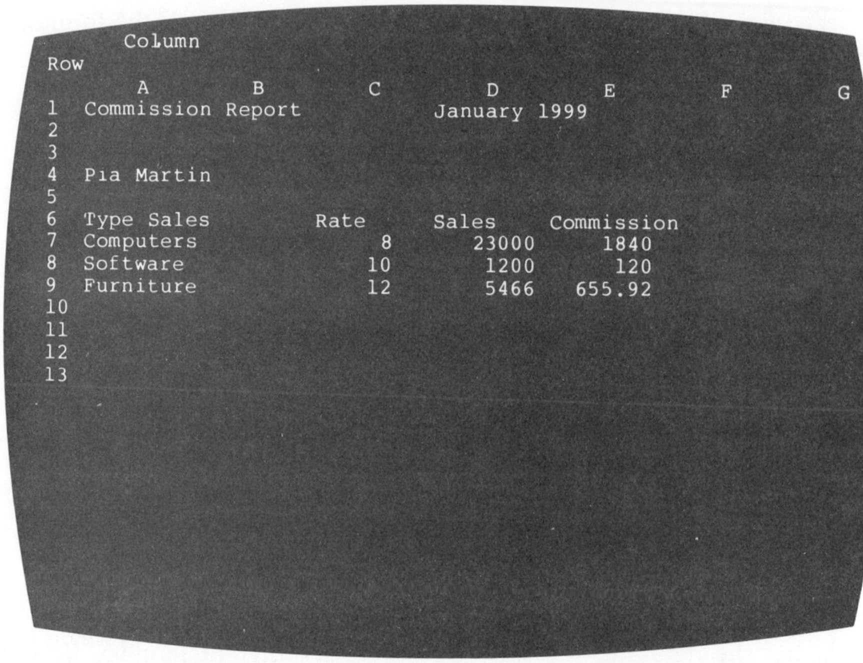

```
        Column
Row
        A         B         C          D          E         F          G
1   Commission Report              January 1999
2
3
4   Pia Martin
5
6   Type Sales           Rate       Sales      Commission
7   Computers             8         23000        1840
8   Software             10          1200         120
9   Furniture            12          5466        655.92
10
11
12
13
```

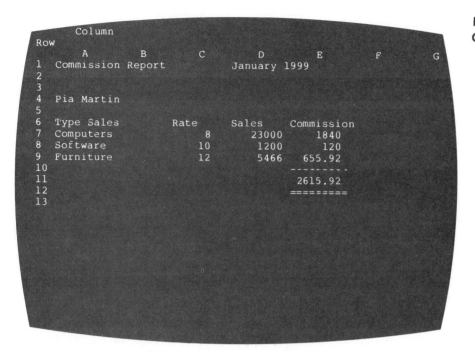

FIGURE 5–14
One More Formula Is Added

```
        Column
Row
          A         B         C         D         E         F         G
1    Commission Report              January 1999
2
3
4    Pia Martin
5
6    Type Sales        Rate       Sales    Commission
7    Computers          8          23000      1840
8    Software          10          1200        120
9    Furniture         12          5466      655.92
10                                           ---------
11                                           2615.92
12                                           =========
13
```

MICROS IN ACTION

A Scott Paper Company accountant reviewed the results and formula used in a spreadsheet. A series of numbers did not seem to be correct. After a short period of time, one formula was found to have an error. The editing capability was used to correct the error and the evaluation was redone in seconds.

The spreadsheet may be used for more than one individual by re-placing the name and the values associated with the second individual. You do not re-calculate. You enter the new data and the electronic spreadsheet produces the results. The output is typed for you so your secretary does not have to type reports.

USER WINDOW

The student set up his accounting homework on a spreadsheet. After one hour he looked up. It was the first time he had ever been able to get a trial balance to balance on the first try. After learning to use the spreadsheet he was able to eliminate his errors and complete most of his assignments in less time and with less effort than required manually.

Editing functions include the capability of:

1. Recalling the formula or label in a cell to make corrections.
2. Inserting/deleting columns or rows.
3. Additional editing features.

Recalling Cells The method used to recall the contents of a cell varies between spreadsheet programs. Once recalled, the information in a cell may be edited in much the same manner as a text file is edited in word processing.

Inserting/Deleting Columns and Rows If you make an error and do not leave enough room on a manual spreadsheet, you will have to copy it over. In an electronic spreadsheet you may insert a column or row when needed with a few simple menu driven instructions. All formulas will be adjusted to the new location of the values upon which they are based.

In a like manner, a column or row may be deleted. If you delete a cell that has the base number or formula in it, you may get an error. The commands used to delete columns or rows are similar between spreadsheets.

Additional Editing Features There are some additional editing features found in many electronic spreadsheets. They include the capability to:

1. Duplicate columns/rows
2. Duplicate a screen in another area
3. Global search and replace
4. Right, left, and center justify

These features make it easier to use a particular electronic spreadsheet, but are not necessary to complete a particular spreadsheet.

Storing and Recalling Spreadsheet programs allow you to save all the information in a spreadsheet or just the labels and formulas. In both cases, once saved, the spreadsheet file may be recalled for use at any time. By editing or overtyping, new data is entered and the analysis is updated for the next period. A spreadsheet saved for future use is often referred to as a **template.** Templates may be purchased on disk or copied out of books for many business applications.

Saving a spreadsheet file is simple and often menu-driven. Table 5–10 is a listing of the commands in the same file menu of Lotus 1–2–3.

Some spreadsheet programs allow you to save a series of many keystrokes in special files called **macros.** These files become routines which may be recalled in total with a few simple keystrokes.

In some spreadsheets you can create your own menus. The /X command is used in Lotus for this task. Table 5–11 is a listing of the options in this menu.

Printing The spreadsheet printing instruction starts with identifying the material to be printed. Usually the number of columns/rows to be printed do not match the standard page format of the printer. There are programs that allow you to print spreadsheets sideways if a better fit can be obtained by this change.

Template:
A spreadsheet or other model saved on disk to be recalled into a spreadsheet or other program as a pattern for future applications.

Macros:
Custom routines which substitute a few keystrokes for many. They may be created by the user and saved on disk as routines that are recalled with a few keystrokes when needed.

TABLE 5–10
/File Menu of Lotus 1-2-3

Command	Function
Save	Store entire worksheet in worksheet file
Retrieve	Restore data from worksheet file
Combine	Incorporate (part of) worksheet file into Current worksheet: Methods: Copy, Add, Subtract use Entire-file or Named-Range only
Xtract	Store range of entries in worksheet file: save Formulas or current values only
Erase	Erase one or more 1-2-3 datafiles
List	List names of 1-2-3 datafiles, report disk space
Import	Incorporate print file into worksheet: treat lines as Text or as Numbers and quoted text
Directory	Change current directory assignment

The printer instructions are menu driven (see Table 5–12) in most spreadsheets, and are specific to a particular spreadsheet program. Many spreadsheet programs allow printing to a file as well as a printer. The file printed is an ASCII file which may be transferred to a word processor or used with the sideways printing program.

Windows

A spreadsheet may be divided into windows as shown in Figure 5–15. It is often useful to have the labels for either column or rows showing in

TABLE 5–11
The Lotus 1-2-3 /X Menu

Command	Application	Notes
/XClocation ~	Call	Continue reading keystrokes at location (cell address, range, or range name). When a /XR command is encountered, return to the point just beyond the /XC location command.
/XR	Return	(Must follow /XC command) Return to reading keystrokes just after the correspoinding /XC location~ command.
/XGlocation ~	Go To	Continue reading keystrokes at location (cell address, range, or range name). No "return" is possible.
/XIformula ~	If-Then	If the formula is TRUE (i.e. has a non-zero value), continue reading keystrokes in the same cell. If the formula is FALSE (i.e. zero), continue to the next cell.
/XMlocation ~	Process a Menu	Allow user to make a menu choice, and branch on the choice. 1-2-3 constructs the menu form the menu range whose upper left corner is location (cell address, range, or range name).
/XLstring~ location~	Label Entry	Displays the specified string as a prompt in the control panel. Accepts an entry from the keyboard, and stores the result as a left justified label (/XL) or as a number (/XN) at location.
/XNstring~ location~	Number Entry	
/XQ	Quit	Enter macro execution and return to Ready mode.

TABLE 5–12
Printer Menu for Lotus 1-2-3

Function	Application
Printer vs. File	Direct output to printer or print file
Range	Range to be printed
Line	Advance printer one line
Page	Advance to top of next page
Options	Page formatting
Headers,Footers	Set page header/footer line
Margins	Left, Right, Top, Bottom
Borders	Graft extra columns/rows to print Range
Setup	Set printer-control characters
Page-Length	Set number of lines
Other	As-Displayed vs. Cell-Formulas:
	Printing of formula texts
	Unformatted vs. Formatted
	Supress headers,footers, page breaks
Clear	Cancel print settings
Align	Reset line-number counter to 1
Go	Print the selected range

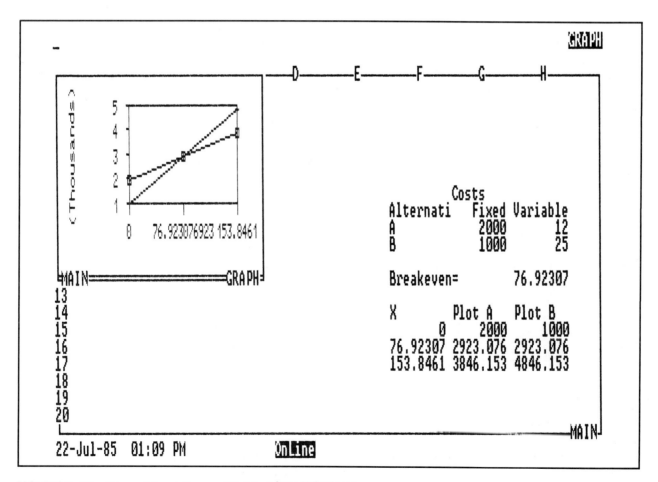

FIGURE 5–15 Spreadsheet Screen Divided into Windows

a window as data is entered into a part of the spreadsheet in a second window. Almost all spreadsheet have this capability.

Interfacing

The capability to transfer spreadsheet results to programs and data from other programs can be important. When you first develop applications with an electronic spreadsheet, the need to transfer data between programs may not seem important. After a number of years you will find yourself with a collection of programs and data in many different formats. You will also find the need to transfer electronic spreadsheet programs into word processing or data base programs. For example, you have a report to prepare based on the output of calculations performed in an electronic spreadsheet. The output of the spreadsheet may be saved as an ASCII file and then transferred into a word processor text file to save you typing.

If an electronic spreadsheet program can read ASCII files, it is generally easy to transfer data in. Only a few programs can read simple ASCII files directly.

Most electronic spreadsheet programs can print files to a disk. This capability usually produces an ASCII file that may be transferred to a word processing program for report preparation.

In addition to simple ASCII files there are a number of other "standard" formats used in spreadsheet work. DIF, data interchange format file, was first developed for the electronic spreadsheet VisiCalc is used by a number of programs to aid in interfacing. DIF files are ASCII files in a specific format. Many spreadsheet programs allow you to save your spreadsheet in DIF.

Integrated Spreadsheet Programs

Integrated programs are often created on the foundation of an electronic spreadsheet program. These integrated programs often include routines for graphics, data base, communication, and word processing. With the growth in the amount of RAM available in microcomputers, the popularity of producing programs with a combination of capabilities has grown.

Lotus 1–2–3 was one of the first programs to combine spreadsheet, graphics, and data base capabilities. Symphony, a product of the same company, has added word processing and communication to the package.

The original version of SuperCalc was a spreadsheet program only. SuperCalc 3 has added some outstanding graphics.

Generally, the cost of a program which integrates a number of capabilities is less than the cost of programs to perform each of the sub-functions. In addition, the transfer of data files between the parts of a program is usually contained in the design of the operation of the program.

THE VARYING CAPABILITIES OF ELECTRONIC SPREADSHEET PROGRAMS

The basic operations of spreadsheet programs is similar, yet each program has unique capabilities. All spreadsheet programs use labels, numbers, and formulas displayed on columns and rows on the microcomputer's monitor. Most operate from a list of functions (a menu) displayed on the microcomputer screen. The main menus of four selected spreadsheets are shown in Figure 5–16.

MICROS IN ACTION

The selection of its spreadsheet program at Scott Paper is determined by its capabilities, not ease of use. The programs, when used, are used so often that a little extra learning time is not as important as performance.

All the spreadsheet menus in Figure 5–16, except Multiplan, are called up by pressing the / key. The Multiplan menu is always on the screen.

Spreadsheet programs tend to be either menu or function key driven. For the beginner or occasional user, the more complete menus are convenient. The experienced user often finds the use of function keys more convenient.

Command cards (cards listing the meaning of the letters in the menu), keyboard overlays (command cards that fit over the keyboard), and key labels (stick-on labels that may be attached to specific keys defining functions) are available for most spreadsheets.

FIGURE 5–16
Spreadsheet Menus

```
Lotus 1-2-3

                                                        MENU
Worksheet Range Copy Move File Print Graph Data Quit
Global, Insert, Delete, Column-Width, Erase, Titles, Windows, Status


Multiplan

COMMAND: Alpha Blank Copy Delete Edit Format Goto Help Insert Lock Move
         Name Options Print Quit Sort Transfer Value Window Xternal
Select option or type command letter



SuperCalc

Enter B,C,D,E,F,G,I,L,M,O,P,Q,R,S,T,U,W,X,A,?



VisiCalc (The Original Spreadsheet)

Command: BCDEFGIMPRSTVW-
```

Spreadsheet programs often have add-on capabilities to perform graphics and data base tasks such as sorting. These add on features often become the determining factor when a spreadsheet selection decision must be made (see Table 5–13).

TABLE 5–13
Comparison of Electronic Spreadsheets

	Lotus 1-2-3	Advanced Visi-Calc	Super Calc 3 Rel 2	Multi-plan
RAM				56K to
Minimum RAM	192K	128K	96K	128K*
Maximum RAM	over 2 MB	1MB	512K	1MB
General				
Number of Columns	256	63	127	63
Number of Rows	2048	254	9999	255
Windows per screen	2	2	2	8
Calculations				
Average	yes	yes	yes	yes
Logarithmic	yes	yes	yes	yes
Percentage	yes	yes	yes	yes
Trigonometric	yes	yes	yes	yes
Auto recalculate	yes	yes	yes	yes
Programming statements	if-then, truc/false, and/or	greater/less than, if-then-else	conditional expression	if-then-else
Editing				
Insert/delete columns/rows	yes	yes	yes	yes
Duplicate columns/rows	yes	yes	yes	yes
Duplicate screen to another area	yes	yes	yes	yes
Global search and replace	no	no	no	no
Right, left, and center justify	yes	yes	R & L	yes
Other Features				
Protect/unprotect indiv. cells, rows	yes	yes	yes	yes
Underline/flashing or inverse video	yes	yes	yes	yes
Vary width of more than one cell	yes	yes	yes	yes
Can $ be displayed	yes	yes	yes	yes
Use commas with numbers	yes	yes	yes	yes
Copy protected	yes	yes	no	yes
Price	$500	$300	$400	$200

(continued on following page)

TABLE 5-13
(continued)

	Lotus 1-2-3	Advanced Visi-Calc	Super Calc 3 Rel 2	Multi-plan
Interfacing				
File Type DIF	x	x	x	
ASCII	x		x	
WordStar			x	
dBaseII	x		x	
Lotus	x		x	
SYLK				x
Add-On Features				
Word processing	No	No	No	No
Graphics	Yes	No	Yes	No
Data base	Yes	No	No	No
Communication	No	No	No	No

SUMMARY

You have learned the importance of the electronic spreadsheet to the business professional and some of the many problems that it may solve. The tasks of the electronic spreadsheet have been defined and some of the more popular ones have been identified. You have had the opportunity to see how simple electronic spreadsheets are to use. The key points learned in this chapter are:

1. The spreadsheet is a business tool. It has been used to solve business problems since the invention of paper and pencil.

2. Electronic spreadsheets save time, increase calculation accuracy, make it possible for managers to perform powerful evaluations, produce final reports, save spreadsheets for future recall and reuse, and do not require a large investment.

3. Electronic spreadsheets require a microcomputer, large amounts of RAM, data entry devices, a monitor, a printer, and usually two disk drives.

4. Electronic spreadsheet programs have some general, configuration, interfacing, and add-on features.

5. Electronic spreadsheet programs solve business problems using labels, numbers, and formulas.

6. Electronic spreadsheets allow you to divide the screen into windows, protect cells, underline, control the size of cells, and control the numerical format.

7. The capability to transfer spreadsheet results to other programs and data from other programs can be important.

8. Some of the more popular programs capable of producing spreadsheets are those with graphics, data base, communication, and word processing capabilities.

9. The basic operations of all spreadsheet programs are similar, yet each has unique capabilities.

Cell
Column
Electronic spreadsheet
Formulas
Labels
Macros
Mathematical operator
Numbers

Precedence
Protected cell
Range
Reference absolute
Reference relative
Row
Spreadsheet
Template

1. What is a spreadsheet?

2. What is an electronic spreadsheet?

3. Which commercial spreadsheet was the first one available for micro-computers?

4. Give an example of a common manual type of spreadsheet.

5. Identify four thing an electronic spreadsheet program gives you the ability to do?

6. What information is entered into an electronic spreadsheet?

7. Define the following electronic spreadsheet terms:
  a. label
  b. numbers
  c. formula
  d. column
  e. row
  f. cells

8. How does the spreadsheet program help you perform a "What if" analysis.

9. Name three applications of spreadsheets in:
  a. Accounting.
  b. Banking.
  c. Finance and economics.
  d. Marketing (transportation and logistics).
  e. Personnel administration.
  f. Quantitative management.
  g. Retail merchandising.
  h. Statistics.
  i. Training.

10. What is mathematical precedence?

11. How might you communicate to an electronic spreadsheet program that you are entering a label?

12. What are the steps required to enter a formula into an electronic spreadsheet?

13. When you enter a formula into an electronic spreadsheet, what appears on the screen?

14. Identify some editing features found in spreadsheet programs.

15. What are some of the additional features found in many spreadsheet programs?

16. How are ASCII files useful in electronic spreadsheet work?

17. What are DIF files?

DISCUSSION AND APPLICATION QUESTIONS

1. Identify several courses you have taken and several you plan to take, in which electronic spreadsheets could help you complete the assignments.

2. Examine advertisements in a microcomputer magazine for electronic spreadsheet programs. What features are now being pushed?

3. From the advertisements reviewed in question 2, determine the amount of RAM that may be used by electronic spreadsheet programs.

4. Use the yellow pages of your telephone book to identify several businesses that have uses for electronic spreadsheet programs. How do you think the programs might be used?

5. Use the yellow pages to find where electronic spreadsheet programs can be puchased in your area.

LABORATORY ASSIGNMENTS

1. Load an electronic spreadsheet into a microcomputer. Enter a label, enter two values, enter an equation based on the values entered, then check the results.

2. Clear the spreadsheet. Enter the number 1 in cell A1 (Row 1 column 1). Enter the formula +A1+1 in cell B1 (Row 1 column 2). Use the copy or replicate routine to replicate the equation for twelve periods.

3. Place the label "Help" in cell A1. Replicate the label into cells A2 through A12.

4. Clear the spreadsheet. Enter the number 3 in cell A1 and the number 10 in B1. Enter the formula +A1+B2 in cell B2. The cell A1 is assumed to be absolute, while cell B1 is relative. Replicate the formula to cells B2 through B12.

5. Clear the spreadsheet. In cells B2, B3, ... B10 enter the values:

$$12 \quad 23 \quad 43 \quad 12 \quad 23 \quad 12 \quad 15 \quad 14 \quad 24$$

In cell B11 enter the label "_____. In cell B12 enter the formula SUM(B2..B10) in the format required by the spreadsheet being used. In cell B13 enter the label " = = = = =

6. Use the data in problem 5. In cell A15 enter the label "Average:". In cell B15 enter the formula
AVG(B2..B10) in the format required by the spreadsheet being used.

7. Use the data in problem 5. In cell A16 enter the label "Standard:". In cell B16 enter the formula
STD(B2..B10) in the format required by the spreadsheet being used.

8. Use the data in problem 5.
   a. Check all calculations by calculator.
   b. Determine if the equation used for standard deviation used n or n-1. (Statistic background recommended).

9. Use the data in problem 5. Use the formulas
MAX(B2...B10) and @MIN(B2,,B10) in the format required by the spreadsheet being used to determine the maximum and minimum values in the data.

PROBLEMS

1. (Education) A class consists of twelve people. Their names and student numbers are:

Number	Student	Student Number
1.	Mary Lenissa	12234
2.	Ivan Petrushian	22445
3.	Stanley Michel	12554
4.	Neal Roberts	43223
5.	Bruce Davis	11447
6.	Kim Aguilar	43556
7.	Kim McCreary	45669
8.	Sven Torgeson	19854
9.	Wayne Bonnana	18888
10.	Anna Spatulski	16431
11.	Jean Angstriech	25647
12.	Chang Ho Quon	54678

Set up a class roll and grade sheet that can be used by the instructor. Identify headings for each column including spaces for roll checking, grades for quizzes, final exams, and course grades.

There are five grading criteria in the class. The first two are reports with a weight of 5% each. The second and third are quizzes with a weight of 10% each. The last is the final exam with a weight of 70%. The class meets twice a week for five weeks.

Identify the formulas used to calculate the student's average for the term, the class average, and class standard deviation. Lay the grade sheet out on a piece of paper in preparation for making an electronic spreadsheet. Identify the location of these formulas.

2. (General) Develop a budget in the form of a spreadsheet for a dual-career couple with the wife working as an accountant for $22,000 per year, and the husband attending graduate school full time at a nearby university. The monthly costs for various budget items are shown:

No.	Item	Monthly Budget
1.	Rent	$344
2.	Food	280
3.	Babysitting	100
4.	Utilities	200
5.	Books	30
6.	Tuition	200
7.	Clothing	200
8.	Travel/Auto	200
9.	Savings or Entertainment	
10.	Miscellaneous	
11.	Gifts/donations	

Using a spreadsheet format lay out the above budget for the year on a month by month basis. Assume that church donations will total $50 a month except during December, when a donation of $300 is planned. Also include a special birthday present for the couple's daughter costing $200 in June. Lay out the above as a spreadsheet, locating all labels and formulas. Identify the formulas needed. The objective is to determine the cash available per month.

3. (General) The couple in problem 2 has a 10 year-old girl who is a member of a youth group. The group is planning a three day, 300 mile trip to the state capital. The costs include:

No.	Item	Cost
1.	Rent on bus	$600
2.	Meals per day per person	18
3.	Camping Fees for the group	50
4.	Museum entrance fees per person	8
5.	Group Insurance	75
6.	Group Camping supplies	50

Lay out a spreadsheet to determine the total cost for the group and to identify the cost per individual if there are 22 children and four adults making the trip. Identify all labels, numbers, and formulas.

4. (General business) A checkbook register contains the following information:

Date	Check Number	Checks issued to or deposits received from	Amount Deposited	Cleared	Amount of Check	Balance
—	—	Original balance		x		2000.00
8/13	202	Rent			150.00	
8/15	203	Utilities			125.36	
8/16	204	Phone			39.87	
8/17	—	Salary check	1500.26			
8/18	—	Gift	12.15			
8/18	205	Cash			175.00	
8/18	206	Food store	97.83			

The bank records show:

Previous Balance	We have added:		We have subtracted:			Current Balance
Statement	Number	Deposits	Number	Checks	Serv Chg	
2000.00	1	1500.26	8	587.01	1.22	2912.03

Checking Account Transactions

Date	Amount	Description
8/19	1500.26	DEPOSIT

CHECKS

DATE..........AMOUNT	
8/15	100.22
8/19	39.87
8/19	5.21
8/19	12.55
8/20	6.33
8/24	175.00
8/25	97.83
8/25	150.00

At the beginning of the period your balance and the bank's balance were the same. There were no outstanding transactions of any type.

Set up a spreadsheet to start with your balance, add the not cleared checks, subtract the unrecorded checks, subtract the not cleared deposits, add the unrecorded deposits, make adjustments for errors in recording and service charges, and produce a final balance to be compared to the bank's.

5. (Accounting) Set up and organize a spreadsheet for the ledger of Western Gas with the following chart of accounts:

Balance Sheet	Debit	Credit
Cash account	5,000	
Accounts payable		7,000
Accounts receivable	1,200	
Building	100,000	
Equipment	59,800	
Reserve for depreciation		30,000
Land	75,000	
Notes payable		55,000
Capital		150,000
Retained earnings		9,000
Supplies	10,000	

Place the accounts in order of current assets, fixed assets, current liabilities, and long term liabilities followed by stockholder's equity.

Locate where all labels and formulas will be and identify these formulas in terms of spreadsheet location.

6. (Marketing) You have a job working for the local computer store to determine the number of spreadsheet users on your campus. A questionaire has been designed. Most questions are designed to be answered with a yes, no, or I do not know. Some questions require the respondent to identify the type of computer or program being used. The questions to be answered by the survey include:

1. Do you know what a spreadsheet is?
2. Are you currently using an electronic spreadsheet?
3. Do you have a microcomputer available?
4. What kind of microcomputer do you use?
5. Do you have an electronic spreadsheet program available?
6. What electronic spreadsheet program do you have?
7. Have long have you had the program?
8. How much did you pay for the program?
9. If you do not have a spreadsheet program are you planning to purchase one?
10. How often do you use your program?
11. Do you plan to purchase a microcomputer? When?

Organize the questions on a spreadsheet. Identify all questions, the numbers you generate, the formulas needed and their location. The objective is to give the store management some idea of how large a market exists for electronic spreadsheet and microcomputers on campus.

7. (Statistics) The formulas for the average and standard deviation of a sample are:

Average = (Sum X(i))/N

Standard Deviation = Square Root((Sum (Average-X(i)))/(N-1))

Set up a spreadsheet for a sample size of 10 to:

1. Find Sum X(i)
2. Identify what N is

3. Find Sum(Average-X(i))
4. Find the average
5. Find the standard deviation

Analyze the following sample data set:

Number	Data
1	12.32
2	12.99
3	13.55
4	16.55
5	11.23
6	12.24
7	13.66
8	12.45
9	12.54
10	12.00

Identify the labels, the numbers, the formulas, and the location of each item.

8. (Accounting/Finance) Lay out a spreadsheet for the preparation of an amortization schedule for the first twelve months of an equal monthly payment mortgage. The mortgage is for $40,000 with a thirty year payout at 12.5% annual percentage rate. Identify the location of all labels, all numbers entered, and all formulas. Specify the formulas needed.

9. (Other Courses) From any course being taken this term or last term, propose a spreadsheet application for the instructor's approval. After approval, layout a spreadsheet for the selected application.

SELECTED REFERENCES

Clark, Roger E. *Executive SuperCalc 3*. Addison Wesley, 1984.

Schrum, Carlton *How to Use VisiCalc/SuperCalc*. Alfred Publishing, 1983.

Weber System Inc. *Lotus 1–2–3 User's Handbook*. Ballantine Books, 1984.

Williams, R.E. *The Power of Multiplan*. Management Information Source.

Williams, R.E. and B.L. King. *The Power of SuperCalc*. Management Information Source.

Williams, R.E. and B.J. Taylor. *The Power of VisiCalc*. Management Information Source.

Williams, R.E. and B.J. Taylor. *The Power of VisiCalc II*. Management Information Source.

Witkens, Ruth. *Managing Your Business with Multiplan*. Microsoft Press, 1984.

Zimmerman, Steven M., Leo M. Conrad and Stanley M. Zimmerman. *Electronic Spreadsheets and Your IBM PC*. Hayden Book Company, 1984.

6

Chapter Outline

Chapter Goals

When you complete this chapter you will be able to:

Understand why data base programs are important to the
 business professional.

Define the tasks of a data base program.

Understand the steps needed to set up and operate a data base
 system.

Identify some commercial data base programs.

DATA BASE

Schnieder-Fleming Insurance

An agent for the Schneider-Fleming Insurance agency identified his needs for microcomputer equipment as:
1. Customer data base file.
2. Word processing—letters, proposals, and contracts.
3. Custom program or spreadsheet client analysis.
4. Communication with the central office.

The data base need was the most critical because the agency research has shown that appointments per phone call and sales per appointment could be increased if the calls could be coordinated with events in the client's lives. Among the more important events were:
1. Birth of a child.
2. Graduation of a family member from high school or college.
3. Obtaining a new job.
4. The purchase or sale of a house.
5. Family member's death.
6. Serious illness of a family member.
7. Marriage (divorce) of a family member.
8. A child's first car.

Sales are also a function of keeping in contact with a client. If contact is not made for one year, the probability of client loss to another agency is increased.

Knowledge:
The assignment of meaning to information by a human being.
Facts:
Something having real demonstrable existence.
Information:
Data that has been processed and recalled from a data base in an organized manner.

A data base is a collection of data used for one or more purposes. An electronic data base program is one that is designed to operate on a computer. A data base program takes care of organizing data for storage disk and usually includes a screen editor that allows data entry and update, and a report generator that produces custom business reports. **Knowledge** starts as **facts** about some business situation, it becomes data when it is entered into a data base. The output of a data base is the act that turns data into **information.** When it is read and used by a human being knowledge is gained.

A young lady was hired as a new car salesperson. She faced the problem of contacting as many friends and acquaintances as possible in order to start building a client group. She started with a list of her high school graduation class and the members of her church.

She used her mother's microcomputer to type a letter. She typed a mailing list of all the names she had collected into the microcomputer for her mail-list data base.

She then proceeded to send all her friends a computer produced letter. This is a simple and effective use of a data base.

Microcomputer users create and maintain data bases for their own personal and business needs by acquiring one of the many data base programs currently available.

These programs vary from **file maintenance** and **report generators** with limited capabilities, to programs that are in effect, very high level, special purpose microcomputer languages in themselves. The **non-procedural language** data base programs can perform almost any data base task, as well as many other tasks.

The data base system found in your microcomputer has a number of functions. First, it is a data storage entry device. The method of organizing the file into which the data is stored must be defined in a setup routine. This is the step that requires the most research and effort. A little extra care and effort in setup greatly adds to the value of a data base in the future as a business problem-solving tool. Once the file is set up and organized, facts must be collected and recorded in the data base as data.

The capabilities of data base systems vary from simple file maintenance to computer languages. Data base programs allow you to search for a particular record with specified characters.

File maintenance:
The entering and updating of data in a data base.
Report generation:
The creation of a formatted report to output information from the data base.
Non-procedural language:
A programming language that does not require programming techniques to be used. It allows the user to send instructions to the computer in English- like statements.

DATA BASE HARDWARE NEEDS

The development and application of microcomputer data bases are dependent upon the capabilities and capacities of the available hardware. The hardware needed for a microcomputer data base includes:

1. RAM
2. Input devices
3. Monitor
4. Printer
5. On-line storage

RAM

Most data base programs, both file maintenance and very high level language programs, have no special RAM requirements. A number of programs which were transferred and re-written from larger computers do have large RAM needs.

Input Devices

Data base input methods include:

1. Keyboard
2. Point of sale (cash register)
3. Light pens
4. Optical character readers
5. Communication programs using other data bases

The most often-used method of data entry, and data base update is the keyboard. Data base programs can be designed to take advantage of many other methods. Point of sales data entry, light pens, and optical character readers are often used for inventory control.

Microcomputer data bases are often used in conjunction with central computer data bases. Communication and transfer of files between the central computer and the microcomputer are common; they will be covered in more detail in the communication chapter.

Monitor

The monitor is used as a primary output device for data base programs. Almost any monochrome or color screen will satisfy the data base user's needs. If the data is to be used for color or high-resolution graphics, a monitor with the required capability is needed.

Printer

Data bases often produce lists and tables. Users of data bases and spreadsheets often have the same need for wide carriage printers. The discussion of printers in chapter 5 applies to data bases as well as to spreadsheets.

On-Line Storage

Data Bases need on-line storage devices that can handle large amounts of storage. As the amount of on-line storage availablilty has increased and its costs decreased, the number of programs and applications of data bases on microcomputers has increased as well. Early data bases on microcomputers were simple due to the limited hardware capacity and software capability. Only when low cost (under $1,000), hard disk devices (over 5 million bytes) and increased RAM (beyond 64K) became available did the number of programs and applications expand.

MICROS IN ACTION

The Schneider-Fleming Insurance agent decided that there should be a master file of all the agency's clients. The maximum number of clients was estimated to be 5,000. The number of characters stored per client was estimated to be 1,000. By multiplying the two numbers together, it was estimated that approximately five megabytes of storage was needed.

To accommodate other applications, a hard disk with a minimum capacity of ten megabytes was specified.

You may not need a hard disk because the size of your data base may fit on a floppy disk system. However, you will find that some data base programs were developed because of the expansion of this market. Table 6–1 lists the capacity of storage on floppy diskettes in microcomputer terms.

Microcomputer Operating System	Floppy Diskettes	TABLE 6-1 Media for Storing Data
Apple DOS	140K	
CP/M	90K up to 760K	
MS-DOS/PC-DOS	160K to 380K, 760K, and 1.2MB	
TRS-DOS(Models I, III, 4)	80K to 180K	

In data base programs using ASCII files, the number of bytes is equal to the total number of characters in the data base including control codes and spaces. Most data base programs use ASCII files. Data base programs using compressed code are able to store more data in the same space as an ASCII file. The storage requirements of files created by a data base program can be determined only from studying its specifications.

Many data base applications are initially set up using floppy disks, then moved to a hard disk as the system grows. Hard disks can store from 5 megabytes to over 500 megabytes of data. The greater the capacity, the greater the absolute cost, but the lower the cost per byte. Laser disks are under development and are expected to have capacities near 500 megabytes.

WHY THE BUSINESS PROFESSIONAL SHOULD KNOW ABOUT DATA BASE PROGRAMS

Information is a resource. Data base help businesses manipulate information. Businesses require many different data bases, for example:

- Accounts payable
- Accounts receivable
- Customer lists
- Lists
- Employee records
- Inventory
- Product information
- Sales records
- Suppliers
- Year to date accounting performance data

The availability of accurate, up-to-date information, can help management earn or save dollars. Management decisions must often be made immediately, and the availability of information from the data base can mean additional profit. Errors in judgment may occur when working without key facts. The cost of creating and maintaining a data base must be balanced with the value of the data to the business.

The question "What is the potential size of the microcomputer college market, if the current price of equipment were reduced by 50%?" cannot be answered by a data base because it is a prediction. The question "What are the current and past sales of microcomputer equipment in different types of colleges in different locations around the country?" can be answered by a data base. Having the answers to the second question can aid a manager in making a better decision about how to service the college microcomputer market.

MICROS IN ACTION

One agent for Schneider-Fleming Insurance set up his own data base. His clients names and their life information needed to provide insurance services were entered into the data base.

The extra work slowed down the number of sales calls at first, but resulted in a good long-term relationship and repeat business from the client base, once it was established.

Some of the data needed were identified as:
1. Name
2. How called (how the individual wants to be addressed)
3. Address
4. Phone number
5. Date of last contact
6. Number in family
7. Names and dates of birth of each family member
8. Approximate date of next life event
9. Home ownership
10. Automobile ownership
11. Unusual or serious illness of a family member.

The principal limitations to the creation of data bases are the needs and imagination of the business professional. Data base design begins with an in-depth understanding of your business needs.

THE LANGUAGE OF DATA BASE

Some basic terms must be understood when learning about data bases. To understand a data base some basic concepts are needed. These concepts include:

1. File management concepts
   a. Files
   b. Records
   c. Fields
2. Data base concepts
   a. Facts
   b. Data
   c. Information
   d. Knowledge
   e. Decision making.

File Management Concepts—File, Record, and Field

A data base file is a collection of similar records. An example of a file is a file cabinet containing all the data pertaining to a group of housing units owned by a real estate investor. A data base file is stored on your disk in the same manner as text or program files.

A **record** is a collection of facts about an **entity.** The rent record form in a file folder in a housing unit file cabinet may contain historical rental facts about a particular housing unit. This form is a record. A collection of forms constitues a file.

A **field** stores data about an **attribute** of the entity. If there is a location to enter the telephone number of the current occupant of a housing unit on the rent record form, this "location" could be considered a field. The telephone number is an attribute. Figure 6–1 illustrates a file, record, and field.

A data base of personnel records may consist of a series of files. In each file may be different job skills. The record or entity would be an individual. The fields in the record would contain the individual's name, sex, pay rate, number of dependents, address, telephone number, etc. The more information in the data base, the more potential applications of the data base. The more information, however, the greater the cost of setup and maintenance.

In many data bases, fields and records contain a fixed number of

Record:
A collection of facts about an entity.
Entity:
Something that has separate and distinct existence.
Field:
A unit of data about an attribute of an entity.
Attribute:
A particular characteristic of interest about an entity.

(a) A File   (b) Record   (c) A Field

FIGURE 6–1   A (a) File, (b) Record, (c) Field

characters or numbers. If the data in a field does not take up the entire field, the remaining space is wasted. Every wasted character cuts down the amount of data that may be stored in a given file, on a given type of computer storage media. When you assign characters to fields you must be careful to balance the loss of information of small fields with the waste of space caused by too large a field. An example of wasted space is a last name field of ten characters with the name JONES in it. JONES uses five characters, the extra space for the five additional characters is wasted.

Data Base Concepts—Facts, Data, Information, Knowledge, and Decision-Making

Definitions of data base terms vary between writers and over time. The meaning of the words facts, data, information, knowledge, and decision-making gives structure to the field of data base management.

The objective of a data base system is to collect facts, store selected facts as data, recall and present the data as information to a knowledgeable worker. The individual may then turn the information into knowledge for decision-making. The system starts with the collection of facts and ends with a decision.

Facts are available everywhere, about everything. The colors of your car and house are facts. Your age and the grade you earned in your last English course are facts. Facts may be considered raw data. Facts do not become data unless they are selected and stored or organized in some manner. Data bases are used to store and organize data for future use.

The data in a data base becomes information when the data is received by a human being in a form that has meaning.

Only a person can have knowledge. Knowledge is the assignment of meaning to information by an individual. You know something about a person or object when the information has meaning. When making a purchase decision, the prices of similar articles is knowledge.

When the value of information is great enough that it pays to create and maintain a data base, then and only then should one be created. The trade-off is the cost of the information versus its value. The low cost of microcomputer data base programs justifies many applications.

The decision to purchase a piece of real estate depends on information. If you are an investor making many such decisions, you may have a need for a personal data base. The value of information about the current real estate market and future trends is great to the investor.

If you are an individual purchasing your first house, then some information is needed. The value of the information is not as great as it is to the investor, but it still has value. Individual home buyers may depend on real estate agents and other professionals for knowledge, rather than set up a system to manage the data themselves.

DATA BASE PROGRAM FEATURES

Data base programs vary from file management-report generators to computer languages. A classification of data base programs helps in the selection of the proper program for your needs. Characteristics of candidate programs may be used to identify a program that matches a need.

The important characteristics of a data base program include:

1. Classification/type
2. Type of index organization
3. Compatibility
4. Other features
   a. File maintenance, report generators, and calculations
   b. Function keys and menus

Classification/Type

Data base programs may be simple file managers, complete languages in which many applications may be created, or something in between. The classification (general type) of data base management programs determines the type of problem the program can solve:

1. File management-report generator data bases
2. Relational data bases
3. Hierarchical data bases
4. Network data bases
5. Free format data bases
6. Multi-user data bases
7. Computer languages.

Most of the data base programs currently available for microcomputers are file management—report generators or relational types.

File Management—Report Generator Data Bases The needs of many business professionals are satisfied by **file management—report generator** data base programs. This type of program is not a true data base; it is often used to create and manage a single file for some single purpose with limited on-line storage capacity. A file management—report generator program controls a file that is organized into records and fields, and produces reports from the data. Figure 6–2 illustrates a file management file layout.

File management—report generators:
Programs designed to store, update, and retrieve business data. These programs are limited to managing simple files with narrow objectives.

Relational Data Bases A relational data base is organized using files, records, and fields in a manner similar to file management systems. Relational data base systems have the additional capability to combine the data from a series of records that have a field with a matching relation-

```
File -- scout masters in a district
    Record --- a scout master
    Fields -- troop/name/street/city/
              zipcode/telephone
```

FIGURE 6–2
File Management File Layout

FIGURE 6–3
Relational Data File Layout

File -- scout masters in a district
    Record --- a scout master
      Fields -- troop/name/street/...
You may join all records that pertain to a
given city.

ship. Relational data bases do not have to be as carefully organized as file management systems, but the poorer the organization, the more slowly the system will operate. Figure 6–3 shows a relational data file layout.

The organization of relational and file management data bases looks the same. The difference is that relational data base programs have a "join" command that allows searching for all individuals with a given characteristic in a specified field, and to combine in a variety of ways the data pertaining to that characteristic. You may produce a list of all individuals in a file who live in the same zipcode area.

Hierarchical Data Bases A data base organized from the top down is called hierarchical. Such a data base does not have to be divided into fields. The hierarchical structure allows us to search the data base without being limited to searching each field. The record contents are not limited by the nature of the search procedures. The file organization determines the location of a record in the hierarchy, not the contents of a file. The organization is similar to the hierarchical organization of MS-DOS files. In the hierarchical system (see Figure 6–4) each record is related to the next higher level by its location.

FIGURE 6–4
Hierarchical Data File Layout

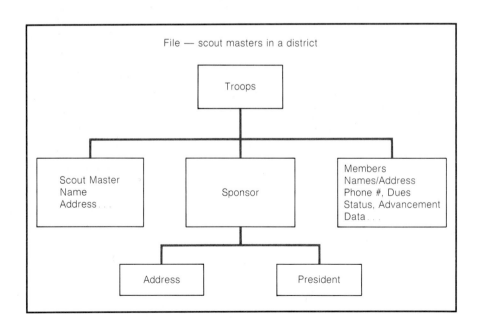

172   Understanding and Using Microcomputers

FIGURE 6-5
Network Data File Layout

File — scout masters, troops, and sponsors

Troops   Sponsors

Scout Master
Name
Address...

A Sponsor
Name/Address
...

Network Data Bases A network (see Figure 6–5) is similar to a hierarchical system, with the exception that it allows for multiple relationships among levels. Microcomputer programs for this type of data base are limited.

Free Format Data Bases Free format data bases (see Figure 6–6) combine different forms of data entry including text, lists, tables, charts, and graphs. Key words located in the stored data base are used to retrieve the material. Programs for microcomputers that handle this type of data base are not readily available.

Multi-User Data Bases The hardware and software technology for multi-user data bases is currently undergoing rapid change. A multi-user data base is one that allows more than a single user access at the same time. This means that two or more microcomputers are connected together and use the same on-line storage device. The problems of two users changing a record at the same time and of file security become more complex when there is more than a single user of a data base.

Computer Languages There are few limits to the problems that may be solved by some data base programs. Complete accounting systems may be created entirely in a data base program. Computer language data base programs fit the definition of a high-level computer language: a set of

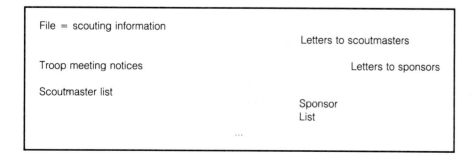

FIGURE 6-6
Data Base Free Format

File = scouting information

Letters to scoutmasters

Troop meeting notices

Letters to sponsors

Scoutmaster list

Sponsor
List

...

near English codes used to give instructions to a computer. These data base programs often include specialized statements which make the creation and use of data bases easier than if a general purpose language were used in their creation.

Types of Index Organization

Indexing schemes reduce the amount of time needed to find data in a data base. Indexing is the manner in which a program orders the records in a file. It is often invisible to the user. The important aspect of record indexing is the amount of time needed to find the data wanted. A sequential search, starting at the beginning of a file, examining each record in turn, and seeking a particular record, quickly results in long delays for even small files, and is not an acceptable method for most data bases. The schemes commonly used for indexing are detailed in the appendix.

Compatibility

The capability to transfer files to and from data bases is a form of compatibility. A data base program is more useful if you are able to transfer files between it and other applications. There are several standards:

1. ASCII, American Standard Code for Information Interchange.
2. DIF, Data Interchange Format (Designed for VisiCalc).
3. SYLK, Symbolic Link (Designed for MultiPlan).

Data base programs that can read and write ASCII files are able to interface with the maximum number of other data base, word processing, spreadsheet, and graphics files.

The DIF, data interchange file, is an ASCII file that is arranged in a special manner. It was developed for the spreadsheet VisiCalc to make the transfer of data between programs easier.

SYLK, Symbolic Link, is a specially formatted ASCII file created to make file transfer with MultiPlan easier.

Your ability to take advantage of new data base programs will be limited if your file cannot be transferred. Retyping a data base is expensive and subject to the introduction of costly errors.

Data base programs are often combined with other programs such as word processing, spreadsheets, communications, graphics, or others. These integrated programs, which include one or more functions, are often selected because the integrated program takes care of file transfer. All parts of the program use the same data file and operate using similar menus or functions.

Some data base programs, such as dBase II and dBase III, include non-procedural programming languages in addition to standard data base features. A program of this nature may be used to create many different applications. You may have to balance your needs for fast results and flexibility. Programmers often find it easier to create complex applications with these very high-level non-procedural language tools. The more a program adds capabilities and approaches a very high-level language, the more difficult it is to learn and use.

Other Features

Microcomputer data base programs aid in data entry, report generation, and in custom calculation of information based on data in the data base. Report generators take the data from the file and produce hard copy using a microcomputer printer. The types of reports produced by data base programs vary from accounting to zoology.

USER WINDOW

Think about the amount of time it would take your university to produce your grade report by hand. Also visualize the potential errors that could be produced in a manual system.

On-screen editors allow you to enter and update data in a data base. No data base remains fixed. Constant update is needed. Most programs allow you to make changes with ease, and to see the changes on the computer's monitor.

One advantage of electronically maintained data bases is that once you have entered the data, you need only update the changes and then press a key to produce a new report.

Data Base Program Function Keys and Menus pfs:FILE uses the function keys on the IBM PC found on the left side of the keyboard in combination with screen selection menus. A menu is a list of different actions that may be taken. For example, in pfs:FILE the screen looks like the one in Figure 6–7.

The pfs:FILE menu allows you to enter the design file (edit) mode, to go to a second menu to define the formats used to produce the page, to print the current file, or to go to a second menu where you can read save, or remove a text file from disk. You may also clear the text from the memory of your computer. This file management program places all the text in the RAM, and it may be cleared with ease.

STEPS REQUIRED IN DESIGNING AND OPERATING YOUR DATA BASE

Microcomputer data base creation requires careful planning. The functions of management are:

1. Planning (including goal setting)
2. Organizing
3. Directing
4. Controlling.

FIGURE 6–7
The PFS:MENU

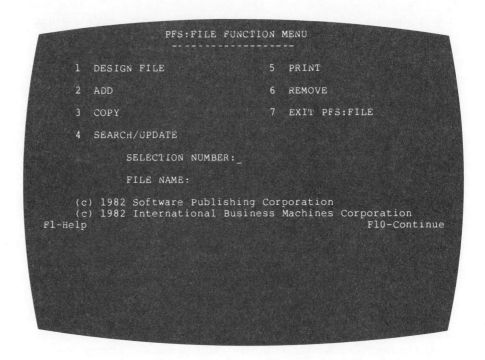

```
                    PFS:FILE FUNCTION MENU
                    ----------------------

    1  DESIGN FILE              5  PRINT

    2  ADD                      6  REMOVE

    3  COPY                     7  EXIT PFS:FILE

    4  SEARCH/UPDATE

          SELECTION NUMBER:_

          FILE NAME:

    (c) 1982 Software Publishing Corporation
    (c) 1982 International Business Machines Corporation
  F1-Help                                         F10-Continue
```

The data base program allows the professional user to:

1. Design the screen format used for data entry
2. Design the reports to be generated
3. Select the facts to be stored
4. Input facts
5. Update the data
6. Generate reports as needed
7. Sort the data
8. Query the data base for specific data.

The business plan and organization determines the data base reports, other outputs, and their frequency. The desired output of a data base determines how it must be designed and operated. Output includes reports and screen displays.

The steps in designing a data base are as follows:

1. Identification of business output needs (reports and other output).
2. Identify the data required, sources, and the input format.
3. Design structure and size for data storage (identify file, records, and fields).
4. Identify what must be done with the input data to generate the reports and output required.
5. Identify data security needs.
6. Select and use data base program to:
   a. Create the data structure.
   b. Design the data input formats.

c. Enter preliminary data.
d. Design procedures for processing the data.
e. Design outputs.
f. Trial run.
g. Evaluate performance.
h. Redesign and repeat steps a-g until satisfied.
7. Operate and manage the data base.

There are constraints on all steps. Some of the facts you need may not be available. In the health business, information on personal health is restricted. Detailed financial facts are also often difficult to obtain.

Business Output Needs

Business needs will dictate the direction of a data base. Data bases are tools for the business professional to accomplish business objectives. The reports and other outputs are the physical manifestations of the business objectives and government regulations. Examples of reports and outputs include a list of customers, employees, church members, property for sale, mailing lists, mailing labels, and automatic addressing of letters.

Figure 6–8 illustrates a report design with records referring to an individual and the following fields:

- Last name
- First name
- How called (how the individual wants to be addressed)
- Phone
- Company
- Address
- City
- State
- Zipcode
- Numerical code
- Alphabetical code

The form in Figure 6–8 was produced according to the specifications in Figure 6–9.

Some microcomputer data base programs are very high-level microcomputer languages, and they are capable of producing customized reports such as general ledgers, income and expense statements, inventory

FIGURE 6–8 The Required Report as Implemented in dBase II

Last	First	Call	Phone	Company	Address	City	Zip	ST	Num	Alp
Prieto	Juan	Smitty	205-555-1212	Able Computer Company	11 First Street	Mobile	12345	AL	1255	99AA
Snodgrass	Mary	Leni.	123-555-1111	AZ Management Services In	4151 Bay Avenue	Atlanta	44445	NJ	5555	A1BB
Conrad	Leo	Dr. Leo	123-555-1116	Imagineering Concepts Inc.	1234 Park Drive	Atlanta	44445	NJ	5556	A2AA
Timbalov	Stephanie	Dr. T	123-555-1111	AZ Management Services In	4151 Bay Avenue	Atlanta	44445	NJ	5555	B2BB
Rockable	Betty	Rocky	333-555-1111	Lost Lane School	55 Byte Drive	Miami	11112	NY	2222	A3CC
Duval	Robert	Bob	333-555-2222	Western Wear Clothes Inc.	12 Label Lane	Miami	11112	NY	2223	A3CC
Kahn	Joe	Joe	205-555-1233	Able Computer Company	11 First Avenue	Mobile	12345	AL	5555	A1AA
Cheng	Thuc	Thuc	333-666-1111	Boston Computer Company	11 First Avenue	Western	11115	AL	5555	A2BB
Anderson	Steve	Mr. Anders	222-444-5555	Eastern Microcomputer Co.	1 Computer Lane	Boston	99995	CA	5555	B6XX
Zimmerman	Carol	Carol	123-555-1111	AZ Management Services In	4151 Bay Avenue	Atlanta	44445	NJ	5555	B2BB

reports, telephone calls, graphic presentations, communication with other computers, and more.

The most common business output from a data base is a report on a piece of paper. Reports are limited by the space available on screen and printer. There are programs that allow you to print sideways on a sheet of paper to overcome the limitations of paper size in a printer (see Figure 6–10).

Figure 6–11 is a 65-column report layout. Sixty-five columns is the default limitation on many word processors. The 65-column limitation was used to illustrate the types of problems that are encountered.

The titles and data are too long for some of the fields. There are no spaces left over to insert blanks between each field. The data will run together. Data base programs are not limited to storing the same information that is printed in a report. Using an output device that handles more than 65 columns or more than a single line for output, both data and title output may be expanded.

```
COL         WIDTH,CONTENTS
001          6,Last Name<CR>
ENTER HEADING: Last<CR>
002          4,First<CR>
ENTER HEADING: First<CR>
003          4,How:Called
ENTER HEADING: Call<CR>
004          9,Phone
ENTER HEADING: Phone<CR>
005          7,Company
ENTER HEADING: Company<CR>
006          7,Address
ENTER HEADING: Address<CR>
007          6,City<CR>
ENTER HEADING: City<CR>
008          1,State<CR>
ENTER HEADING: St<CR>
009          4,Zip<CR>
ENTER HEADING: Zip<CR>
010          4,Num:Code<CR>
ENTER HEADING: Num<CR>
011          3,Alp:Code<CR>
ENTER HEADING: Alp<CR>
012          <CR>
```

FIGURE 6–9   Defining Fields in dBase II

The four-digit numeric and alpha-numeric codes are assumed to be needed by the business objective. Most data base programs differentiate between numeric data and alpha-numeric or character data. They may represent an income level, a credit rating, a health problem type, a preference in cars, computers, copiers, types of TV sets, or cameras. The data is shown in Figure 6–12.

The limitation of 65 columns reflects the users' decision to design a report that would fit on normal width paper. Most data base programs allow you to enter a greater number of characters in a given field than are printed.

Examine each field to see if the output would be useful for a business application. Since the space is limited the data printed will not be useable for many applications. As a user you must determine your output needs and the limitations of the equipment used and then make a careful trade-off between them if a conflict occurs as in this case. Some fields are fixed, such as the telephone number and zipcode. The code fields must also be shown in their entirety. Some data base systems allow you to add spaces and the extra characters in phone numbers and zip codes that make them more readable. The layout of a report requires a lot of carful counting and consideration of each output.

FIGURE 6–10
Sideways Printed Report

(last 5 months projected)

	Aug.	Sep.	Oct.	Nov.	Dec.
	405,075	567,516	554,109	575,362	617,345
	116,213	127,423	124,687	175,298	135,083
	42,052	46,284	48,219	50,045	57,225
	50,999	50,417	50,372	55,058	60,118
	614,339	791,640	777,387	855,763	869,771
	236,225	230,128	219,613	218,449	220,123
	8,449	9,207	8,763	8,789	8,884
	14,880	14,501	13,435	11,238	12,433
	36,738	30,777	41,122	43,972	42,873
	296,292	284,613	282,933	282,448	284,313
	17,817	18,552	19,001	19,224	17,335
	61,085	60,135	59,245	61,444	60,187
	1,046	1,030	1,555	1,322	1,088
	79,948	79,717	79,801	81,990	78,610

Data Required, Sources, Input Format, Design Structure, and Size

The data base output defines the need for input. The report in our example includes the last name, first name, how called (for personal letters), phone number, company name, address, city, state, zipcode, and two codes for customer information. These facts must be found someplace. Sources include salesperson reports, other data bases, and copies of orders. Once located, the data must be entered into the data base. Figure 6–13 illustrates a typical input screen for these facts.

The facts, once obtained, must be entered into the data base. Most entries will be through the keyboard onto a form designed and displayed on the screen. Some data may be entered directly from other data bases

FIGURE 6–11
Definition of Field Size For 65 Column Report

Last Name	First Name	How Called	Phone	Company	Address	City	St	Zip	Numeric Code	Alpha Code
7	5	5	10	8	8	7	2	5	4	4

```
O | Last    First How Phone       Company Address City    StZip   Num Alph  | O
  | Name    Name Calle                                    Code Code Cod     |
O | Prieto Juan Smitt2055551212Able Com11 FirstMobile AL12345125599AA       | O
  | SnodgraMary Leni 123555l111AZ Manag4151 BayAtlantaNJ444455555Al BB      |
O | Conrad Leo  Dr. L1235551116Imaginee1234 ParAtlantaNJ444455556A2AA       | O
  | TimbaloStephDr. T1235551111AZ Manag4151 BayAtlantaNJ444455555B2BB       |
O | RockablBettyRocky3335551111Lost Lan55 Byte Miami  NY111122222A3CC       | O
  | Duval  RoberBob  3335552222Western 12 LabelMiami  NY111122223A3CC       |
O | Kahn   Joe  Joe  2055551233Able Com11 FirstMobile AL123455555A1AA       | O
  | Cheng  Thuc Thuc 3336661111Boston C11 FirstWesternAL111155555A2BB       |
O | AndersoSteveMr.An2224445555Eastern 1 ComputBoston CA999955555B6XX       | O
  | ZimmermCarolCarol1235551111AZ Manag4151 BayAtlantaNJ444455555B2BB       |
```

FIGURE 6–12
The 65 Column Report

Some report generators truncate as shown. Others print the entire contents of a field, and wrap-around the output when it does not fit in the space available.

by **downloading** the data electronically. Data may also be **uploaded** to a data base from a microcomputer.

The data entry screen format must usually be defined by the data base user. Figure 6–14 shows how the screen format is defined in dBASE II and III. The same care used in laying out the output format pays dividends when defining the input format. The data entry task is made easier by a careful layout. Following the layout of the source documents if there is a consistent one is often useful.

Downloading:
The transfer of data from another computer into yours.
Uploading:
The transfer of data from your computer to another computer.

Operations

The operations needed in the simple example are sorting, querying, report generation, and some addition. Most data base programs provide all these capabilities with the exception of addition. You must examine the business requirements, determine what you plan to do with the data, and then eliminate from consideration all data base programs which do not have the capabilities required.

Security

Management has a professional, social, moral, and legal obligation to control the quality and use of the data in their data base. A data base must be protected from both internal and external contamination and

```
O
O      RECORD # 00003
O      LAST:NAME  :Conrad            :
       FIRST      :Leo         :
O      HOW:CALLED:Dr. Leo    :
O      PHONE      :123-555-1116:
O      COMPANY    :Imagineering Concepts Inc:
       ADDRESS    :1234 Park Drive          :
O      CITY       :Atlanta:
O      STATE      :NJ:
       ZIP        :44445:
O      NUM:CODE   :5556:
O      ALP:CODE   :A2AA:
```

FIGURE 6–13
Screen Input

Data Base   **181**

FIGURE 6–14   dBase II and
dBase III File Organization
Specification

```
..............
dBase II


Enter TODAY'S DATE AS MM/DD/YY
   or RETURN for none:

*** dBASE II    Ver 2.3      6 Jan 82
 .CREATE
ENTER FILENAME:B:FIRST
ENTER RECORD STRUCTURE AS FOLLOWS:
   FIELD    NAME,TYPE,WIDTH,DECIMAL PLACES
001          Last:Name,C,15
002          First,C,10
003          How:Called,C,10
004          Phone,C,12
005          Company,C,25
006          Address,C,25
007          City,C,7
008          State,C,2
009          Zip,C.5
010          Num:Code,N,4,0
011          Alp:Code.C,4
012              _

 ..............

dBase III

c:filespec.dbf                        Bytes remaining: 3881
                                      Fields defined:     11

   field name type      width dec    field name type      width dec
   ----------------------------      ---------------------------
 1  LASTNAME   Char/text  15
 2  FIRST      Char/text  10
 3  HOWCALLED  Char/text  10
 4  PHONE      Char/text  12
 5  COMPANY    Char/text  25
 6  ADDRESS    Char/text  25
 7  CITY       Char/text   7
 8  STATE      Char/text   2
 9  ZIP        Char/text   5
10  NUMCODE    Numeric     4
11  ALPCODE    Char/text   4
12
```

misuse. Equipment must be protected from damage and theft. A data base with contaminated data may lead to decisions that hurt both the individuals whose data is in the data base and the company. The misuse of data by both employees and outsiders can damage all involved. The loss of equipment is the least crucial loss although it does cost the company dollars.

Data may be contaminated by the entry of bad data. This can happen in the normal course of business, and management must develop methods to detect and purge bad data.

Data contamination can also occur when an employee who is unhappy enters bad data to damage the company. If your system uses telephone communication input, an unauthorized outsider may break into your system and enter bad data. The bad data could result in millions of dollars of funds being transferred to an account out of the country, or your company could injure someone because of the bad data, and you could find yourself on the receiving end of a lawsuit.

The destruction of data may be caused by individuals who are part of your organization or external to it, or by some electronic power or hardware failure. Good backup procedures help protect you against these problems. With good backup procedures it is not difficult to replace data that has been destroyed. It is often less costly to have all your data destroyed than to have it polluted or misused.

USER WINDOW

Diane knew Robert kept his report in his personal computer. Advance knowledge of his presentation would be of great value. One week before the meeting she worked late, walked over to Robert's desk, turned on his computer, found his report, printed a copy, and . . . .

For individual users of microcomputers, data security may mean locking up the floppy diskettes when they are removed from the microcomputer, locking up the microcomputer if using a hard (fixed) disk system, adapting a software protection scheme, using passwords and account numbers, or a combination of these measures.

The security problem becomes more complex when there is a number of users of the same microcomputer with a fixed non-removable hard disk. If you have an automatic answering telephone device on your microcomputer or use the microcomputer as part of a network, you will have the same security problems as a large computer timesharing system.

Suggested security procedures include:

1. Long passwords to make exhaustive searches difficult.
2. Passwords containing random characters.
3. Limiting the number of trials to three or less.
4. Invisible passwords during operation.
5. Careful administration of passwords.
6. Multi-level system: One password for read only; second password for read and write.
7. Change passwords often (monthly).
8. Create special operating procedures for when your security system is attacked.
9. Holding area for new data—data check before it is added to the data base.
10. Limiting remote access to read only or input to holding area only.
11. Dial back devices.
12. Logs of data use and access.

It is difficult to protect yourself completely from other computer users who wish to break into your system when it is on line with an auto-answer telephone device and in an unattended mode. Timesharing managers spend many hours developing schemes to protect their computers from outsiders. If you are concerned with data security, we recommend that you not use an auto answer device.

Your company is responsible for what is in the data base and for the use of that data. Social attitudes toward information about individuals recorded in data bases are changing, along with the laws governing the use of such information. You must make sure you operate within current legal and moral constraints. It is important to enter accurate data into your data base, and to carefully control the data's distribution.

Selecting and Using Data Base Programs

The business objective determines the size of the file, record, fields, and the type of record/field (fixed or variable). Most data base programs require that each record and field be a fixed size. Fixed size records and fields waste space. Programs often have fixed records and fields because it is easier for the programmer to create other capabilities with these limitations.

Variable size fields often mean larger data bases may be maintained in the given amount of on-line storage. The business need for large data bases must be balanced with the data base programs capability to manipulate the data.

The selection of a data base program is the matching of business needs with program capabilities. The business needs include output requirements, data required, sources, and the input format, structure and size for data storage, operations, data security, and the management procedures planned for the systems' operation.

Operating and Managing the Data Base

To be useful to the business user a data base must produce results that are:

- Relevant
- Accurate
- Reliable
- Timely
- Available
- Secure
- Flexible
- Economical

The relevancy of the output of a data base often depends on how it is managed and operated as much as on the selection of the data base program. Only the business user can determine if the facts contained in a data base are of value in a given business situation.

The expression "garbage in garbage out" has been picked up for popular use in the computer field. "garbage in garbage out" (or GIGO) refers to the necessity of carefully controlling and selecting the facts that go into a data base to make sure the information wanted is available when requested. The facts entered into a data base must be both accurate and measured in a consistent manner for the facts to be reliable for making business decisions.

If a data base requires constant update, management must make sure the updates are made. Old data may often have no value or even a negative value in a given business decision making situation.

One reason for the growth of microcomputer data bases is that they provide the professional with a method of getting the information needed to perform. The facts stored in the data base are readily available. There are "user friendly" data base programs designed to make it easy for the computer beginner to get started. But "user friendly" programs also tend to be "abuser friendly" programs, that is, unauthorized individuals can break in and get information out of such systems.

A data base program must be flexible. Business exists in an ever-changing environment. Business objectives change as the environment changes. Data bases must change and adapt to the changing business objectives. This means a continuous management commitment to operating and directing the data base.

Information has value. It costs money to create and manage a data base. If at any time the value of the information generated by a data base is less than the cost of operating the system, the continued existence of the data base must be questioned.

VARYING CAPABILITIES OF DATA BASE PROGRAMS

All data base programs make it possible to create, maintain, and use data bases, but there are many data base programs available. Table 6–2 is comparison of some of the more popular data base programs.

TABLE 6–2   Comparison of Data Base Programs

Hardware	pfs:FILE pFS:REPORT	Lotus 1-2-3	DataStar ReportStar	dBase III
RAM	128K	192K	96Kb	256K
Hard disk	Yes*	Yes	Yes	Yes
Sub-dir				
*Newer versions only				
General				
Family	Yes	Package	Yes	Stand alone*
Backup of Program	Limited	Limited	Unlimited	Limited
Fixed Fields	No	Yes	Yes	Yes
Fixed Records	No	Yes	Yes	Yes
File Mgt	x	x		
Relational			x	x
*dBase III is part of a family, but primarily it is a stand-alone package.				
Calculations				
Math	Limited	Yes	Yes	Yes
Data Entry And Update				
Automatic File Backup	No	No	Yes	No
Sort	Not data	Yes	Yes	Yes
Index	No	No	Yes	Yes
Search	Yes	Yes	Yes	Yes

(continued on following page)

TABLE 6–2 (continued)

Merge Files	Yes	Yes	No	Yes
Change File Definitions	Yes	Yes	Yes	Yes
Other Features				
User Documentation	Good	help screens	Training	Tutorial available
Technical Documentation	Minimum	Minimum	Yes	Yes
Technical Pocket Reference	No	Yes	Yes	No
Compressed Print	Yes	Yes	Yes	Yes
Interfacing				
Read ASCII Files	No	Yes	Yes	Yes
Price	139	495	395	695

SUMMARY

You have learned how and why the business professional needs and uses data base programs. You have learned what tasks the data base program can perform for you and the steps needed to set up and operate a data base system. You have learned about some of the commercial data base programs. You have learned how easy data base programs can solve simple file management and report generation tasks. Some of the important points you have learned are:

1. A data base is a collection of data used for a series of different purposes.

2. Data base programs solve business problems.

3. The development and application of microcomputer data bases is dependent upon the capabilities and capacities of the available hardware.

4. There are some basic terms that must be understood when learning about data bases.

5. Data base programs vary from file management—report generators to computer languages.

6. Data bases are classified as file managment, relational, hierarchical, network, free format, or multi-user.

7. Indexing schemes reduce the amount of time needed to find data in a data base.

8. The capability to exchange files between data bases is a form of compatibility.

9. Microcomputer data base programs aid in report generation and in custom calculations of information based on data in the data base.

10. Microcomputer data base creation requires careful planning.

11. Business needs dictate the direction of a data base.

12. Errors will be made when entering data into a data base. There are easy methods for updating and correcting errors.

KEY TERMS

Attribute
Data
Data base
Data base management program
Facts
Fields
File

File maintenance
File management—report genera-
tor
Information
Knowledge
Non-procedural language
Record
Report generation

REVIEW QUESTIONS

1. Define the following key terms.
   a. Facts
   b. Data
   c. Information
   d. Knowledge
   e. Data base
   f. Data base management program
2. What is file maintenance and report generation?
3. Give some examples of input devices used to enter data into data bases.
4. Why did the number of microcomputer data base programs and applications start to increase?
5. Give some examples of data bases used in business.
6. What is a data base file, a record, a field, an attribute?
7. Name the classification (general type) of data base programs.
8. What is a file management—report generator program?
9. What is unique about a relational data base program?
10. What is a hierarchical data base?
11. What is a network data base?
12. What is a free format data base?
13. What is unique about a multi-user data base?
14. What is indexing? What is a sequential search?
15. Identify some standard file transfer formats used for data base files.
16. What are the decision making areas of management?
17. Identify the steps in designing a data base.
18. What is the relationship between reports and business objectives?
19. How is data base output related to the input?
20. What is uploading/downloading?

21. What may result from contaminated data?

22. What is the trade-off between user friendly and abuser friendly designed programs?

DISCUSSION AND APPLICATION QUESTIONS

1. Identify some data bases where you would expect to find information about yourself listed.

2. Identify some data bases maintained by your university.

3. Identify some data bases maintained by your religious organization.

4. Identify some data bases maintained by your local government.

5. Visit a local business and identify some data bases it maintains.

LABORATORY ASSIGNMENTS

1. Obtain a copy of the data base program available in your microcomputer laboratory and set up the example on page 25 as a data base.

2. Create your own data base, by entering the text found on page 25.

3. Print a copy of the material in the data base you have just created.

4. Sort the data according to the first field and print the results. Sort the data according to zipcodes and print the results.

5. If your data base has the capability, design a custom form and print the output specified in 3 and 4 above.

6. Create a data base with records that have three fields:

Fields:	*Name*	*Zipcode*	*Dollars*
	Alphabetic	Alphabetic	Numeric
	20 characters	5 characters	12 spaces

If capable, instruct the data base to sum the number of dollars.
Enter the following data:

- Anderson   36605   23.44
- Angstriech   12345   125.22
- Conrad   54321   2.33
- Prieto   54545   12.33
- Cheng   15995   22.75
- Osborne   02698   12.55
- Patcher   001122   2.11

a. Print a report using the data as entered.
b. Sort by name and print a report.
c. Sort by zipcode and print a report.
d. Sort by amount owed and print a report.

1. (General Business) Set up a data base for inventory control with the following fields:

- Stock number
- Description
- Wholesale unit cost
- Quantity on hand
- Quantity on order
- Reorder point
- Sales this month
- Sales year to date

Enter the following data:

Stock Number	Description	Wholesale Unit Cost	Quantity on Hand	Quantity on Order	Reorder Point	Sales Month	Sales Year to Date
15525	RS-232 cable	9.55	8	12	12	5	36
15684	Parallel cable	8.22	15	0	12	9	44
14871	Null modems	20.11	2	0	1	0	8
12322	Cable ends	1.00	22	30	24	12	78
23232	Cable tool	5.22	5	6	5	3	22

Produce reports of entire inventory and stock numbers with orders outstanding.

2. (Clubs) Use your data base to set up a club membership recordkeeping procedure. Each member must be listed, with telephone number, the academic division, dues status, and attendance record.

Some data base programs may be used to solve the same type of problem that may be solved using spreadsheet programs. If you have a program such as dBase II or III, you may solve all of the problems in Chapter 5. Below are some additional problems of this type.

3. (Educational) Create a data base for a class roll:

Number	Name	Student Number	Exam #1	Exam #2	Final Report
1.	Mary Prieto	11122			
2.	Leo Anderson	12345			
3.	Fred Prieto	54123			
4.	Bill Cheng	15487			
5.	Jean Beitel	78451			
6.	Carol Baker	02635			
7.	Fred Osborne	11223			

Add equations to find the sum, average, and standard deviation of each grading criterion, each student, and for the total class effort.

4. (General Business) A checkbook register contains the following information:

Date	Check No.	Checks issued to or deposits received	Amount Deposit	CL Amount Check	Balance
—	—	Original balance			1,225.22
9/1	210	Rent		150.00	
9/2	211	Utilities		101.00	
9/3	212	Telephone		31.22	
9/6	—	Salary check	1,500.26		
9/7	213	Cash		160.00	
9/11	214	Food store		102.33	

The bank record shows:

Balance last Statement	We have added: Number	Deposits	We have subtracted: Number	Checks	Service Charge	Balance
1,225.22	2	2,000.26	6	644.55	1.22	2579.71

Checking Account Transactions

Date	Amount	Description
9/6	1,500.26	Deposit
9/8	500.00	Deposit

Checks

Date	Amount
9/2	150.00
9/5	101.00
9/8	31.22
9/8	100.00
9/12	160.00
9/15	102.33

At the beginning of the period your balance and the bank's balance were the same. There were no outstanding transactions of any type.

Set up a data base program to start with your balance, add the not cleared checks, subtract the unrecorded checks, subtract the not cleared deposits, add the unrecorded deposits, make adjustments for errors in recording the service charges, and produce a final balance to be compared to the banks.

5. (Accounting) Set up and organize a data base to enter a chart of accounts, a debit and credit field. Add the capability to sum both the debits and credits.

Chart of Accounts	Type	Liquidity	Debit	Credit
Cash account	A	L	9,200	
Accounts receivable	A	L	1,200	
Accounts payable	L	C		1,400
Retained earnings	E	T		2,000
Capital stock	E	T		4,000
Supplies	A	L	500	
Building	A	F	12,000	
Build-reserve for Depreciation	A	F		4,000
Trucks	A	F	8,000	
Truck-reserve for Depreciation	A	F		3,000
Equipment	A	F	22,000	
Equip-reserve for Depreciation	A	F		6,000
Notes payable	L	C		8,000
Loans payable	L	T		24,500

Under type A is an asset, L is a liability, E is for stockholders equity.
Under liquidity L is for liquid, C is for current, T is for long-term, and F is for fixed.
Use the codes to help sort the data base into a good presentation order.

SELECTED REFERENCES

Atkins, Robert W. and Walter L. Mazur. "The Dayflo Architecture." *Byte* pp. 155, 156, 159, 160, 162.

Atkinson, Chuck. *Inventory Management for Small Computers.* Dilithium Press, 1982.

Austin, Sandy. "In Search of the Perfect Data Manager", Business Computer Systems. September 1984, pp. 91, 92, 96, 99, 100.

Capron, H.L. and Brian K. Williams. *Computers and Data Processing.* 2nd ed. The Benjamin/Cummings Publishing Company, Inc., 1984.

Cooke, Rick, and John Brandon. "The Pick Operating System." Byte, pp. 177, 178, 180, 182, 187, 188, 190, 192, 196, 198.

Grillo, John P. and J.D. Robertson. *Data and File Management for the IBM Personal Computer.* Wm. C. Brown Company Publishers, 1983.

Hines, Douglas V. *Office Automation.* John Wiley & Sons, 1985.

Krajewski, Rich. "Databases." *Byte,* p. 135.

Krajewski, Rich. "Database Types." *Byte,* pp. 137, 138, 140, 142.

Lipton, Russell. "Organizing Data: File It Under DBMS." *Business Computer Systems,* September 1984, pp. 25, 26.

Mandell, Steven L. *Computers and Data Processing.* 3rd ed., West Publishing Company, 1985.

McNicholas, Charles W. *Data Base Management With dBase II.* Reston Publishing Compnay, Inc., A Prentice-Hall Company, 1984.

Potter, George B. "Data Processing An Introduction." Business Publications Inc., 1984.

Shapiro, Ezra. "Text Databases." *Byte,* pp. 147-150.

Veit, Stanley S. *Using Micro-Computers in Business.* Hayden, 1984.

7

Chapter Outline

Chapter Goals

Upon completion of this chapter you will be able to:

Understand why microcomputer graphics are important to the business professional.

Define the capabilities of microcomputer graphics.

Identify the more popular graphics programs.

Use some of the capabilities of microcomputer graphics.

GRAPHICS

Graphics:
Pictorial representation of data.
Business graphics:
Pictorial representation of business data. Analytical: Line, bar, pie, and XY (scatter) charts. Presentation: Illustrations that combine art and photography.

The microcomputer is a tool for the creation of graphic displays on screen, paper, film, and other media. **Graphics** involve picture creation and processing. Microcomputer **business graphics** includes the creation of line, bar, pie, and XY (scatter) charts for businesses using a microcomputer. The microcomputer and its graphic programs can help you create, edit, store, retrieve, display, and print graphic presentations more quickly and easily than any manual method.

Business data may be taken from the files of spreadsheets, data bases, word processors, or entered directly into graphics programs from the keyboard. Many spreadsheet and data base programs have graphic capabilities built in. Some word processing programs are able to produce data to be used for graphics generation and, when matched with a printer, can produce graphic charts both on screen and as hard copy. There is also a wide selection of stand-alone graphics programs.

A full range of capabilities to produce graphics in both monochrome and color is available. Color printers, plotters, and screen cameras (see Figure 7–1 and 7–2) make producing color graphics almost as easy as black and white.

HARDWARE FOR GRAPHICS

Business graphics require a minimum of special hardware devices. To perform graphics on a microcomputer the minimum hardware includes:

1. Monitor with the resolution match to the business need.
2. Enough RAM for the program and any special data storage.
3. Input devices.
4. Printers.
5. On-line storage devices.

Monitor

The monitor is the principal output device for microcomputer graphics. The number of pixels that a monitor can use becomes critical for this application.

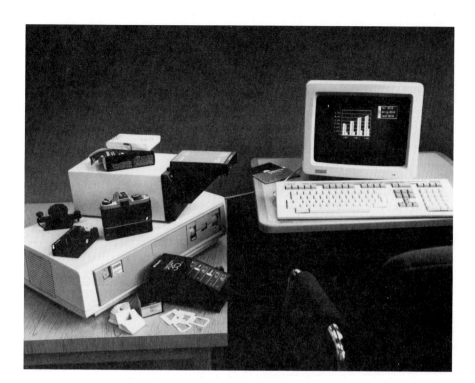

FIGURE 7–1   Polaroid
Palette Computer Image
Recorder

FIGURE 7–2   Polaroid
Palette Computer Image
Recorder with 35mm
Camera

Printed circuit boards may be purchased for driving the many special monitors, both high- and ultrahigh-resolution for presentation graphics. Some presentation graphics pc-boards may be used to **digitize** a picture. When a picture is digitized a **bit map** is created. This type of graphics is often referred to as **raster graphics.**

For business graphics a high-resolution monitor is needed (see Figure 7–3). Pictures look even better on ultrahigh-resolution systems, but are not required for professional results.

There are a number of ways to obtain a hard copy of the graphics produced on a monitor. One is to use a camera which directly copies the screen or one which works indirect such as the shown in Figure 7–4. Another way is to copy the screen onto a printer or plotter printer.

RAM

Business graphics may be performed on most microcomputers without excessive amounts of RAM. Some programs, such as Lotus 1-2-3, that combine business graphics with other functions, require more RAM than stand-alone packages.

Presentation and engineering graphics often require extra RAM. These applications could not be developed until the amount of available RAM grew to over one-half megabyte.

Input Devices

The keyboard is the most common method of data input. Some business graphics programs use the mouse, joy stick, digitizing pad, Koala Pad, and even a television camera. Many graphic programs can use computer results generated in spreadsheet and data base programs as inputs.

FIGURE 7–3 Princeton Graphic System ColorView Graphics PC-Board

Printers

Dot matrix, laser, ink jet, plotter, or similar printers may be used to copy microcomputer screen graphics. A printer that allows you to control each individual dot must be used. Figure 7–5 shows a color printer that allows the user to control individual dots.

Usually the number of dots produced by a printer does not match the number of dots (pixels) on most microcomputer screens. The quality of hard copy is the function of the number of dots per square inch a printer can produce. Most dot matrix printers do not have as many dots per square inch as the microcomputer screen. The laser printer has many more dots per square inch than you can currently get on most microcomputer screens. To take full advantage of a laser printer, you must produce your results directly on the laser printer without using the screen. There are also a number of quality color printers available.

Plotter printers (see Figure 7–6) are programmed in a manner similar to the technique used in the creation of graphics on a microcomputer screen. Plotters use ballpoint and felttip pens to produce their images. They are slow, but may be controlled directly by the microcomputer through special programs. It is not necessary to create an image on the screen and then copy it onto the plotter.

Screen graphics do not look the same when copied by plotter printers or other devices because the height to width ratio is and media is

**FIGURE 7–5   Epson JX-80
Color Printer**

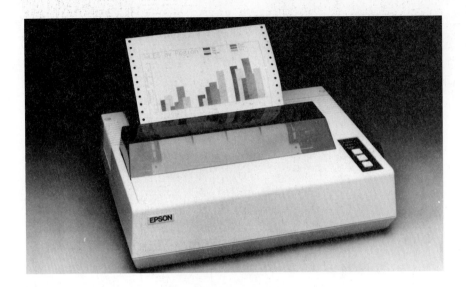

different. Sometimes the best way to obtain a copy of the screen is to use a screen camera.

A graphics utility routine called by typing the word GRAPH-ICS<CR> before loading BASIC is available under MS/PC-DOS. This graphics utility allows you to use the PrtSc option to make both a text and graphics copy of the screen when using programs written in BASIC on a dot matrix printer such as the Epson FX and MX series.

On-Line Storage Devices

Business analytical graphics have no special on-line storage needs, although some engineering and business presentation graphics programs have large data storage requirements.

WHY THE BUSINESS PROFESSIONAL SHOULD KNOW ABOUT MICROCOMPUTER GRAPHICS

Microcomputer graphics are a tool for the professional to use in accomplishing business objectives. Microcomputer graphics are a professional tool used to accomplish business objectives. The magic of microcomputer graphics is that the business professional, with no art training or skill, may produce quality presentations with little effort.

Just as microcomputer word processing programs help the business professional produce professional documents, microcomputer graphics programs help produce professional illustrations.

Microcomputer graphics may be classified into the following groups:

1. Business graphics (analytical and presentation)
2. Engineering/scientific graphics

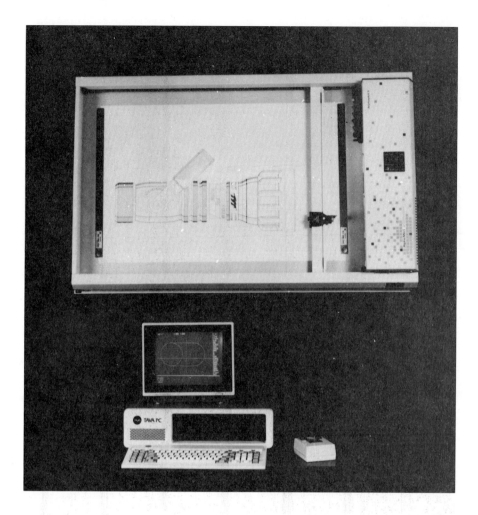

FIGURE 7–6 Alphaplot II Plotter Printer

BUSINESS GRAPHICS

Business graphics include the following:

1. Analytical graphics
   a. Line Charts/Graphs
   b. Bar Charts
   c. Pie Charts
   d. Scatter graphs- XY charts
2. Presentation graphics
   a. Enhancements for presentation
   b. Static and dynamic displays.

Pictures, charts, and text may be combined for both static and dynamic presentation of business data (see Figure 7–7). The objective of this type of graphics is custom output for specific groups. Software packages are available for the creation of slides, transparencies, hard copy, and video images.

FIGURE 7–7   Video
Capture System PC-EYE

Engineering/scientific, design, and manufacturing graphics are important to the business professional in a technical business. Often the technical staff will take over the use of this type of graphics.

Other graphics include line charts, flow charts, and statistical analysis.

Graphics for Business Objectives

Microcomputer-produced graphics may be subject to more missuse than other presentation methods, because the program reduces the training and experience required of the user. An untrained individual may control the creative process without outside help.

MICROS IN ACTION

Jean King and Associates require specialized custom presentations for specific business objectives. They prepare slides using screen copy equipment for meetings and hard copy for stockholder reports and similar publications. They also use graphics slides, films, and television tapes for audiovisual presentations.

Business graphics have two objectives:

1. To project expected relationships for decision-making; to evaluate and demonstrate past relationships between variables.

2. To control ongoing business operations; to find and demonstrate growth trends and deviations.

Figure 7–8 illustrates a XY chart showing the relationship of two **variables.**

Microcomputer Business Analytical Graphics

Microcomputer business analytical graphics include line, bar, pie charts, and XY scatter diagrams. Business charts and graphs may be created by the microcomputer from data generated by programs, input from data bases, or created in the digitizing process. We have classified business charts and graphics as follows:

1. Line charts/graphs
   a. Stratum graphics
   b. Percentage or index graphs
   c. Double y axis scale charts
2. Bar Charts
   a. Regular vertical
   b. Stacked bar charts
   c. Cluster bar charts
   d. Horizontal bar charts
   e. Range graphs (high-low-close)
   f. Percent bar charts

Variable:
A quantity that may assume any one of a set of values. There are two types of variables: Independent—variables that change by themselves, such as time; Dependent—variables that depend on a second variable(s), such as sales per month, that depend on the month of the year.

FIGURE 7–8 XY Chart

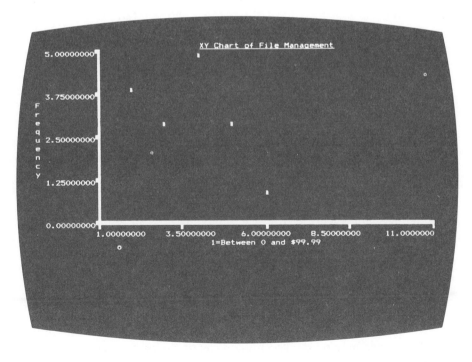

3. Pie charts
   a. Regular
   b. Exploded
4. Scatter graphs- XY charts

Graphics are a tool of the business user to communicate information to a targeted individual or group. The tool selected depends on the capabilities available, the targeted group, and the information to be communicated.

You must know who the target group is, what their educational and training level is, and what type of graphics may best be used to communicate information to them. The nature of some data limits your selection. For example, the pie chart may be understood by most individuals, but may appear cluttered when applied to month-by-month sales of two products for a year.

The final selection of a technique to match a data set and an information communication objective is a professional decision that must be made with care. You may wish to try several alternate presentations before making a final selection. The microcomputer makes it easy to develop these alternate presentations.

Line graphs are excellent for displaying financial and daily, weekly, monthly, quarterly, and yearly data. It is possible to plot more than a single relationship on the same chart for comparison purposes.

Line graphs may be distorted by not plotting from a base of zero. The business objective of matching data presentation to communicate information to a target group must be kept in mind when preparing a graph. Distortion may or may not help in obtaining the objective.

A line graph is similar to an XY graph (see Figure 7–9). In the line graph you are able to control the x scale (horizontal) while in an XY graph it is done for you. Figure 7-10 shows what can happen in a line graph where the scale is not assigned properly.

The X scale is illegible. The same chart as a line graph with the X scale controlled is shown in Figure 7–11. Many programs will also give you the option of controlling the Y scale.

Stratum graphs are also referred to as surface charts or band charts, when the difference between two variables is highlighted. In a graph of this nature, each variable is placed on top of the lower one. If the lowest variable has large peaks and valleys, it will be difficult to evaluate the upper variables. The band chart (see Figure 7–12) is similar to the stratum chart in that it shows the difference between variables.

If the scale of the vertical axis is in terms of percentage, you have a frequency scale (Figure 7–13) or a percentage scaled graph as shown in Figure 7–14.

Graphs may be prepared with multiple scales for different variables. Such methods allow the comparing of trends that are thought to have some relationship.

Bar charts are commonly used to illustrate business data. The common type of bar chart is the vertical or column bar chart. Figures 7–15 and 7–16 illustrate simple bar charts.

Bar charts may be stacked one on top of the other (see Figure 7–17).

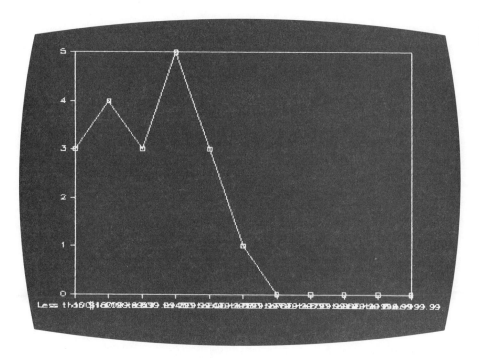

FIGURE 7–9   Plotting
Three Variables

You may add costs to gross profits to produce a revenue or sales bar chart as shown.

Bar charts can be drawn in clusters, rather than as stacked illustrations. Figure 7–18 illustrates this type of chart.

FIGURE 7–10   Graph With
Illegible X Scale.

FIGURE 7–11   X Scale
Controlled

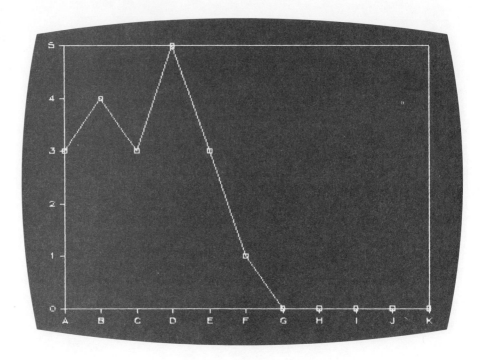

Bar charts may be drawn horizontally as well as vertically. The selection of this format is useful for a change of pace to get the attention of the reader.

FIGURE 7–12   Band
Graph—Break-even

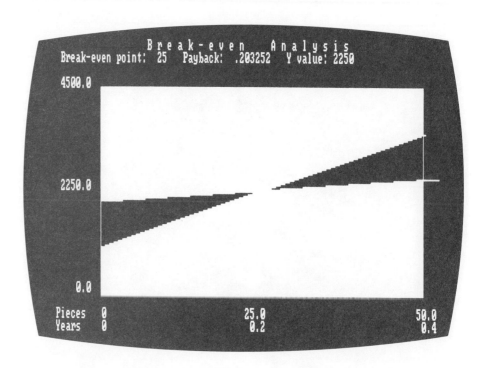

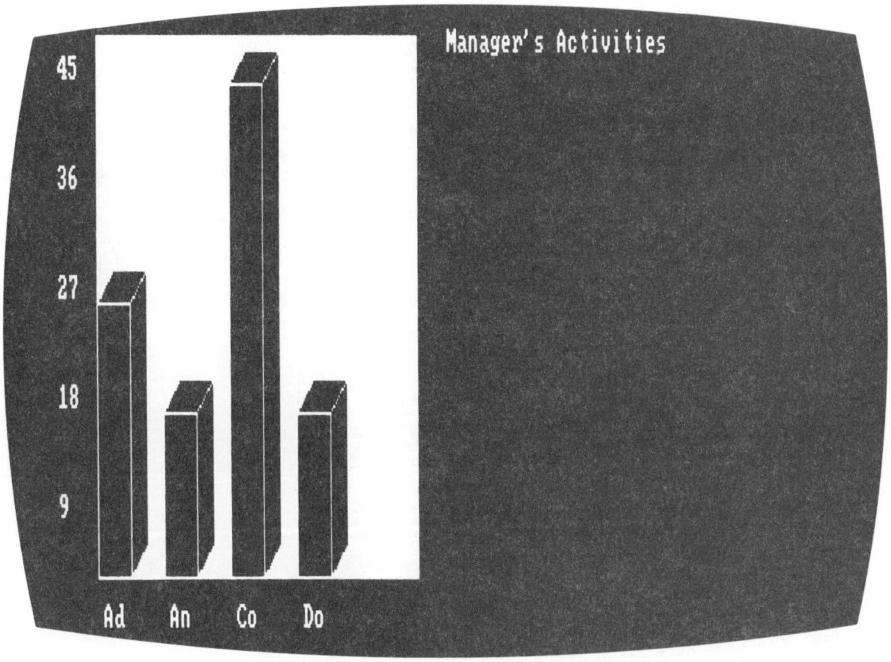

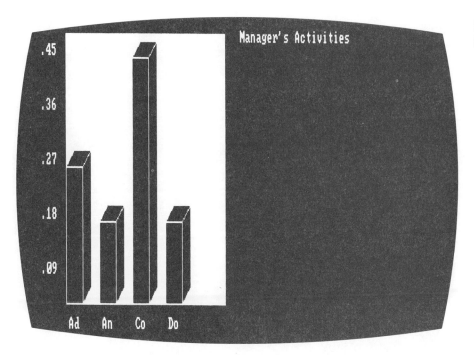

FIGURE 7–13 Frequency
Scale—Bar Chart

The high-low-close chart used to plot stock market prices, is also known as the range chart. Figure 7–19 is an example of this type of chart.

FIGURE 7–14 Percentage
Scale—Bar Chart

FIGURE 7–15   Bar Chart
Vertical

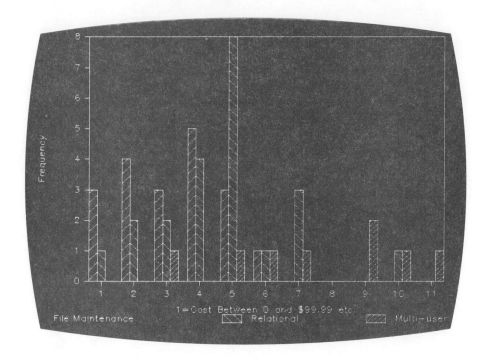

Pie charts are popular and widely used for business applications. Figures 7–20 and 7–21 show two types of pie charts. Pie charts and bar charts may be designed to illustrate the same information, however, bar

FIGURE 7–16   Bar Chart
Horizontial

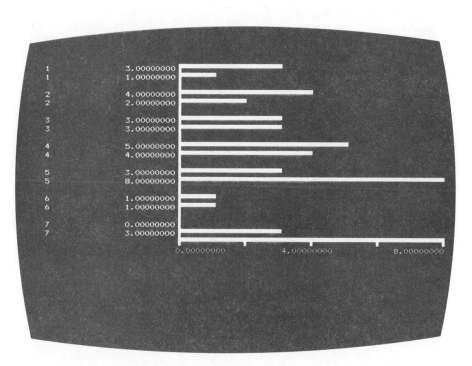

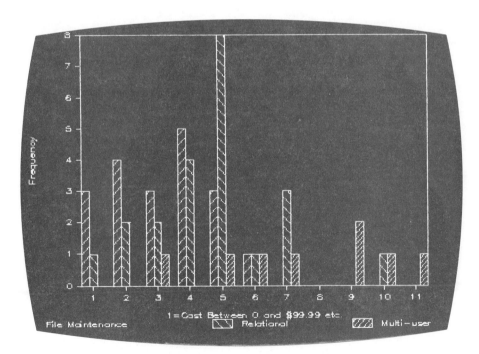

FIGURE 7–17 Stacked
Bar Chart

charts may be used to handle a wider range of variables through the use
of colors and different shading.

The analysis of time data, such as the monthly sales of a product for

FIGURE 7–18 Clustered
Bar Chart

FIGURE 7–19   Range/High-Low-Close Chart

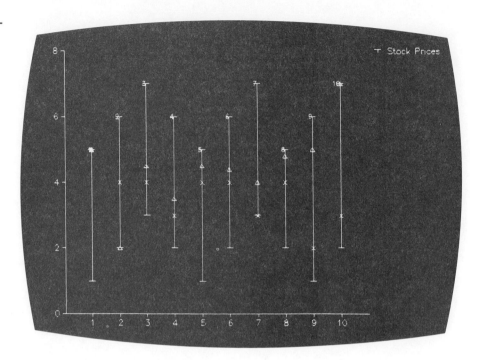

FIGURE 7–20   Regular Pie Chart

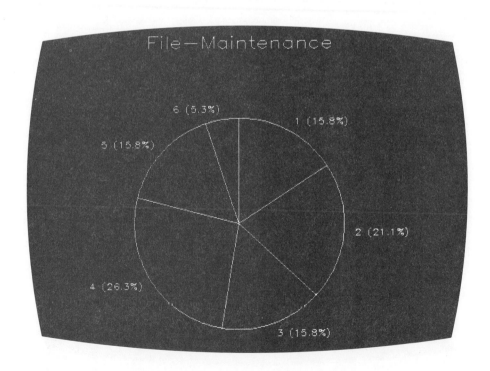

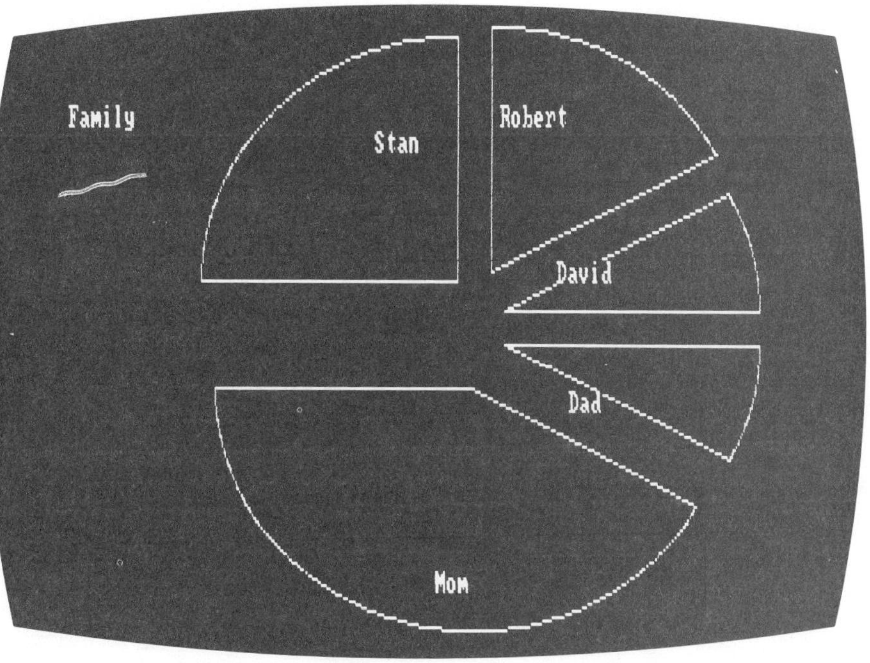

FIGURE 7–21   Exploded
Pie Chart

three years, often results in a scatter diagram showing a series of points over time. Figure 7–22 shows this type of chart.

BUSINESS PRESENTATION GRAPHICS

Professional presentations are like marketing; you must sell your ideas and yourself. The number of programs available to aid the professional in preparing slides, transparencies, and other special effects is growing rapidly. The nature of these programs cannot be classified because they are just now being developed. There are free-hand drawing programs and symbol library programs that make the creation of organization charts, electronic drawings, computer flow charts, and many other special applications easy. Figure 7–23 illustrates how graphics may be combined into data base.

MICROS IN ACTION

Jean King and Associates has found the exploded pie chart to be one of the most popular presentations for fundraising campaigns and government presentations. They also use bar charts and line charts.

The microcomputer can produce both static (fixed images) and dynamic (moving images) displays. Dynamic images are valuable for mar-

FIGURE 7–22   Scattered
Graphs

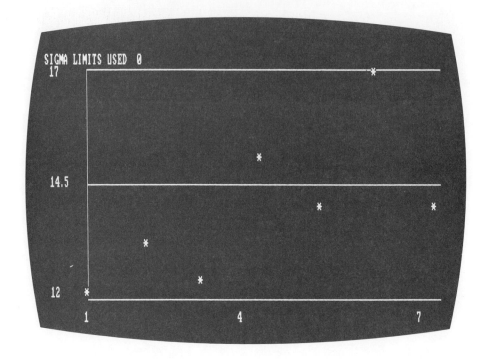

keting presentations and training of persons of all ages. Some microcomputers may be linked with videodiscs for interactive training.

ENGINEERING SCIENTIFIC GRAPHICS

Engineering/scientific, design, and manufacturing graphics are available to the business professional.

Engineering/scientific, design, and manufacturing applications include the following:

1. CAD—Computer Aided Design
2. CAM—Computer Aided Manufacturing
3. CADD—Computer Aided Design And Drafting.

CAD, computer aided design, describes the software and hardware available to help an individual with a design task. The microcomputer may produce a 3-D image of an object, and then with little effort, rotate the object so the designer can see it from a different point of view. With the addition of a CAD data base, an engineering evaluation of the design can be produced. There are many software packages devoted to different design problems available for microcomputers.

CAM, computer aided manufacturing, refers to controlling production equipment with your computer. The operation of a machine tool can be programmed to perform a variety of operations that can be accomplished more quickly and more accurately than by their human counterpart.

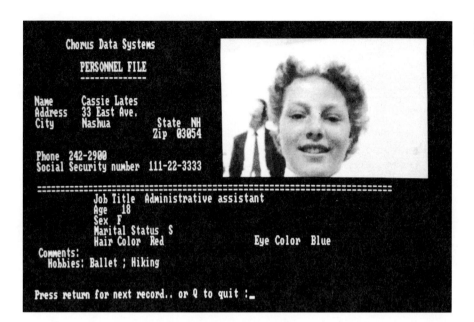

FIGURE 7–23   Data Base with Photo

CADD refers to computer aided design and drafting. Not only can the microcomputer help the engineer see what the product looks like, it can also be used to produce the many working drawings needed to transfer the idea into a product. Microcomputers can produce and update drawings with great accuracy in less time than is possible by humans.

COMPARING BUSINESS GRAPHICS PROGRAMS

Business graphics are available in stand-alone programs and as routines in spreadsheet and data base programs. Listed in Table 7–1 are some of the graphics programs available for MS-DOS microcomputers.

TABLE 7–1
Business Graphics Programs

Programs
BPS Business Graphics
Boardroom Graphics
Business Graphics System
Chart-Master
Context MBA
Encore
Fast-Graphs
Giraph
GrafTalk
GraphPlan
GraphPower
Graphwriter
KeyChart
Lotus 1-2-3

(continued on following page)

TABLE 7–1 (continued)

	Programs
	pfs:Graph
	Sign-Master
	SuperCalc 3

Business graphics are found in stand-alone programs and as part of other spreadsheet and data base programs. Many of the stand-alone programs can exchange data files with integrated programs. Table 7–2 compares selected stand-alone and integrated programs.

**TABLE 7–2
Stand-Alone Graphic Programs**

	Chart-Master	pfs:Graph	Super Chartman II	KeyChart
RAM	128K	64K	192K	128K
Monitor				
Color	x	x	x	x
Monochrome	x	x	x	x
Disk drives	2	1	1	1
Printers				
Anadex				
Epson		x	Parallel	
IBM/Gra		x	Parallel	
IDS		no color	Parallel	
Itoh		x		
NEC		x		
Plotters	Serial	x	Serial	x
Printer				
Color	x		x	x
Program				
Backup	limited	limited	limited	Yes
Files ASCII				x
dBase II			x	
DIF	x	x	x	
Multiplan				
SuperCalc				
1-2-3	x	x	x	
Charts				
Line				
Line/				
Bar	x	x	x	x
Line/		x	x	x
Area	x	x		x
Bar Horz	x		x	x
Stacked	x	x	x	x
Vert	x	x	x	x
3-D			x	
Pie	x	x	x	x
Exp	x		x	x
Pie/Bar	x		x	x
Scatter	x			
XY		x		x
Price	$375	$140	$400	$375

Integrated (Spreadsheet)Packages with Graphics

	Lotus 1-2-3	SuperCalc 3 Rel 2	Encore!
RAM	192k	96K	256K
Monitor			
Color	x	x	
Monochrome		—without graphics—	
Disk drives	2	1	2
Disk drives	2	1	2
Printers			
Anadex	x	n.a.	n.a.
Epson	x	x	x
IBM/Gra	x	x	x
IDS	x		
Itoh	x		
NEC	x		
Plotters	x	x	
Printer			
Color	x	x	n.a.
Program	limited	no	limit
Backup			
Files ASCII	x		x
dBase	x		
DIF	x		
Multiplan			
SuperCalc		x	
1-2-3	x		
Charts			
Line	x	x	x
Line/Bar			
Line/		x	x
Area			
Bar Honz			x
Stacked	x	x	x
Vert	x	x	x
3-D			
Pie	x	x	x
Exp		x	
Pie/Bar			
Scatter	x		x
X-Y	x	x	
Price	$500	$400	$700

You have learned why microcomputer graphics are important to the business professional and how they are defined. You learned about some of the more popular business graphics programs. You have learned how easy it is to use microcomputer graphics. The key points in this chapter are:

1. The microcomputer is a tool for the creation of graphic displays on both screen and paper.

2. Microcomputer graphics are a tool for the professional to use in accomplishing business objectives.

3. You must always keep the business objective in mind when using microcomputer graphics.

4. Business graphics require quality monitors, a printed circuit board to run the monitor, and a dot matrix printer with dot addressable graphics or a plotter to produce business graphics.

5. Microcomputer business graphics include line, bar, pie charts, and XY scatter diagrams.

6. Presentation, engineering/scientific, and other graphics are important to the business professional.

7. Professional presentations are like marketing; you must sell your ideas and yourself.

8. Engineering/scientific, design, and manufacturing graphics are available to the business professional.

9. The business professional needs to produce line and other special types of charts.

10. Business graphics are available in stand-alone programs and as routines in spreadsheet and data base programs.

KEY TERMS

Bit mapped   Pixels
Business graphics   Raster graphics
Digitizing   Variable
Graphics

REVIEW QUESTIONS

1. What are graphics? What are business graphics?

2. Identify some of the sources of data for business graphics.

3. What are pixels?

4. What is meant by digitized, bit mapped, and raster graphics?

5. Identify the magic of microcomputer graphics.

6. Identify the classification of microcomputer business graphics.

7. Identify the types of business graphics.

8. The concept of a variable is important to graphics. What is a variable?

9. Identify the types of business graphics.

10. What does the selection of a graphics presentation depend upon?

11. Identify each of the following and what type of graphics they are: CAD, CAM, and CADD.

1. Using magazines and newspapers find an article on microcomputer graphics and report on its observations.

2. Find an article on the use of television cameras and computer graphics. What do you think the future developments in this area will be.

3. Find an article in either computer magazines or industrial publications on the use of computer generated backgrounds for movies and television. What potential use do these capabilties have in business?

4. Detail the value of microcomputer generated graphics in presentations in other courses and in reports for other courses.

5. If your school has an engineering or industrial drafting department visit that department and report on the computer aided design capabilities available.

6. Contact your art department and visit them if they have any computer aided capabilities of interest.

1. Enter the following data into your graphics program and prepare a pie and bar chart:

Classsification	Amount
David	20
Robert	10
Stanley	19
Steven	22
Carol	55

2. Use your spreadsheet calculation capabilities to calculate the value of SIN(X) for values of X from -10 to $+10$ in increments (steps) of 0.1. Plot the results using an XY chart.

3. Change the equation in number 2 to SIN(X)/X and plot the results using an XY chart.

4. Change the equation in number 2 to 10*X + 20 and plot the results using an XY chart.

5. Change the equation in number 2 to X 2+2*X+12 and plot the results using an XY chart.

6. For one of your other classes prepare a graphics presentation using the plotting capabilities of the microcomputer.

7. Obtain some economic facts on your city or area. Prepare some charts and graphs to present this data to your class.

SELECTED REFERENCES

Conklin, Dick. *PC Graphics: Charts, Graphs, Games and Art on the IBM PC.* John Wiley and Sons, 1983.

Cuellar, Gabriel. *Graphics Made Easy for the IBM PC/XT.* Prentice-Hall, 1984.

Ford, Nelson. *Business Graphics for the IBM PC.* SYBEX, 1984.

Fowler, John. *The IBM PC/XT Graphics Book.* Prentice-Hall, 1984.

Harold, Fred G. *Introduction to Computers With BASIC.* West Publishing Company, 1984.

Hearn, Donald, and M. Pauline Baker. *Computer Graphics for the IBM Personal Computer.* Prentice-Hall, 1983.

Hopper, Grace M. and Steven L. Mandell. *Understanding Computers.* West Publishing Company, 1984.

Long, Larry. *Introduction to Computers and Information Processing.* Prentice-Hall, 1984.

Volkstorf, J. Edward. *Graphics Programming on the IBM Personal Computer.* Prentice-Hall, 1983.

Chapter Outline

Chapter Goals

When you complete this chapter you will be able to:

Understand why microcomputer communication is important to the business professional.

Understand some theory, the steps needed to set up, and how to operate a communication session.

Understand the role of some of the special microcomputer communication hardware.

Name and identify the tasks performed by communication within a microcomputer system and between microcomputers.

MICROCOMPUTER
COMMUNICATION

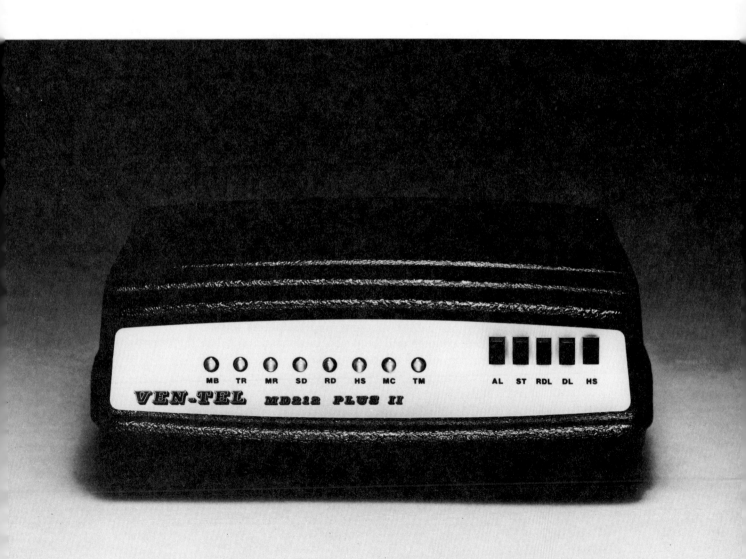

Gleem Paint Center in Mobile, Alabama is a retail store approximately 50 feet by 200 feet in size with an inventory of over $100,000 in paint, and painting supplies. An analysis identified their microcomputers needs as:

Inventory control
General ledger
Accounts payable
Accounts receivable

Inventory control was identified as the most important. Each month a physical inventory had to be taken for cost control. Each item in the store had to be counted and the records updated, then a value calculated.

The needed microcomputer equipment included:

A desk top microcomputer.
A printer.
An lap microcomputer and bar code reader.

The Epson HX-20 and IBM PC were selected so data could be communicated between them.

Communication is the transfer of data and/or (microcomputer) instructions from one computer to another or to peripherals. Microcomputer communication within a system is similar to communication between different microcomputer systems. This chapter deals with data and instructions between the parts of a microcomputer system and between individual microcomputers.

Microcomputer communication is necessary when data exists on one computer that is needed on another computer or peripheral or when instructions must be sent from one device to another.

The hardware needed for communication between microcomputers and their parts or between microcomputers and other microcomputers includes the cables used to connect the parts of a system, special communications cables, modems, and telephone lines.

This chapter will help you understand and use the communication capabilities of the microcomputer.

COMMUNICATION HARDWARE

The microcomputer requires a communication port for input and output to a second device. Computers communicate with the world through ports:

Input Ports	Output Ports	Input/Output Ports
Keyboard	Monitor	RS-232C
Bar code reader	Printer (Parallel)	(Communication)

Input Ports	Output Ports	Input/Output Ports
Joy sticks	IEEE 488(lab equipment)	(Printer)
Voice recognition	Voice synthesis	(Plotter)
Koala Pads		(Device control)
		Disk drives
		Hard drives

Some ports are for input or output, others for both. The RS-232C port is commonly used for communication, and can be used both for input and output. The microcomputer must have an RS-232C port for most communications discussed in this chapter. Figure 8–1 shows the ports at the read of a microcomputer.

The ports of a microcomputer may be designed to send, and/or receive data. Often, even those ports that you most likely would assume are one way only are actually both sending and receiving. For example,

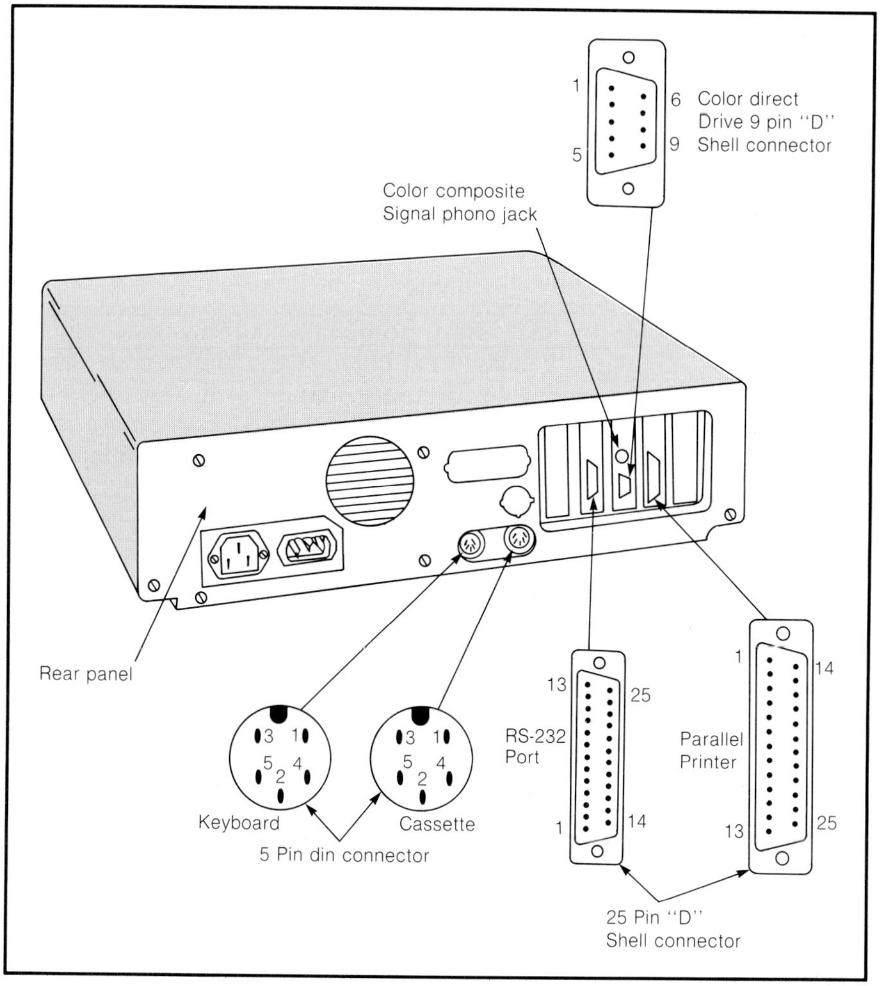

FIGURE 8–1   Ports of a Computer

the parallel port is typically a conduct to the printer. This port usually receives input on the status of the printer. Notice how the microcomputer waits for the printer to perform its task, no matter how slow it is. The microcomputer is receiving information from the printer at the rate of flow of data the printer can handle.

Each port on a microcomputer seems to require a special connector. The RS-232C and Centronics parallel connectors are quasi-standard. The use of differently styled plugs with different numbers of active lines for varied purposes is often used by the manufacturer to make it difficult to make errors when connecting equipment. This practice usually means that special cables are needed for each application.

USER WINDOW

The three connectors in the back of the Model I Radio Shack computer were all the same. Three dots of correction fluid were placed on the tape recorder port, two on the video port, and one on the power port. The cables were marked to match. The amount of time to set up the system was reduced by half.

Special communication hardware devices are available for using the telephone, connecting to a central computer, and connecting two microcomputers together. Some of these devices fit into the expansion slots, while others are external.

Modems

Modem:
A device to connect the microcomputer to the telephone. It changes binary codes to sound for telephone transmission and then back again.

The built-in or add-on RS-232C serial port connects the microcomputer to a **modem.** A modem is a device that changes the binary code generated by the microcomputer to a sound so it may be sent over telephone lines to a second modem that changes the sounds back to binary code. The word modem comes from the tasks it performs, to MOdulate and DEModulate. Some microcomputers have internal modems.

Answering microcomputer-modems send their code on one frequency, while the originating microcomputer uses another. This is why one microcomputer must be the originator and the other the answer.

A modem may be a direct connect modem or it can use an acoustical coupler. A direct connect modem is connected directly into the telephone line (see Figure 8–2). It works well in a home where telephones may be easily disconnected. An acoustical coupler is a device that cradles the telephone receiver (see Figure 8–3). It may be used anywhere: your office, a telephone booth, or your home.

Baud rate:
Usually refers to the transmission rate. 1200 baud is 120 characters per second.

Most acoustical couplers are limited to 300 baud, while direct connect modems can often handle 300, 1200, 2400, and even 4000 baud. Modems with the capability of using faster **baud** are more expensive and are currently under development. Direct-connect modems are less likely to cause errors than are acoustical couplers.

In lap and briefcase microcomputers, it is common to find internal modems. These microcomputers are designed to be carried to remote locations for the communication of information back to a desktop microcomputer or central computer.

Modems may be simple devices for connecting the microcomputer to telephone lines, or smart devices that dial automatically, control the log-on information, and answer the telephone when called. Smart modems must be direct connect.

One advantage of smart modems is that you may use the microcomputer to call other microcomputers automatically in the middle of the night when long distance telephone costs are at their lowest. The microcomputer may be instructed to send a series of prepared files for processing the next day, and then break the connection. The smart modem also allows the microcomputer to answer incoming calls and receive and store messages, as well as send automatic messages.

Special programs are needed for both the automatic send and receive functions. This feature opens the microcomputer to all the security problems of the national data base operator. Users of auto-answer modems may have unwelcome users break into their systems and damage files or obtain confidential information.

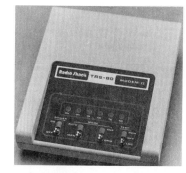

FIGURE 8–2
Direct Connect Modem

Cables and Null-Modems

Another way to use the communication capabilities of briefcase and lap computers is to collect information in their fulltime or low power memories for transmission to desktop computers through the use of direct wired connections and a null-modem. **A null-modem** is a way of wiring microcomputers together, making them think a modem is being used to connect them when there is none. Baud rates of up to 9600 are commonly used for null-modem file transfer with the proper software.

Null-modem:
Device that makes the computer behave as if it is connected to a telephone to allow communication between computers.

Mechanical and Electronic Switching Devices

More than a single printer may be connected to a microcomputer with the aid of switches. The first time many microcomputer users think of controlling a printer as a communication task is when a second printer is needed. This need may arise when a letter-quality printer is needed for correspondence, and a dot matrix printer is needed for business graphics.

FIGURE 8–3
Acoustical Modem

> ### MICROS IN ACTION
> Gleem Paint Center had the option of using a modem or null-modem to connect the HX-20 with the IBM PC. Since both were at the same location, a null-modem was selected. After a little experimentation, the printer cable of the HX-20 was found to work as if it were a null-modem to connect the two microcomputers together.

If one printer is parallel and the other serial, it is possible to connect one to each port and instruct the microcomputer which port to use for each task. MS/PC-DOS microcomputers equipped with more than one serial port may control one device per port. When both printers use the same communication port, both may be connected at the same time with a switch. Connecting and disconnecting a cable will soon damage the

FIGURE 8–4   Switch

connection on either cable or microcomputer, or both if a switch box is not used (see Figure 8–4).

There are switches available for both parallel and serial controlled devices. Most switches are mechanical, while others use electronic switching. The need for electric power generally indicates the presence of electronic switching.

Serial devices use 25 pin connectors, but may use as few as 3 active pins. Since the actual pins used for specific purposes are not standard, you must be careful when purchasing switches to make sure they work for the purpose intended, with the cables available.

Most devices are interchangeable among brands, but there are exceptions. Cables and switches may be used to connect different brands of peripheral devices and microcomputers, but you may need to learn about your system and how it works.

In addition to connecting two printers to one microcomputer, it is possible to connect several microcomputers to a single printer. It is also possible to connect one or more microcomputers together to form a simple network for the exchange of files and programs. Usually the data sent must be converted to ASCII code before being sent from one microcomputer to another.

WHY THE BUSINESS PROFESSIONAL MUST LEARN ABOUT MICROCOMPUTER COMMUNICATION

Knowledge of communication procedures helps the user get the most from each part of a microcomputer system. Business users need electronic data and instruction communication when:

1. There is a need for high-speed data and instruction transfer.

2. The data at both ends of the transfer is needed ready for computer use.
3. The cost of electronic transfer is less than alternate means.
4. One part of the microcomputer system must control a second part.
5. An external device must be controlled.
6. Data is being collected by an external device.

Need for Speed

Data and/or instructions may be sent over regular telephone lines from one microcomputer to another. Auto-answer modems provide the capability of answering the telephone to microcomputers without human assistance. Microcomputers may be left on standby waiting for messages that may be sent at any time by other microcomputers. Business transactions depend on timely communication. A late letter or contract can mean a lost sale.

Need for Computer Data

Entering data into a computer is time-consuming and subject to errors. If data is already in a form usable to a computer, it is wasteful to transfer it to hard copy and re-enter it into a computer.

Data and/or instructions in one microcomputer may be required in a second microcomputer at a different location. If the computers use the same disk format the data and instructions may be sent on diskette. If the formats do not match, the data and instructions may have to be sent using either telephone or direct wire transfer.

Low Cost

The cost of a telephone call from one microcomputer to another may be the most economical method of transferring data and instructions. Data and instructions sent this way are usually in the form needed for printing or using by the second microcomputer.

Controlling the Parts of a Microcomputer System

Data and instruction transfers from a microcomputer to its printer, disk drives, monitor, and hard disk are the same as or similar to the data and instruction tranfers between two microcomputers. For example, to be able to use all the capabilities of a printer, the user must know what instructions are needed to make the printer perform a task, and how to get the microcomputer to send these instructions.

Many printers can boldface, underline, subscript, superscript, produce extra large type, produce small type, change fonts, and do many other things. Some programs make it easy to perform these tasks while others make it difficult or impossible. The business user must know:

1. The business need.
2. What the device can do.
3. What the program can do.

The accomplishment of a business result depends on the capability of the device and program. If the device can, but program cannot accomplish a desired result the business user must find new programs or ways to change the available program to get the job done. If the device cannot do the job, it must be replaced with a device that can.

Controlling External Devices and External Data Collection Devices

Microcomputers can communicate with **analog devices** that measure continuous changes in voltage. A special interface such as the IEEE-488 is required to allow a computer, that is a binary device, to understand an analog device. Laboratory equipment, machine monitors, and other data collection devices are often designed to operate as analog devices.

With external devices, the microcomputer can control the temperature in a room, the lights in a house, the flow of liquid in an experiment, and many other things in both an office and industrial plant. In many cases the microcomputer must first be able to determine facts about the process being controlled, in order to make feedback adjustments needed to control the process.

Analog devices:
Devices used to monitor real-world conditions such as temperature, sound, and movement. These devices use continuous voltage rather than the binary coding system of the microcomputer.

COMMUNICATION THEORY, BACKGROUND, AND PROGRAMS

The user must understand some of the theory and know some of the terms and programs to obtain the most benefit from the communication capabilities available. The business user needs the microcomputer to perform a specific task or set of tasks. If a system cannot be purchased ready to perform a needed task, one must be assembled from products supplied by a number of different vendors. To match different vendors' products, the communication procedures often require configuration. The user who does the configuration must know some theory and terms and must be knowledgeable about the programs available. Some things the business user must study are:

1. The nature of communication between two smart devices.
2. Serial and parallel connections.
3. Communication parameters (asynchronous or synchronous).
4. Communication parameters (ASCII).
5. Other communication parameters.
6. Communication programs.

Microcomputer Communication—Two Smart Devices

Communication between microcomputers and from microcomputers to peripherals is the transfer of meaningful data and instructions in the form of bits. Bits may be part of a standard coding system, such as ASCII, or a custom code of a particular system.

When the devices at both ends of the communication link are smart. Often, one device will try to outsmart the other and cause communication failure. It is best to let one communication partner standardize on the communication parameters (speed and other settings), then adjust the second partner to fit the needs of the first.

Serial and Parallel Connections

The most common method of connecting two microcomputers together, or a microcomputer and a peripheral, is by serial or parallel cables. The standard serial communication port is the RS-232. A serial RS-232C port uses a standard connector with 25 pins, not all of which are active. In serial communication, data is transmitted one bit at a time through a single wire to a specific pin.

MICROS IN ACTION

Gleem Paint Center selected the Epson HX-20 because bar code readers were available. Inventory data is collected by the HX-20/bar code reader and stored in its CMOS memory for printing or communication at some later time.

Serial RS-232C communication is used for both peripherals and between microcomputers. It may be used to connect additional devices to a telephone to allow a microcomputer to communicate over telephone lines.

Parallel (Centronics) connections are commonly used for printers and other peripherals. Figure 8–5 illustrates different types of connectors. Parallel connections transmit all the bits used along a set of wires at the same time. Many devices may be connected in either serial or parallel. Most microcomputers use both types of connections. There are additional connections and ports to communicate with the keyboard, bar code readers, and other devices.

Asynchronous or Synchronous

There are two types of computer communication:

1. Asynchronous
2. Synchronous

FIGURE 8–5 (a) Male and Female RS-232C Plug; and (b) Male and Female Centronics Parallel Plug

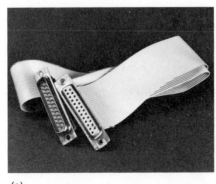
(a)

(b)

Asynchronous is commonly used on microcomputers. Only during data transmission, is timing critical in **asynchronous communication.** **Synchronous communication** requires continuous timing.

In asynchronous communication, the microcomputers control the timing only when a character is sent. Communication may start at any time and end at any time. During the period when a character is being sent, the timing is important.

Synchronous communication requires that the timing of the transmission from the beginning of to the end of a communication session be synchronized, coordinated. Synchronous communication is used predominantly with central computers.

Asynchronous communication: Communication that requires timing only when a bit is being transmitted.

Synchronous communication: Communication that requires continuous timing.

Communication Using ASCII

ASCII is the standard used by most of the microcomputer industry. ASCII uses seven-bits, the decimal numbers from 00 to 127, to define specific characters and control codes (see Table 8–1).

TABLE 8–1   American Standard Codes for Information Interchange—ASCII

Binary No.	Decimal No.	Character	Binary No.	Decimal No.	Character
0000000	000	control	1000000	064	@
0000001	001	control	1000001	065	A
0000010	002	control	1000010	066	B
0000011	003	control	1000011	067	C
0000100	004	control	1000100	068	D
0000101	005	control	1000101	069	E
0000110	006	control	1000110	070	F
0000111	007	Bell	1000111	071	G
0001000	008	backspc	1001000	072	H
0001001	009	tab	1001001	073	I
0001010	010	Line fd	1001010	074	J
0001011	011	control	1001011	075	K
0001100	012	form fd	1001100	076	L
0001101	013	carr ret	1001101	077	M
0001110	014	control	1001110	078	N
0001111	015	control	1001111	079	O
0010000	016	control	1010000	080	P
0010001	017	control	1010001	081	Q
0010010	018	control	1010010	082	R
0010011	019	control	1010011	083	S
0010100	020	control	1010100	084	T
0010101	021	control	1010101	085	U
0010110	022	control	1010110	086	V
0010111	023	control	1010111	087	W
0011000	024	control	1011000	088	X
0011001	025	control	1011001	089	Y
0011010	026	control	1011010	090	Z
0011011	027	Esc	1011011	091	[
0011100	028	control	1011100	092	\
0011101	029	control	1011101	093	]
0011110	030	control	1011110	094	ˆ
0011111	031	control	1011111	095	—

(continued on following page)

TABLE 8–1   (continued)

Binary No.	Decimal No.	Character	Binary No.	Decimal No.	Character
0100000	032	blank	1100000	096	`
0100001	033	!	1100001	097	a
0100010	034	"	1100010	098	b
0100011	035	#	1100011	099	c
0100100	036	$	1100100	100	d
0100101	037	%	1100101	101	e
0100110	038	&	1100110	102	f
0100111	039	'	1100111	103	g
0101000	040	(	1101000	104	h
0101001	041	)	1101001	105	i
0101010	042	*	1101010	106	j
0101011	043	+	1101011	107	k
0101100	044	,	1101100	108	l
0101101	045	−	1101101	109	m
0101110	046	.	1101110	110	n
0101111	047	/	1101111	111	o
0110000	048	0	1110000	112	p
0110001	049	1	1110001	113	q
0110010	050	2	1110010	114	r
0110011	051	3	1110011	115	s
0110100	052	4	1110100	116	t
0110101	053	5	1110101	117	u
0110110	054	6	1110110	118	v
0110111	055	7	1110111	119	w
0111000	056	8	1111000	120	x
0111001	057	9	1111001	121	y
0111010	058	:	1111010	122	z
0111011	059	;	1111011	123	{
0111100	060	<	1111100	124	:
0111101	061	=	1111101	125	}
0111110	062	>	1111110	126	~
0111111	063	?	1111111	127	special

The codes from 00 to 31 are mostly control codes. Some microcomputers and printers use different control codes. There is a degree of inconsistency in how the codes from 00 to 31 are used by different printers and microcomputers. Line feed (10) and carriage return (13) are quasi-standard. However, some microcomputers only use carriage return (13). When communicating from one microcomputer to another it is common to get double line feeds or none when because of this inconsistency. Programs can often solve these problems.

Esc code (27) is widely used to send special instructions, but again it is not universal. Common end-of-file markers in CP/M and MS/PC-DOS are usually 26, while in TRS-DOS zero is used.

Using a seven-bit character with one **stop bit,** the first bit is a **start bit** telling the receiving computer that asynchronous communication is about to start. The next seven-bits are the ASCII code. The next bit is usually the **parity bit,** and the last bit is the stop bit.

Stop bit:
The bit that tells the second micro-computer the character is complete.

Start bit:
The bit that tells the second micro-computer a character is being sent.

Parity bit:
Error checking bit.

The microcomputer often sends an eight-bit binary number to the second device. An eight-bit binary number can produce decimal numbers from 00 to 255. There are no standards for the numbers over 127. Screens and printers often use **high bit** numbers for graphics and control purposes.

High bit:
The last bit in a binary number. High bit numbers are the decimal numbers that can only be created when the last bit is used.

MICROS IN ACTION

Gleem Paint Center's Epson HX-20 was equipped with a serial port into which could be connected a serial printer or a microcomputer such as the IBM PC.

The IBM PC, equipped with a communication program is instructed that a communication device was sending data. The program will then capture the data and store it on the IBM PC's diskettes as an ASCII data file.

The inventory data needed by Gleem Paint Center can be collected and stored with minimum effort and errors.

Communication Parameters

Combinations of hardware and software are used to set the communication parameters. There are a number of **parameters** that must be agreed upon before two computers can communicate using ASCII asynchronous communication. These parameters include:

1. Who will originate and who will answer
2. The baud rate
3. The **character size**
4. Parity
5. The number of stop bits
6. The use of full or half duplex.

Parameter:
A variable value. Parameters are values that must be set before communication can occur.

Character size:
The number of bits per character.

When communicating between a central computer and a microcomputer, the usual convention is for the central computer to **answer** and for the microcomputer to be the **originator.** The computer that answers is sometimes referred to as the host, while the originator is called a terminal. Some programs limit the hardware they are used on to one role. Many programs allow the computer to answer or originate. It makes no difference which is which betweem microcomputers, but one microcomputer must answer and one must originate. Communication will not occur otherwise.

Answer:
Modem setting in asynchronous communication. One partner must answer, the other originate.

Originate:
Modem setting in asynchronous communication. One partner must originate, the other answer.

Baud rate is the speed of transmission during the communication of a character. Both computers in the communication process must be using the same baud rate setting. (The definition of the term "baud rate" has undergone changes-current usage is given.)

Common baud rates for telephone communications are 110, 300, 1200, 2400, and 4800. A baud rate of 300 means 300 bits are sent per second. Since ten bits are needed for each character (start bit, seven bits for ASCII code, parity bit, and stop bit), this results in a rate of 30 characters per second. A baud rate of 1200 means 120 characters are sent per second during communication. For most communication involving humans, the use of 300 baud is satisfactory. For large file transfers, faster baud rates are required. A twenty page single space report consists of approximatly 3500 characters including blanks. This report would take two minutes at 300 baud and three quarters of a minute at 1200 baud.

Parity aids in finding transmission errors. Parity may be odd, even, or none. Adding up the bits contents (0 or 1) you will get an odd or even number. Using even parity, the parity bit is adjusted so the sum of the ten bits is even. When the receiving computer finds the sum is not even, it knows a transmission error has occurred and will ask for a retransmission of the character. Parity must be matched.

In asynchronous communication the number of stop bits may be one or two. The most common is one. Communication may occur even if the number of stop bits is not matched.

Full-duplex is like telephone communications. Both parties can send or receive at the same time. **Half-duplex** is like CB or ham radio communication. One party talks, then tells the second they are finished. Each party must tell the other to take "over" when transmission is complete.

Setting Up Communication Parameters

Setting up communication parameters in communication programs varies from detailed step-by-step procedures to a single-step process. In some communication programs, it is menu driven. The advantage of the step-by-step process is that you can control each parameter individually. Data Capture, a communication program, is used to illustrate this approach. PC-Talk III, another popular communication package, is used to illustrate a single-step approach. The matching task often involves some trail and error before a match is obtained.

Data Capture Setting up communication parameters in the communication program Data Capture is a menu-driven task. Figure 8–6 shows the initial screen display of this program.

The program has built-in default values of the communication parameters. If your needs match the parameters, you will be ready to start the communication process.

When first using a program it is important to read the information on the screen and documentation which comes with the program carefully. The only function key used by Data Capture is F10. As shown in

Full-duplex:
Both communication partners can send and receive at the same time.
Half-duplex:
One communication partner can send and the other receive at any given time.

FIGURE 8–6   Starting Data Capture

```
Duplex = Half Baud = 300      Drive = A:  Capture = BUFFER  Lines =0
Transmit = On Echowait = OFF  Linefeed = Off Line fill = On Prompt =10
---------- SOUTHEASTERN SOFTWARE --- DATA CAPTURE/pc-------------
ENTER/RECEIVE -Press F10 for Menu
```

Figure 8–6, it is the key that calls the menus where you can set the communication parameters.

Since long distance telephone calls can be expensive, it is best to check the parameter settings before proceeding. If you find it necessary to set the parameters it will usually require five or more steps. Data Capture gives the user many controls beyond setting parameters which are menu driven in a manner similar to setting the parameters.

Figure 8–7 demonstrates some of the additional capabilities of Data Capture. For example, you may instruct the program to turn on a "C)apture Buffer to store in RAM the characters which are being sent or are received. This discussion is limited to the menu selections needed for setting the communication parameters.

PC-Talk III PC-Talk III is available for MS/PC-DOS microcomputers. It does not require you to walk through a series of menus for the setting of the communication parameters but rather does it all in one step. Figure 8–8 shows the initial screen of this program.

The help menu of PC-TALK III is examined in Figure 8–9.

Setting communication parameters is a single step. Figure 8–10, is PC-TALK III's menu for setting the communication parameters.

Communication Programs

Communication capability depends on both hardware and software. Like all other capabilities of a microcomputer, a program is needed to make things happen. There are many communication programs available.

FIGURE 8–7   Additional
Capabilities

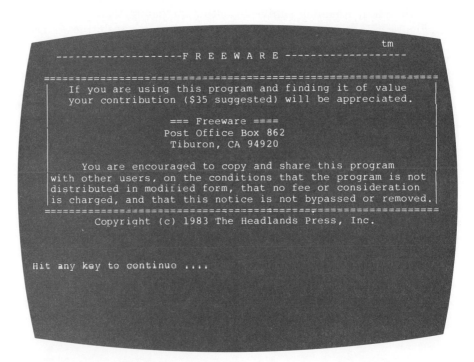

```
Duplex = Half Baud = 300       Drive = A:  Capture = BUFFER  Lines =0
Transmit = On Echowait = OFF  Linefeed = Off Line fill = On Prompt =10
---------- SOUTHEASTERN SOFTWARE --- DATA CAPTURE/pc-------------

Toggle Menu

Select One of the Following:

  C)apture Buffer (ON/OFF)
  D)isk drive (A:/B:)
  E)chowait (ON/OFF)
  F)ill Empty Lines (ON/OFF)
  H)alf/Full Duplex
  L)inefeed (ON/OFF)
  P)rinter (ON/OFF)
  R)emote System Prompt Character
  S)uppress Directory (ON/OFF)
  T)ransmit (ON/OFF)

  WHICH > ? (Press <_| To Exit Menu )
```

They are sold as individual programs or may be purchased as part of a data base, spreadsheet, or combination program package.

Programs are available for most CP/M and MS/PC-DOS microcomputers. There are three types of programs:

1.   Dumb terminal programs

FIGURE 8–8   Starting
PC-Talk III

```
                                                          tm
-------------------F R E E W A R E -------------------
==================================================================
|    If you are using this program and finding it of value    |
|    your contribution ($35 suggested) will be appreciated.    |
|                                                             |
|                === Freeware ====                            |
|                Post Office Box 862                          |
|                Tiburon, CA 94920                            |
|                                                             |
|    You are encouraged to copy and share this program        |
|with other users, on the conditions that the program is not  |
|distributed in modified form, that no fee or consideration   |
|is charged, and that this notice is not bypassed or removed. |
==================================================================
        Copyright (c) 1983 The Headlands Press, Inc.


Hit any key to continue ....
```

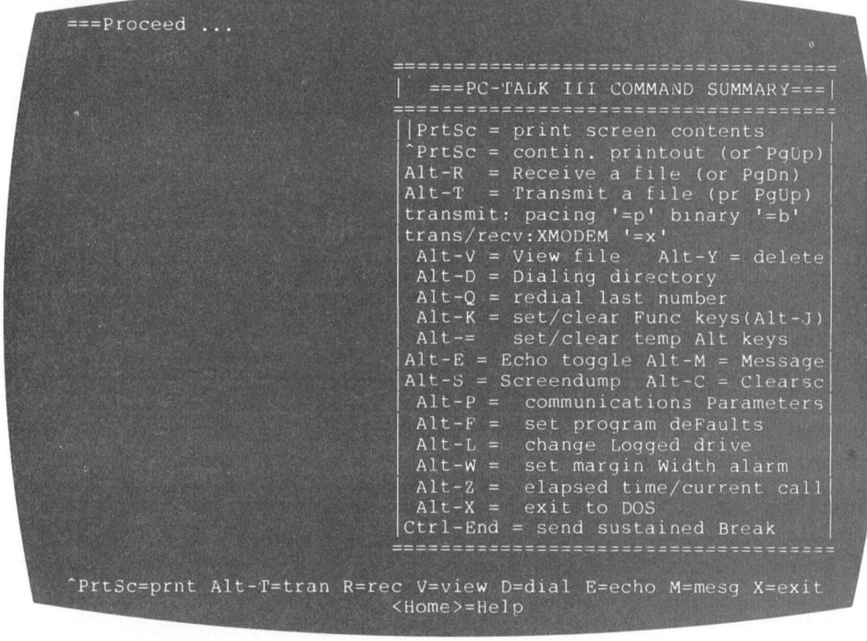

FIGURE 8–9   Help Menu

```
===Proceed ...                                                    o

                      ===================================
                     | ===PC-TALK III COMMAND SUMMARY=== |
                      ===================================
                     ||PrtSc = print screen contents    |
                     ^PrtSc = contin. printout (or^PgUp)
                     Alt-R  = Receive a file (or PgDn)
                     Alt-T  = Transmit a file (pr PgUp)
                     transmit: pacing '=p' binary '=b'
                     trans/recv:XMODEM '=x'
                      Alt-V = View file    Alt-Y = delete
                      Alt-D = Dialing directory
                      Alt-Q = redial last number
                      Alt-K = set/clear Func keys(Alt-J)
                      Alt-= set/clear temp Alt keys
                     Alt-E = Echo toggle Alt-M = Message
                     Alt-S = Screendump  Alt-C = Clearsc
                      Alt-P =  communications Parameters
                      Alt-F =  set program deFaults
                      Alt-L =  change Logged drive
                      Alt-W =  set margin Width alarm
                      Alt-Z =  elapsed time/current call
                      Alt-X =  exit to DOS
                     Ctrl-End = send sustained Break
                      ===================================

    ^PrtSc=prnt Alt-T=tran R=rec V=view D=dial E=echo M=mesg X=exit
                          <Home>=Help
```

2. Smart terminal programs
3. Automatic originate and answer programs.

A **dumb terminal** program is one that allows the microcomputer to communicate under the supervision of a human being. When informa-

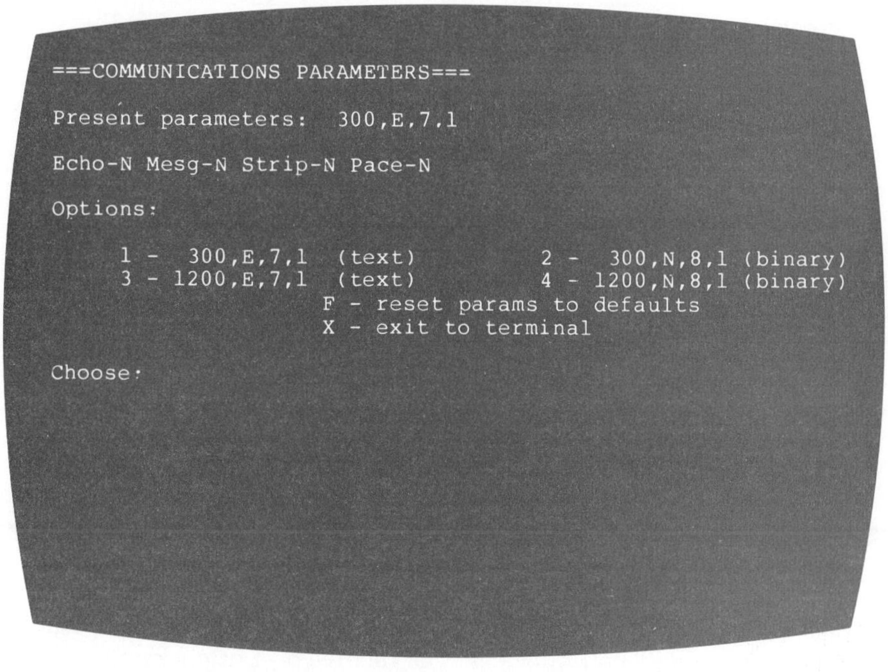

Dumb terminal:
A terminal that can only communicate under the control of an individual.

FIGURE 8–10   PC-Talk III Communication Parameters

```
===COMMUNICATIONS PARAMETERS===

Present parameters:  300,E,7,1

Echo-N Mesg-N Strip-N Pace-N

Options:

    1 -   300,E,7,1 (text)        2 -   300,N,8,1 (binary)
    3 -  1200,E,7,1 (text)        4 -  1200,N,8,1 (binary)
                     F - reset params to defaults
                     X - exit to terminal

Choose:
```

Smart terminal:
Terminal that can be used to transfer data files between computers.

tion is typed, it is sent. The information returning is displayed on the microcomputer screen.

A **smart terminal** program allows the opening of a disk file and the transfer of its contents out from the RS-232C port (uploading). It also allows the capture and storage of data received (downloading). In addition, the program can control the printer to obtain hard copy of the material sent or received. Some microcomputer-dumb terminal combinations also allow printed output.

When combined with smart modems, that can dial or answer a telephone automatically, a program may instruct the microcomputer to make its own communication connection at defined times for the transfer of files. This helps take advantage of off-time telephone rates to reduce costs.

MICROS IN ACTION

Gleem Paint Center's Epson HX-20 did not require a communication program. A standard communication program was needed for the IBM PC to capture the data when sent by the HX-20.

COMMUNICATION WITH PERIPHERALS

The disk operating system is a communication controller. The microcomputer system is a communication network. Peripherals are controlled using the same codes and communication hardware that may be used to communicate between microcomputers. You may connect two microcomputers or a microcomputer and a peripheral using the same cables. There will often be slight differences in how the cables are connected.

When documenting the operation of a program, it is possible to connect a microcomputer in place of a printer and capture the data as it is printed.

USER WINDOW

A Radio Shack Modem 100 briefcase microcomputer and its built-in word processor were used to write part of a term paper while in a study hall. Upon returning home, at serial RS232 cable was connected between the Radio Shack Model 100 and an IBM PC serial port. An IBM communication program was told to capture and save the text as it was sent by the built-in communication program of the Model 100.

Off-Line Data Entry Devices

Some microcomputers have special capabilities that add to their usefulness as remote data entry devices. The relative cost of pocket, briefcase, lap, and desktop microcomputers results in an on/off-line situation similar to that of microcomputers and large central computers. The smaller, low-cost microcomputer may be used as off-line equipment relative to the desktop microcomputer.

COMMUNICATION BETWEEN MICROCOMPUTER SYSTEMS

Modems, null-modems, and diskettes can be used to communicate between microcomputers. For example, a microcomputer can be connected to a second microcomputer using two modems and the telephone system. All communication parameters must be matched, except that one modem must be set on answer and the other on originate, and one microcomputer must be a host while the other is a terminal.

A program set in the terminal mode does not reflect code that is sent to it. A host program does. If a communication setup results in double letters being printed on screen, it is possible that the second computer is reflecting code back when it should not be. If typing information results in no characters on the screen, the computer at the other end may not be reflecting code when it should be. The duplex setting may also result in the same problem. Often there is more than one way to solve any communication mismatch.

The use of null-modem connections is common for the transfer of files between microcomputers that cannot read or write on matched diskette formats and that are in the same location. This method of file transfer is slower than direct disk reading and subject to errors. Since ASCII is a seven-bit standard, control codes contained in the eight-bit may or may not be transferred correctly.

Read-Write-Format Programs

Communication, the transfer of data files from one microcomputer to another, may occur using direct disk transfer. MS/PC-DOS is one of the few disk operating systems that includes the disk format as part of its standard. Most MS/PC-DOS microcomputers can exchange diskettes with each other, but there are exceptions. Some microcomputers with quad-density disk drives have problems reading diskettes produced on microcomputers with double-density disk drives, due to slight variations from design specifications.

Diskettes with foreign formats may be read in one microcomputer by another with special programs. For example, programs are available for

Radio Shack TRS-80 Model I, III, and 4 microcomputers with double-density drives to read, write, and format single-sided diskettes using the MS/PC-DOS format. Models of Epson, Kaypro, Osborne, and other microcomputers operating under CP/M have programs available that allow the reading, writing, and formatting of diskettes with many different formats, including MS/PC-DOS.

The amount of time required to transfer a file using direct disk transfer programs is a little longer than to transfer a file between two diskettes using the same format in a given microcomputer. The transfer of files is usually without error.

Even files transferred error-free often require some editing. If you transfer an ASCII file from one microcomputer to another, you will likely not have problems. A WordStar file transferred from an Apple IIe under CP/M to the IBM PC or back will most likely transfer without error. So will a dBase II file. You will have more problems transferring a file between two different programs on the same microcomputer than between the same program on two different microcomputers.

A program written in a high-level language such as BASIC is better transferred by saving it as an ASCII file on the first microcomputer, then moving it back to machine program code after transfer. It will usually work if there are no special capabilities used on the first microcomputer that are not available on the second. BASIC programs may be written to run on a number of different microcomputers if the code selected is consistent with all machines. The transfer of machine language programs is possible, although it is unlikely they will work once transferred.

Other Special Communication Procedures

The ham radio community has been involved in microcomputers since the early days. Many "hams" were the original hardware hackers. The electronic theory and concepts of ham radio and microcomptuers are closely related.

Ham operators have developed hardware and software that allow the microcomputer to produce both Morse Code and standard ASCII code, and to transmit such code by radio signals. Federal regulations limit the manner in which the microcomputer may be used for "over the air transmission" using continuous wave (CW) communications.

For international business that requires long distance transmission, ship-to-shore and ship-to-ship, the use of the microcomputer is increasing. As the capabilities increase in this area, more and more business uses will be developed.

COMPARING COMMUNICATION PROGRAMS

The features needed in a communication package are a function of the hardware used. Most communication programs will work with a variety of modems and hardware configurations. Some are designed to work

TABLE 8–2   Communication Software

Hardware Features	Crosstalk XVI Microstuf Inc.	Data Capture /pc Southeastern Software	PC-Talk III Headlands Press Inc.	Smartcom II Hayes Microcommputer Products
Memory Req.	128K	128K	64K	192K
Drives Req.	1	1	1	1
General Features				
Copy Protect	No	No	No	No
Baud Rates	110-9600	110-19,200	110-9600	300, 1200, 2400
Duplex Full	X	X	X	X
Half	X	X	X	X
Auto Answer	X	X	X	X
Dialing	X	X	X	X
Re-dial	X		X	X
Keyboard	X	X	X	X
Other Features				
Menu Driven	X	X		X
Function Keys	X	X	X	
Directory	X	X	X	X
Price	$195.00	$120.00	$35.00	$245.00

with specific configurations. Some hardware configurations require specific packages. Features such as auto-dialing, auto-answering, and the maintenance of a directory require a combination of both hardware and software. See Table 8–2 for a comparison of communication software.

SUMMARY

You have learned why microcomputer communication is important in business, some communication theory, the steps needed to set up, and how to operate a communication session. You have reviewed the role of some of the special communication hardware and have been introduced to the tasks performed by communication withing a microcomputer system and between microcomputer systems.

The difficulties of setup and the ease of use of communication have been introduced. The key points in this chapter are:

1. Communication is the transfer of data and instructions from one computer type device to another.
2. Communication capability depends on both hardware and software.

3. The microcomputer requires a communication port for input and output to a second device.

4. A modem is a device that connects a microcomputer to a telephone. Some microcomputers have built-in modems.

5. Microcomputers may be connected with special cables for the transfer of files.

6. More than a single printer can be connected to a microcomputer with the aid of switches.

7. Knowing about communication helps the user get the most from each part of a microcomputer system and make different microcomputers work together as a system.

8. The business user must understand some of the theory, know some of the terms, and be familiar with various programs to obtain the most benefit from the communication capabilities available.

9. Smart devices are at both ends of the microcomputer communication partnership.

10. The most common method of connecting two microcomputers together, or a microcomputer and a peripheral, is by serial or parallel cables.

11. Asynchronous communication requires timing when data is transmitted. Synchronous communication requires continuous timing.

12. The ASCII standard is important for the communication process.

13. Combinations of hardware and software are used to set the communication parameters.

14. Setting up communication parameters is menu driven in some communication programs.

15. The disk operating system is a communication controller.

16. Some microcomputers have special capabilities that add to their usefulness as remote data entry devices.

17. Modems, null-modems, and diskettes may be used to communicate between microcomputers.

18. Communication, the transfer of data files from one microcomputer to another, may occur using direct disk transfer.

19. The microcomputer can help the ham radio operator communicate.

KEY TERMS

Answer	Modem
ASCII	Null-modem
Asynchronous communication	Originate
Baud rate	Parameter
Character size	Parity bit
Download	Smart terminal
Dumb terminal	Start bit
Full duplex	Stop bit
Half duplex	Synchronous communication
High bit	Upload

1. Identify some ports found on microcomputers.

2. What is a modem?

3. Identify the two types of modems.

4. What is a null-modem?

5. Detail the reasons why business users need electronic data and instruction communication.

6. What must the user know in order to communicate using microcomputers?

7. Define microcomputer communication.

8. What is ASCII?

9. What is serial communication? What is parallel communication?

10. What is asynchronous communication? What is synchronous communication?

11. Identify the start bit, parity bit, and stop bit in asynchronous communication.

12. In asynchronous communication how many bits are needed for each character?

13. What communication parameters must be set?

14. Define these communication terms:
    a. Originate
    b. Answer
    c. Character size
    d. Full duplex
    e. Half duplex

15. What are the three types of communication programs?

16. What is downloading and uploading?

17. Why is off-line operation of microcomputers of interest to the business user of microcomputers?

18. When can a microcomputer read diskettes with foreign formats?

1. In ASCII what is the code for a blank? Identify the code numbers necessary to reproduce your name.

2. Find advertisements for communication programs in a magazine and identify what is available and what it costs.

3. Examine advertisements for modems. Identify their features and costs.

4. Find advertisements for internal and external modems. Compare the features of the two devices.

5. Identify where in your local area you would purchase special communication cables.

LABORATORY ASSIGNMENTS

1. Examine the equipment in your laboratory. Idenitfy what communication hardware and software is available and what would be necessary to allow you to communicate between two of the microcomputers available.

2. If hardware and software are available use two microcomputers connected with a null-modem wire to configure one to originate and one to answer. Establish communication.

3. If hardware and software are available use your communication program to transfer an ASCII data file from one microcomputer to another.

4. If hardware and software are available use your communication program to transfer an ASCII program file from one microcomputer to another. Use the program after it is transferred. Explain why the program performed as it did after transfer.

5. If hardware, telephone line, and software are available establish telephone communication between two microcomputers.

6. If hardware, telephone line, and software are available use your communication program to transfer an ASCII data file from one microcomputer to another.

7. If hardware, telephone line, and software are available use your communication program to transfer an ASCII program file from one microcomputer to another. Use the program after it is transferred. Explain why the program performed as it did after transfer.

SELECTED REFERENCES

Buckwalter, Jeff T. *Understanding Data Communications*. Alfred Publishing, 1983.

Flanders, Dennis. *Communicatons and Networking for the IBM PC*. Prentice Hall, 1983.

Glossbrenner, Alfred. *The Complete Handbook of Personal Computer Communications*. St. Martin's Press, 1983.

Kruglinski, David. *The Osborne/McGraw-Hill Guide to IBM PC Communications.* Osborne/McGraw-Hill, 1984.

Melin, Michael, and Michael Mikus. *Connections: The Micro-Communications Guidebook.* The Book Company, 1984.

Nichols, Elizabeth, Joseph Nichols, and Keith Musson. *Data Communications for Microcomputers.* McGraw-Hill, 1982.

Chapter Outline

Chapter Goals

When you complete this chapter you will be able to:

Understand why microcomputer communication with central
    computers is important to the business user.

Understand some theory, the steps needed to set up, and how
    to operate a communication session.

Understand the role of some of the special communication
    hardware.

Name and identify the tasks performed by communication
    with central computers.

Understand some of the difficulties of setup and the ease of
    use of communication.

COMMUNICATIONS WITH CENTRAL COMPUTERS

Dean Witter

Dean Witter is a large financial services brokerage firm owned and operated by Sears. They have offices in all major cities and in many smaller ones.

In the local offices, the professionals who advise and place orders for the public are called account executives. The account executive's potential needs for a microcomputer were identified as:

1. Communication with F.A.S.T. (Financial Action Service Terminal) System.
2. Maintenance of a client's data base.
3. Special application program and spreadsheet analysis of client's needs.
4. Word processing.

The F.A.S.T. system is a dial up service operated by Dean Witter for both the account executive and individual clients. Clients may access their own data files, enter into the company's research files, learn what is available, and obtain an up-to-date value at any time using their own microcomputer.

Minicomputer:
Medium-size computer, larger and more expensive than a microcomputer, but smaller than a mainframe.

Mainframe:
A large computer. Originally all computers were mainframe computers. Most require technical expertise to operate.

Communication is the transfer of data and instructions from one computer type device to another, and the interactive use of a larger computer using a second computer. The need for microcomputer communication with central computers exists for reasons similar to the needs of microcomputer-to-microcomputer communications. The central computer may be a microcomputer, although it is usually a large computer (**minicomputer** or **mainframe**) that has some capabilities beyond those found in a microcomputer. At times it is useful to use the microcomputer as a terminal to use the larger central computer.

The business professional has a need to communicate between a microcomputer and a central computer when:

1. Data or instructions are in the microcomputer and are needed in the central computer.
2. Data or instructions are in the central computer and are needed in the local microcomputer.
3. The microcomputer is used as a terminal for a central computer.

Electronic mail is an example of the need for data transfer to a central computer and back. A memory area in the central computer is reserved for mail and messages. The sender uses a microcomputer to upload a message to the central computer. The second party checks the "mail box" to determine if any messages have been sent and, if so, downloads the message. The job of the central computer is to act as the middleman.

Electronic mail:
The transmission of letters, memos, and other messages by one microcomputer to another computer.

The lack of standards and rapid technical improvements has resulted in a slower than expected growth of **electronic mail** and other communication applications. The professional user must use the same type of communication procedures that were outlined in chapter 8. The knowledge is technical, and difficult to learn and use for some individuals. The technical knowledge needed after the initial setup is completed is minimal.

The hardware needed for communication between a central computer and a microcomputer is similar to the hardware needed to communicate between microcomputers. Many microcomputers come with the capability to communicate included. If not available, the addition of asynchronous communication capability to microcomputers is relatively simple and low cost.

WHY THE BUSINESS PROFESSIONAL MUST LEARN ABOUT COMMUNICATION BETWEEN A MICROCOMPUTER AND CENTRAL COMPUTER

The central computer has capabilities and data storage capacity that are not available on microcomputers. Microcomputers can solve many of the problems of the business professional, but there are problems that may require a larger computer. Usually a large central computer is needed because of a combination of factors.

1. Speed—they are faster than microcomputers.
2. Size—they can handle files and data bases that are larger than those possible on microcomputers.
3. Programs—special programs are available only on selected central computers.
4. Data management—security and other data management tools are generally better on central computers.
5. Number of users—a central data base may service a number of users at the same time.

Speed

Because the design of large computers is different from that of microcomputers, it is difficult to make a direct comparison of the speed. The speed of a computer is a function of the speed of the central processor, the activities performed by the central processor, the operating system of the computer, as well as many other design aspects. No matter how speed is measured, the larger computers are faster and may be used where such speed is needed. Microcomputers may be used to collect data and then transfer that data to the central computer for the routine that requires the extra speed.

Size

The amount of RAM available in microcomputers has increased from 64K to over three million . In some microcomputers the additional memory can be used only for selected purposes, so the actual increase may not be as large as it may appear.

The size of on-line storage devices has increased from 50K to over 100 megabytes. The most common size of hard disks is currently 20 megabytes.

Even with these increases in internal and on-line capacity, the microcomputer still does not have as much memory available as the large central computers do. In addition, when large data bases are created, the speed of the larger central computers may be needed to handle the massive amount of data involved.

Electronic libraries **(national data bases)** are available that may be called to research many different topics. Some of the available data bases are listed in Table 9–1.

**TABLE 9–1
Selected National Data Bases**

Name of Data	Base General Function
Accountant's Index	Corresponds to hard copy of the Accountant's Index.
Commerce Business Daily	U.S. Department of Commerce-corresponds to printed Commerce Business Daily.
CompuServe	General features including electronic mail.
Dow Jones News	Provides searcher access to Wall Street Journal stories, Dow Jones News Service, and Barron's. Dow Jones records date to 1979.
F.A.S.T. (Financial Action Service Terminal)	Financial and stock quote services.
Source	General features including electronic mail.
WESTLAW	Data base for lawyers to research legal cases.

Most data bases charge fees for joining and usage.

Electronic libraries (data bases) allow business researchers to complete projects in minutes, transfer the results, and generate reports without the production of hard copy until the final report.

Using the Source Communication involves two computers. One of the most popular communication partners is the Source. The Source may be called directly or through the use of a national telephone network service, such as Telenet. Using Telenet, you must first log on to the telephone network (so you can be charged), then log on to the Source. You must make arrangements to purchase both services before you can use them (the Source will bill you for access charges).

The Source is designed to support many combinations of communication parameters. The communication parameters that work for our system on the Source are: eight-bit characters, one stop bit, no parity, and full-duplex. In addition, the Source is in the answer mode, so you must be in the originate mode. The program parameters and your modem must be set to match one of the combination of parameters support by the Source. Most microcomputer equipment will work with the parameters as shown, but some will need to be set differently.

Assuming you have configured the program as outlined in chapter 8 to match the Source, the next step is to dial one of the national network services and connect the telephone line to your modem.

Making the Connection (Hand-Shake) When initial contact is made you may have some spurious characters will appear on your screen. The inital should look like the one in Figure 9–1.

You must have several codes to use the system. Figures 9–2 and 9–3 illustrate the screens which require the entry of codes.

The Source is used by calling to the screen a series of menus either directly or through some other menu. The initial menu is started by typing MENU<CR>. You may go directly to any menu if you know where you are going and its name. Figure 9–4 illustrates the Sources's main menu.

Figure 9–5 is the Education and Careers menu while Figure 9–6 details the services available through this menu.

The Source has a help menu which may be called at almost anytime. The help menu aids the user who has forgotten how to use the system. Figure 9–7 is the help menu.

Programs

The rule "Find the software and then select the computer" still applies when selecting a central computer service. There are many programs developed only for specific central computers that may be needed by the microcomputer user. When one of these programs is needed the purchase of time on a central computer is a logical choice.

FIGURE 9–1
Starting the Source

FIGURE 9–2
Making the Connection

```
xxx xx CONNECTED
Connected to THE SOURCE
>°
```

Programs for analyzing large data sets may be limited to a particular computer due to:

1. Program size

FIGURE 9–3

```
id xxxxxx xxxxxx<CR>
TCF068 (user 18) logged in Saturday, 01 Dec 84 10:17:32.
Welcome, you are connected to THE SOURCE.
Last login Friday, 30 Nov 84 13:07:16.

(C) COPYRIGHT SOURCE TELECOMPUTING CORPORATION 1984.

THIS SYSTEM WILL NOT BE AVAILABLE FROM 4 AM
TO 6 AM (EDT) ON  12/01/84 FOR MAINTENANCE.

Pick the Heisman Trophy winner. Type
SPORTS for details.

Reader's Digest Gives You A Chance
To Earn $250. See NEW for details.

Have You Expressed Your Opinion About
The Source Business Magazine? If Not,
Type BIZDATE For Details.
-> CHAT -OFF

-> MAILCK
Your Mailbox is empty at this time.
->
```

FIGURE 9–4
Source's Main Menu

```
THE SOURCE MAIN MENU

1   NEWS AND REFERENCE RESOURCES
2   BUSINESS/FINANCIAL MARKETS
3   CATALOGUE SHOPPING
4   HOME AND LEISURE
5   EDUCATION AND CAREER
6   MAIL AND COMMUNICATIONS
7   PERSONAL COMPUTING
8   INVESTOR SERVICES

Enter item number or HELP _
```

2. Data set size
3. Computer speed.

FIGURE 9–5
Making a Selection

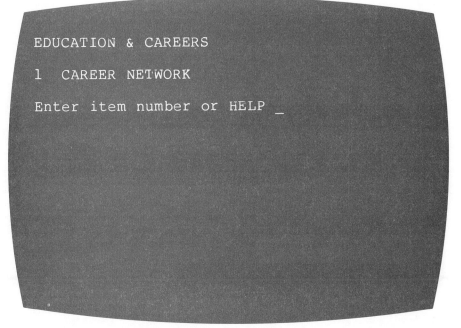

```
EDUCATION & CAREERS

1   CAREER NETWORK

Enter item number or HELP _
```

FIGURE 9–6
After the Selection

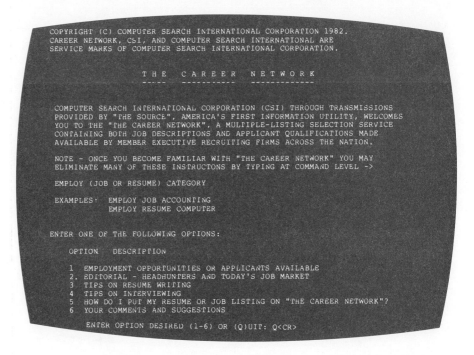

```
COPYRIGHT (C) COMPUTER SEARCH INTERNATIONAL CORPORATION 1982.
CAREER NETWORK, CSI, AND COMPUTER SEARCH INTERNATIONAL ARE
SERVICE MARKS OF COMPUTER SEARCH INTERNATIONAL CORPORATION.

               T H E   C A R E E R   N E T W O R K
               -----   ----------   -------------


COMPUTER SEARCH INTERNATIONAL CORPORATION (CSI) THROUGH TRANSMISSIONS
PROVIDED BY "THE SOURCE", AMERICA'S FIRST INFORMATION UTILITY, WELCOMES
YOU TO THE "THE CAREER NETWORK", A MULTIPLE-LISTING SELECTION SERVICE
CONTAINING BOTH JOB DESCRIPTIONS AND APPLICANT QUALIFICATIONS MADE
AVAILABLE BY MEMBER EXECUTIVE RECRUITING FIRMS ACROSS THE NATION.

NOTE - ONCE YOU BECOME FAMILIAR WITH "THE CAREER NETWORK" YOU MAY
ELIMINATE MANY OF THESE INSTRUCTONS BY TYPING AT COMMAND LEVEL ->

EMPLOY (JOB OR RESUME) CATEGORY

EXAMPLES:  EMPLOY JOB ACCOUNTING
           EMPLOY RESUME COMPUTER


ENTER ONE OF THE FOLLOWING OPTIONS:

   OPTION   DESCRIPTION

   1  EMPLOYMENT OPPORTUNITIES OR APPLICANTS AVAILABLE
   2. EDITORIAL - HEADHUNTERS AND TODAY'S JOB MARKET
   3  TIPS ON RESUME WRITING
   4  TIPS ON INTERVIEWING
   5  HOW DO I PUT MY RESUME OR JOB LISTING ON "THE CAREER NETWORK"?
   6  YOUR COMMENTS AND SUGGESTIONS

      ENTER OPTION DESIRED (1-6) OR (Q)UIT: Q<CR>
```

Data Management

Data is a valuable asset of a business. The security and use of data must be controlled. The protection schemes available for some microcomputer

FIGURE 9–7
The Help Menu

```
-> HELP<CR>
BE GLAD TO!

- STC CUSTOMER SUPPORT MAY BE REACHED VIA MAILBOX...........TCA088
     OR AT OUR TOLLFREE NUMBER................................800-336-3330
- FOR THE LATEST ANNOUNCEMENTS FROM THE SOURCE, TYPE........NEW
- FOR A LISTING OF SYSTEM COMMANDS, TYPE....................HELP SYSCOM
- FOR THE MAIN INDEX TO THE SOURCE CONTENTS, TYPE...........HELP LIBALL
- TO ENTER THE SOURCE MAIN MENU, TYPE.......................MENU
- FOR AN INDEX TO BUSINESS AND FINANCIAL SERVICES, TYPE.....HELP BIZDEX
- FOR AN INDEX TO ONLINE INFORMATION ON PROGRAMMING & THE
     EDITOR, TYPE...........................................HELP ADAPPR
- FOR A LIST OF ALL HELP FILES AVAILABLE TO YOU, TYPE.......HELP LIST
->
```

data bases are limited. In many situations, using a central computer as a central **file server** gives management tools needed to ensure such security and control needed over the company's memory, its data base.

Number of Users

It is difficult to separate the need for many users to access a data base from speed, size, and security factors. The large central computer or some type of network with a central file server (subject of chapter 10) is needed to perform this task.

COMMUNICATION THEORY, BACKGROUND, AND PROGRAMS

The business professional must understand some of the theory, know some of the terms, and be familiar with some programs to obtain the most benefit from the central computer communication capabilities available.

When communicating with a central computer, knowledge of communication parameters is important because the microcomputer user must be able to match the parameters used by the central computer. Most of the terms and concepts are the same as those discussed in chapter 8, except that most communication uses telephone lines, so only the screen of the microcomputer can be seen. Some of the things the user must know are:

1. The nature of communication between a central computer and microcomputer.
2. Communication parameters (asynchronous-ASCII-or synchronous-EBCDIC).
3. Communication parameters and programs.

Microcomputer Communication with Central Computers

Communication between microcomputers and central computers is the transfer of meaningful data and instructions in the form of bits. The bits may be part of a standard coding system, such as ASCII, **EBCDIC**, or the custom code of a particular system. It is possible to purchase an interface device that allows microcomputers using ASCII to communicate with a central computer using EBCDIC. These devices are called **emulators** if they are internal to the microcomputer, and interfaces if they are external. Microcomputers equipped with emulators are often joined together into a company network.

When communication is between a microcomputer and a central computer, the central computer's communication parameters will usually be set, and the microcomputer will have to be adjusted to make the communication process work.

Asynchronous or Synchronous

Both asynchronous and synchronous communications are used between microcomputers and central computers. Often central computers can only communicate using synchronous communications, and interface devices are needed to convert asynchronous to synchronous and back between the two computers.

> ### MICROS IN ACTION
>
> Dean Witter's F.A.S.T. system is designed to be used with a variety of microcomputers. The standard used is asynchronous using ASCII. There are no special limitations on the microcomputer equipment, modems, and programs needed to communicate with the system.

Many microcomputers produce (asynchronous) ASCII only, while most central computers produce (synchronous) EBCDIC only. Modems convert between digital and analog, change synchronous to asynchronous, and convert ASCII to EBCDIC and back.

Communication Parameters and Programs

Communication between microcomputers and central computers requires the same parameters and programs as other microcomputer communication. Asynchronous ASCII signals look the same no matter what hardware and software is used. The microcomputer user must set the parameters to match the central computer. Most central computers are set in the answer mode so the microcomputer user must set the microcomputer to originate. In most cases, the software package need not have the capability to answer when communicating with a central computer. If file transfers are not needed the microcomputer user may need only a dumb terminal program.

> ### MICROS IN ACTION
>
> Dean Witter's F.A.S.T. computer is the host. The microcomputer owned by the client or account executive is the terminal. The terminal may be either dumb or smart.

COMMUNICATION HARDWARE

Most of the microcomputer hardware used for communication with central computers is the same hardware as that used for communication with other microcomputers. Some special hardware is available for special applications.

The RS-232C port is used for communication with central computers. Modems and null-modems are used as they are in communication between microcomputers. Special printed circuit cards may be added to microcomputers to give them additional capabilities.

Emulators and Interfaces

The microcomputer may be made to work like custom devices with the addition of internal or external hardware and special software. For example, the microcomputer, plus a special printed circuit board and software, can emulate an IBM 3270. An IBM 3270 is a terminal that can be connected to an IBM mainframe computer. It has special communication and graphics capabilities.

Central computers do not do their own communicating directly. They often use **collectors** that interface with devices having special characteristics. Microcomputer manufacturers make interfaces that act like collectors. These devices are limited to specific mainframe-microcomputer combinations.

CENTRAL COMPUTER COMMUNICATION

The business problem is to determine what is best done by the microcomputer as a stand alone unit, and what is best done by the central computer.

Timesharing started with the use of large mainframe computers in the mid 1960s. The idea was to allow the user access to the central computer by way of terminals. This service allows individuals to process data in **real time,** rather than as part of a **batch run.** The original terminals were capable of operating only when connected to the central computer.

The dial-up terminal was developed for the timesharing computer. Business people quickly realized that microcomputers could act as terminals for central computers.

Collector:
An interface that collects messages from a number of devices, organizes the messages, and then forwards them to the central computer.

Real time processing:
To process data and instruction as they are transmitted to the computer. The user works interactively with the computer.
Batch run:
A scheduling system which requires computer tasks be collected and given to a central controller who then runs them as a single job-batched together.

USER WINDOW

Never say never in microcomputers. Three years after connecting a Model I Radio Shack as a terminal to an IBM-360, the microcomputer user was told by the system's operator it could not be done.

The economic problem is to balance the cost of on-line processing with off-line processing. The original business computers (late 1950s, early 1960s) were so expensive that great efforts were made to create and use off-line machines for sorting, printing, and other services.

The on-line/off-line problem still exists. The difference is that the off-line equipment is now a low-cost smart microcomputer. The microcomputer can do many of the tasks of a central computer at lower cost.

As a business professional you will have to answer the question "What is the best way to do the job: microcomputer or central computer?" Your answer will vary as the capabilities and costs of the two alternate approaches continue to change.

In addition to performing many of the tasks of the central computer and acting as a terminal for the central computer, the microcomputer may be the central computer.

National Data Bases

Institutions may maintain their own data bases, use those established as commercial services, or both. Among the national data base systems available are:

1. Source
2. CompuServe
3. Dow Jones News/Retrieval Service.

The procedure for logging on, getting started, in all systems are similar to the Source. The Source was one of the first data base systems, and offers over 1,200 features and programs. It is owned and operated by Reader's Digest. It offers current stock information with custom calculation of your own portfolio, and an executive job search data base.

The Source was one of the first systems to offer electronic mail. To use this service, both senders and receivers must be members of the Source, and receivers must check their own mail box with their own microcomputers. There is no limitation on which microcomputer is used, since the communication uses standard asynchronous ASCII. One feature of electronic mail service by the Source is the capability to send up to 200 messages at one time, to be fowarded at specific times.

MICROS IN ACTION

Dean Witter's F.A.S.T. system is similar to other data base programs. It is available to the account executives and clients of Dean Witter only.

CompuServe is another data base service that has been operating for a number of years. It offers services similar to those of the Source. CompuServe has electronic mail, a bulletin-board, news, weather, magazines, wire services, directory, and more. News services, such as the one for Commodities, are updated every twenty minutes. The cost of use during business hours is much greater than during off hours.

Dow Jones News/Retrieval System is a news and financial data base service for up-to-the-minute information on stocks and bonds. You may research a company in depth and maintain a stock portfolio for automatic update.

There are specialized data bases in law, advertising, aviation, medicine, engineering, and many other fields. You will find books listing these data bases in your library or at your local bookstore.

Electronic Mail

Electronic mail is the use of the computer to send messages through a computer network. Currently, you have the choice of electronic messaging (computer-to-computer transmission) or computer-generated mail (computer-input, terminal-output). Mail may be sent using an internal company system or through one of the commercial electronic mail carriers such as MCI, ITT, Western Union, Telex, or one of the electronic bulletin board systems.

Internal company networks may consist of a microcomputer with an auto-answer telephone modem and a communication program that can save any message received. The system is turned on after business hours, and all messages received are printed the next morning and fowarded as needed.

Some commercial electronic mail services provide a local toll-free telephone number. The user is expected to compose the letter off-line and upload it to the electronic mail service. There is usually an on-line charge to discourage on-line composition. The commercial service will save a message for downloading to the receiver's microcomputer, foward it by first-class mail, overnight mail, or hand deliver a printed copy of the message for various charges. Electronic mail is not seen as a substitution for a personal letter. It is a way to reach someone who is not available by phone, to send out mass mailings, or to get a document delivered rapidly.

Setting up to use electronic mail requires knowledge of the communication parameters and how to use the program available on your microcomputer to match the settings with the electronic mail service. EasyLink, the electronic mail service of Western Union, comes with many manuals including a training manual. The manual is well written, but the volume of material is liable to turn off all but the most determined potential user.

If your company has a central computer or a microcomputer with a modem that will automatically answer the telephone, you may set up your own electronic mail service. The ability to standardize the parameters and software used internal to an organization makes the creation of a internal electronic mail service easier than a commercial service in many circumstances.

Computer Conferencing

Computer conferencing is similar to telephone conferencing, except that microcomputers and a central computer are on both ends of the communication partnership. Many systems accept text, graphics, and voice. Using your own resources or a data base service such as the Source, you can set up a "PARTICIPATE" communication network. This allows individuals in different physical locations to "meet," using microcomputers. The advantage of this type of meeting over the telephone is that text, graphics, and voice may be transferred. If you have a microcomputer with a communication program that can capture and save what is received, you may transfer the material to your diskettes for future use.

Other Computer Data Bases and Bulletin Boards

There are specialized computer data bases servicing almost every industry and community. Many local retail microcomputer stores will run bulletin boards for their customers and potential customers.

Forum80 is a bulletin board found in many local communities. It was originally set up by TRS-80 microcomputer owners, but usually serves all users. You will find some business information, but mainly hobby information, in this type of bulletin board.

The Microcomputer as a Remote Data Entry Device

In the 1960s, computer systems were designed carefully to use off-line equipment for sorting and preparing data. The computer card was the popular input-ouput and data storage medium at that time, and there was equipment for sorting, collating, and separating decks of computer cards, depending on the need.

USER WINDOW

The supermarket clerk picks up his microcomputer with built-in bar code reader. Inventory is taken in four hours, rather than the usual twelve, with this add-on device.

The reason for off-line operation was the high cost of computer time, and the relative low cost of the off-line equipment that could do the preparation. Today, the microcomputer may be used to prepare data off-line from a mainframe computer. The best balance between the use of microcomputers and mainframes is constantly changing, as the costs of the alternatives change. Look at the use of different types of computer equipment as alternate methods of solving problems. Select the lowest cost method that does the best job for your organization.

USER WINDOW

A survey is taken to determine the potential market for a product in a selected city. The data is coded and typed into a microcomputer. The microcomputer is connected to the telephone line and the data is transmitted to a central computer for addition to a data base, and for analysis and evaluation.

The concept of selecting the most economical balance between on-line and off-line use of different size computers depends on the capability to transfer data, text, and other files between the computers. Communication between dumb terminals and a computer does not involve the transfer of files. Microcomputers may act as dumb or smart terminals. The capability to transfer files is one of the characteristics which differentiates dumb and smart terminals.

MODEMS

Modems come with custom features and their own programs. Most modems work with many different communication packages. Some modems come with their own software. The price is often not a measure of the features available. See Table 9–2 for a comparison of several modems.

TABLE 9–2 Asynchronous Direct Connect Modems

Features	Acess 1-2-3 Novation	Smartlin II Business Comp. Net.	Smartmodem 1200B Hayes Microcomp.	Volksmodem 12 Anchor Automation
Speed 300	x	x	x	x
1200	x	x	x	x
Internal	x	x	x	
External			x	x
Duplex Full	x	x	x	x
Half		x	x	x
Includes				
Program	Yes	Yes	Yes	No
Auto answer	x	x	x	x
dial	x	x	x	x
redial	x		x	x
Price	$595.00	$199.95	$599.00	$299.00

SUMMARY

You have been introduced to the importance of microcomputer communication with central computers to the business professional. You have learned that microcomputer-to-central-computer communication is similar to microcomputer-to-microcomputer communication.

The key points in this chapter are:

1. Communication is the transfer of data and instructions from one computer type device to another and the interactive use of a larger computer using a second computer.

2. The central computer has capabilities and data that are not available on microcomputers.

3. The business professional must understand some of the theory, know some of the terms, and be familiar with some programs to obtain the most benefits from the central computer communication capabilities available.

4. Most often communication between a central computer and a microcomputer occurs over telephone lines or in a network.

5. Asynchronous (ASCII) communication is common on microcomputers while synchronous (EBCDIC) communication is common on central computers.

6. Communication between microcomputers and central computers requires the same parameters and programs as other microcomputer communication.

7. Most of the microcomputer hardware used for communication with central computers is the same hardware as that used for communication with other microcomputers. Some special hardware is available for special applications.

8. The microcomputer may be made to work like custom devices with the addition of internal or external hardware and special software.

9. The business problem is to determine what is best done by the microcomputer as a stand-alone unit, and what is best done by the central computer.

10. Institutions may maintain their own data bases or use those established as commercial services.

11. Electronic mail services are available.

12. Computer conferencing is similar to simple telephone conferencing except that microcomputers and a central computer may be on both ends of the communication partnership rather than human beings.

13. There are local data bases for use by individuals for local needs.

14. The concept of on-/off-line equipment developed in the 1960s is applicable to the use of the microcomputer as an off-line data entry device for large computers.

KEY TERMS

ASCII	File server
Asynchronous	Interface
Collector	Mainframe computer
EBCDIC	Minicomputer
Electronic mail	National electronic data base
Emulators	Synchronous

REVIEW QUESTIONS

1. What are mainframe and minicomputers?

2. When does the microcomputer user need to communicate between a microcomputer and a central computer?

3. Identify one reason why electronic mail has been slow to grow.

4. Define electronic mail.

5. Why does the microcomputer user need a large central computer.

6. What is a national electronic data base?

7. What it Telenet? How is a data base such as the Source contacted using Telenet?

8. What is on the Source's main menu?

9. Identify and explain the following key terms:
   a. ASCII
   b. EBCDIC
   c. Emulators
   d. Interfaces

10. What is asynchronous and synchronous communication?

11. How is communication organized in central computers?

12. Identify some of the services offered by CompuServe.

13. What is required to set up electronic mail?

DISCUSSION AND APPLICATION QUESTIONS

1. Why is ASCII a key concept in both microcomputer-to-microcomputer and microcomputer-to-central computer communication?

2. Examine some microcomputer magazines and report on the type of modems and their costs now being advertised.

3. Contact some electronic mail services and report on the nature of the services being offered and their cost.

4. If your central computer has a mailbox service find out about it and report on its operation.

5. From magazines and other sources find out about emulators and collectors. Report on their capabilities, costs, and availability.

6. Contact a national data base and report on their services and the cost of these services.

LABORATORY ASSIGNMENTS

To perform communication laboratory assignments your microcomputer needs to be equipped with a modem or a null-modem. You must have the correct communication software, and the communication partner identified must be available.

1. Use your microcomputer to communicate with the university's central computer. Report on the problems and initial log-on screens. What communication parameters were used?

2. Use your microcomputer to communicate with a local data base. Report on the problems and initial log-on screens. What communication parameters were used?

3. Use your microcomputer to communicate with a national data base. Report on the problems and initial log-on screens. What communication parameters were used?

4. Send a text file created on your microcomputer to a different brand microcomputer.

SELECTED REFERENCES

Cameron, Janet. "Electronic Mail Gallops into the Future," *Computerworld on Communications*, November 1984, vol. 1, no.1. p. 71.

Campbell, Joe. *The RS-232 Solution*, Sybex Books, 1984.

Edelhart, Mike and Davies Owen. *OMNI Online Database Directory*, Collier Books, Macmillan Publishing Company, 1983.

Glossbrenner, Alfred. *The Complete Handbook of Personal Computer Communications*. St. Martin's Press, 1983.

Lesko, Matthew. "Low-Cost On-Line Databases," *Byte*, pp. 167, 168, 171, 172, 174.

Schwaderer, David. *Digital Communications Programming on the IBM PC*, John Wiley and Sons, 1984.

10

Chapter Outline

Chapter Goals

When you complete this chapter you will be able to:

Understand why local area networks are important to the business professional.

Understand some of the theory of local area networks.

Understand the role of some of the special local area network hardware.

Understand some of the difficulties of setup and the ease of use of local area networks.

LOCAL AREA NETWORKS

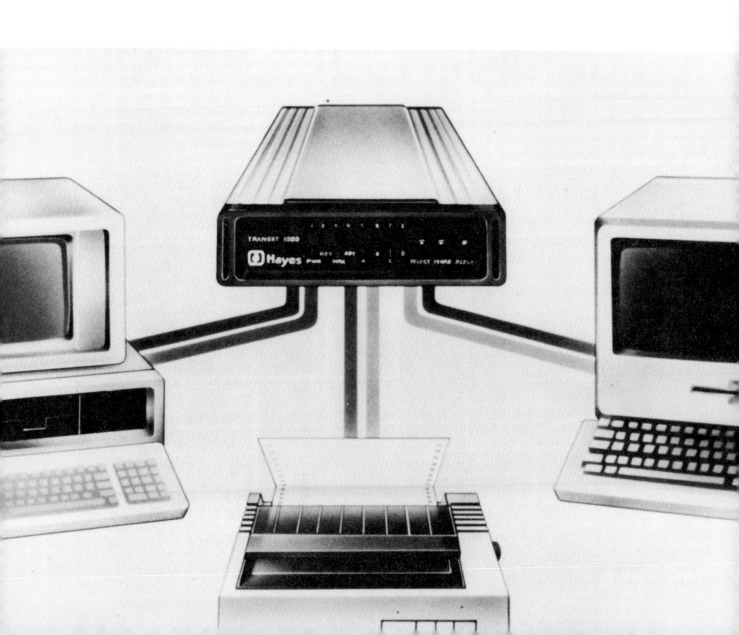

LAN:

Local Area Networks. A series of microcomputers connected together sharing peripherials, files, and programs.

A local area network **(LAN)** allows a company to tie a series of microcomputers together to form a system for the purpose of sharing peripherals, files, and programs. The cost of expensive peripherals, such as letter-quality printers, may be spread among a number of users rather than carried by a single user.

The most basic network is one that uses a mechanical or electronic switching device to connect microcomputers and peripherals together. The connection of microcomputers to peripherals form networks. These

FIGURE 10–1
A Local Area Network

networks are considered a limited case only. Figure 10–1 illustrates a local area network of microcomputers in operation.

It is often necessary for several individuals to use the same file. By having a network, all users can get to the files. The latest version or update is always available and there is no need to transfer diskettes among individuals. The LAN accomplishes the communication objective of making data available to several users at different locations.

LANs allow a single copy of a program to be used by many individuals. The program may be stored in a central area along with the common data files. When needed, the program is called up.

The large central computer has long been used as the core of networks for the sharing of data, programs, and peripherals. A network of microcomputers may be used in place of a central computer in situations in which the speed, programs, and other special capabilities of the larger computer are not needed. The current interest in LANs is due to the drop in the cost of networks, programs, terminals, wiring, and all other aspects of networks. Technical improvements and cost reductions are making LAN a solution for many more business problems.

Because the technology is new, there is no single accepted LAN standard. For example, the type of cable used varies from twisted wire pairs such as those in telephone wires to the use of fiber-optic cables. Often many different types of cables, including telephone lines, will be combined in a single network.

The three aspects of a LAN are:

1. Physical transmission media and transmission techniques.
2. LAN topology (logical arrangement of stations).
3. Access methods.

WHY THE BUSINESS PROFESSIONAL MUST LEARN ABOUT LANS

LANs mean cost savings in equipment, better control of data files, and the sharing of expensive programs. LANs are needed in business situations in which sharing must occur. Small businesses may need only personal computers that work alone. As a business grows, however, and more individuals use microcomputers, sharing may be the best alternative for company growth.

In large corporations there is a need for both stand-alone work stations and coordination between individual microcomputer users. Data management and security are important in situations in which a number of users need to use and update the same data file constantly.

In small companies where cash is short, the sharing of peripherals may be the most important reason for a LAN. In larger companies, the sharing of data and program files may be more important.

RELATED CONCEPTS AND BACKGROUND

Networking is part of the growth of technology that is occurring in many aspects of microcomputers. A precondition for the general use of microcomputer based local area networks was the availability of microcomputers with speed adequate enough to perform more than one thing at a time, that is, with the capability for **multi-tasking.**

A special type of network may be created by using the microcomputer's capability for **multi-use.** In a multi-user environment, all users share the same microprocessor. This means the system need only have dumb terminals, but many use both smart and dumb terminals. Standard RS-232C, asynchronous serial communication may be used in this type of network.

The capability for multi-using is part of the hardware and operating system. It is not found in all microcomputers. Software is available that adds this capability in some microcomputers.

Multi-using is not a solution to all business problems. If only one person uses a microcomputer, or if the microcomputer used does not have to share data bases, multi-using may not be needed.

The cost of this feature, relative to the cost of operating two stand-alone microcomputers, is in a state of change. For small offices, a central microcomputer with a limited number of terminals may be an economical solution to computer usage in the future. The terminals often will not have all the capabilities of the stand-alone microcomputer. The operation of a terminal in a network is similar to the operation of a microcomputer, except that data and instructions may be sent and received from other work stations in the network.

A **central file server** program which makes a microcomputer into a central file server is often used in a local area network to control the access of individual work stations to the files stored in the ''large'' central storage device (hard disk). The central file server handles problems that occur when several users are trying to update a file at the same time. The central file server is often designed to handle the problem of file security keeping selected users from using specified files.

It is possible to connect a series of microcomputers together with the addition of hardware and software that allow the sharing of data and instructions between them.

The control, such as limiting users, that management may exercize with central file servers approaches that of a large central computer. Data management of central data files is critical in many business situations.

Local area networks may be stand-alone networks or part of a larger system. You may have several different types of networks tied together with an interface device, and then, through another interface device, tied into a large central computer. The objective of networks is to carry out the concept of on-/off-line balancing of costs and benefits from different devices.

The central data storage device may be a hard disk with 10 Megabytes of memory or more. Generally, LANs are designed for computers to communicate within an organization, using direct-wire connections with special interface devices for communication across telephone lines. When a LAN uses telephone lines, the operator will encounter many of the security problems of the timesharing mini and mainframe computer operator.

There are some copyright problems yet to be solved in the sharing of

Multi-tasking:
The capability of the microcomputer to perform more than one task at the same time.

Multi-use:
Microcomputers and programs that allow more than one user to share the same microprocessor.

Central file server (program):
Program that controls the access to files by individual work stations in a LAN.

commercial programs. The technical developments in local area networks have progressed faster than the legal and moral solutions to the use of software on more than one microcomputer.

Some multi-user networks are created by the addition of a program to a microcomputer system. Most local area networks are combinations of hardware and software that must be matched to create the network.

PHYSICAL TRANSMISSION MEDIA

There are four popular cables used for connecting networks. Cost limitations, performance, and speed determine the best selection. The microcomputer is connected to a local area network through a port. This port may be built-in or created with the addition of a special purpose printed circuit board to the microcomputer.

There are four popular types of cable used for microcomputer networks, in addition to the standard serial and parallel cables already discussed. They are:

1. Twisted-pair wire cable
2. Baseband coaxial cable
3. Broadband coaxial cable
4. Broadband optical-fiber.

The lines used to connect telephones, called twisted-pairs, can be used for networks. Networks using this type of wire are often designed around a central switching station. Generally this type of network is the least expensive, has the lowest speed (approximately 1Mbps—one million bytes per second), and is limited in the distance data can be sent to approximately 200 feet.

MICROS IN ACTION

Burnett-Wilson General Contractors selected a twisted wire paired network because the distances between terminals were limited, and the maximum number of terminals were not expected to go beyond four.

Baseband coaxial cable networks are medium speed, between 1Mbps and 10Mpbs, depending on the physical type of cable. This type of cable is used by PC Net and Ethernet (two popular commercial networks). A baseband coaxial cable is similar to cable television wiring. The baseband is limited to allowing one terminal or microcomputer to transmit at a time. The single bus can handle only a single user at a time. Distances are limited to a few thousand feet without the use of repeaters. A repeater is a device similar to an amplifier that inputs a weak electrical impulse, then fowards a stronger impulse. The installation cost of baseband coaxial cable is generally higher than that of twisted wire pairs or broadband cabling.

Broadband coaxial cable can handle many transmissions at one time, even different kinds of transmissions. Speeds of from 1Mbps to 10Mbps in each of up to 30 channel pairs are common. (For communication, a channel pair is needed to transmit information in both directions.) Optical-fiber cable is becoming more popular for broadband applications. Broadband cable can extend for miles with the use of inexpensive amplifiers.

A system built around one type of cable is easy to control and understand. Hybrid systems requiring a mixture of cables, interfaces, collectors, and telephone lines can become complex and technical.

LAN TOPOLOGY

The arrangement of stations relative to each other and relative to a central file server, fall into some simple classifications. LANs are often perceived to be a central communications network among individuals and machines in a local office. LANs require flexibility in adding and changing hardware devices to keep the system current as technological changes occur. A LAN may need to be interfaced with mainframes or other LANs. Some popular **LAN topology** configurations include **central switching stations, communication buses, communication rings or circles,** and **point-to-point communication** (see Figure 10–2).

LAN topology:
The relative physical and logical arrangement of stations in the network.

Central switching station:
The central microcomputer connected to a series of stations in a LAN.

Communication bus:
A LAN layout around a bus which serves as a channel of communication.

Communication ring or circle:
Layout of LAN where the stations are connected in a ring or circle.

Point-to-point LAN:
Layout of LAN topology where each station is connected directly to other stations.

> ## MICROS IN ACTION
>
> Burnett-Wilson, General Contractors selected a central file server with terminals. For the central file server an IBM-AT was used. IBM-PC's were selected for the terminals. Users of central controller or terminals may read and write from files stored on the IBM-AT hard disk.

ACCESS METHODS

Access methods determine how stations communicate with the other physical parts of the network. The availability of a LAN depends on the existence of an operating system that can control a number of units. UNIX and UNIX derivatives have been the principal operating system supporting LANs in the past. MS/PC-DOS 3.1 is also capable of operating a LAN.

Access method:
The scheme used by the operating system to control the communication between work stations in a LAN.

The **access method** is the scheme used by the operating system to control the individual work stations right to transmit. Access control is either centralized or distributed. In a centralized system, a central file server checks on the activities of all stations and controls the transmissions. In a distributed system, each station participates in controlling the LAN.

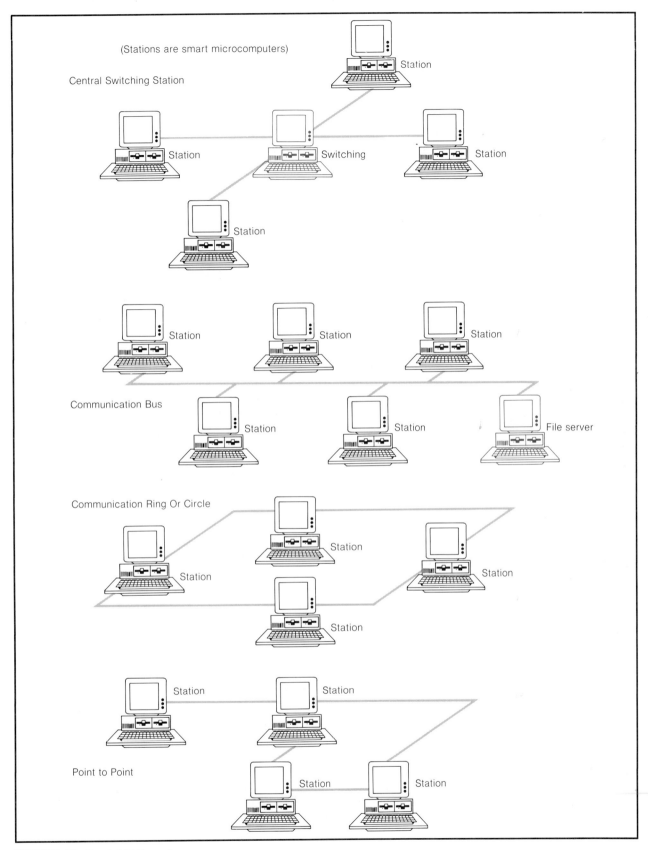

(Stations are smart microcomputers)

Central Switching Station

Station

Station

Switching

Station

Station

Communication Bus

Station

Station

Station

Station

Station

File server

Communication Ring Or Circle

Station

Station

Station

Station

Point to Point

Station

Station

Station

Station

FIGURE 10–2   LAN Topology

The access control techniques include:

1. CSMA/CD
2. Token-passing

CSMA/CD (Carrier Sense Multiple Access/Collision Detect) operates similar to a party-line telephone system. The line is checked by the work stations program to see if it is being used. If it is not, transmission proceeds. All stations are able to read the messages sent, and must have software to check and see if the message is addressed to them. There is no central control microcomputer because the control is exercised by the individual stations. Ethernet was one of the first systems to use this approach to networking.

Token-passing is a common method of transmission control when a circle network is used. Each station checks to see if a given transmission is for them and, if it is not, passes the message along to the next station.

Broadband coaxial systems use modems to control the frequencies of transmissions. A modem is needed to translate the microcomputer transmission to a special frequency and back. More than a single user may transmit at one time because modems divide the cable into channels.

Networks may be created with a variety of cables and with the addition of telephone connections. A central problem in creating such a network is the timing of each cable subsystem. A large file being transferred over one of the slower links can create bottlenecks, that can tie up the entire system. The creation, maintenance, and organization of networks are tasks that often require engineering skills.

The data management needs of an organization may determine the type of local area network which may even dictate the selection of a large central computer rather than a microcomputer system. Capabilities such as securing (locking) files and records from individual users is important. These capabilities are built into some local area network systems.

COMPARING LANS

The number of variety of local area networks is growing. The number of local area networks available has increased as the capability of microcomputers has grown. Some of the more popular ones are shown in Table 10–1.

TABLE 10–1   Local Area Networks

Architecture Features	Omninet	Davong MultiLink	Easinet	PC Network
	Corvus Systems	Davong Systems	Esprit Systems	IBM
Topology	Bus	Star	Ring	Bus
Cable	Twisted Pair	Coaxial Baseband	Twisted Pair	Coaxial Broadband

TABLE 10–1 (continued)

Architecture Features	Omninet	Davong MultiLink	Easinet	PC Network
	Corvus Systems	Davong Systems	Esprit Systems	IBM
Data LRates MMbps	1.0	2.5	1.0	2.0
Access Method	CSMA/CA	Token Passing	Token Passing	CSMA/CA
Interface (Gateway to mainframe)	Yes	Yes	No	Yes
Software Features				
File Locking	Yes	Yes	No	Yes
Record Locking	Yes	Yes	No	Yes
Electronic Mail	Yes	Yes	No	Yes
Remote Access	No	No	No	Yes
Capacities Features				
Maximum stat	63	255	254	72*
Cable length Maximum	1,000 feet	2,000 feet	500 feet	2,000*** feet

*Additional stations with special cables.
**Longer distance with special cables.

SUMMARY

You have been introduced to the use of local area networks to solve the business problem of communication between microcomputer users. The key points to remember are:

1. Local area networks can increase the productivity of the business user.
2. LANs means cost saving in equipment, better control of data files, and the sharing of programs.
3. Networking is part of the growth of technology that is occurring in many aspects of microcomputers.
4. There are four popular cables used for connecting networks. Cost limitations, performance, and speed determine the best selection.
5. The arrangement of stations relative to each other and relative to a central file server falls into some simple classifications.

KEY TERMS

Access method	File server
Bus	LAN
Central file server (program)	LAN topology
Central switching station	Multi-tasking
Communication bus	Multi-user
Communication ring	Point-to-point

REVIEW QUESTIONS

1. What is a local area network?

2. What are the three aspects of LANs?

3. What is multi-tasking? Why is it of interest when establishing a LAN?

4. What is multi-user?

5. What is a central file server program?

6. What are the four types of cables used for microcomputers networks?

7. What is LAN topology?

8. Identify the layout of a central switching station, communication bus, communication ring or circle, and point-to-point communications.

9. What is a LAN access method? Which two are reviewed in the text?

DISCUSSION AND APPLICATION QUESTIONS

1. Examine magazines and other sources for articles about the legal aspects of sharing programs on microcomputers in a network.

2. Examine the license agreement that comes with one or more pieces of software. What is the significance of these agreements to LAN operations?

3. Investigate the present methods of controlling the access of individual work stations to a given data record to prevent or allow more than a single individual to update a file at the same time.

4. If possible tour a local area network and report on its operation. Identify the type(s) of cables used and the topology.

5. Interview a business person who has set up a LAN. Report on the problems involved with such a set up.

6. Interview a professional who has used electronic mail. Report on the interview.

LABORATORY ASSIGNMENTS

1. If a local area network is available use one of the work stations to load a program from your work station's on-line memory, recall a data file from one of the other stations or central file server a data file. Update and use the data file. Transfer it back to a second station or central file server using a new filespec.

2. If a local area network is available use one of the work stations to load a program from one of the other stations or central file server. Use the program.

SELECTED REFERENCES

Allen, Roger. "LANs Stake Their Claim and Opt for Coexistence," *Electronic Design*, vol. 45, March 1984, p. 26.

Duca, James, R. "Local Area Networking Provides Link for Today's Office," *The Office*, vol. 95, February 1982, p. 113.

Flatman, Alan V. "Low-cost local network for small systems grows from IEEE-802.3 standard," *Electronic Design*, vol. 32, July 1984. p. 187.

Glossbrenner, Alfred. *The Complete Handbook of Personal Computer Communications*, St. Martin's Press, 1983.

Gruhn, Marty. "Battle of the LANs," *Office Administration and Automation*, vol. 45, March 1984, p. 26.

Marshal, Martin. "Ethernet gets two bad report cards," *Electronics*, vol. 45, March 1984, p. 88.

11

Chapter Outline

Chapter Goals

When you complete this chapter you will be able to:

Understand the need for data file transfer software between application programs.

Understand the need for software to integrate the operations and data files used.

THE INTEGRATION OF
OPERATIONS AND
DATA FILES

**International Software
Consultants, Inc.**

International Software Consultants, Inc. is a small vertical marketing and consulting firm specializing in the area of:

Job cost accounting for the construction industry.
Student administration for educators.

They also act as system integrators to aid firms in combining different software packages. As a part of this effort, ISC has developed the capability to move data files between programs on the same, as well as on different microcomputers. They have purchased and developed a number of specialized transfer programs.

Most of the personal productivity increase obtained from using the microcomputer is due to the general application programs that were reviewed in earlier chapters:

1. Word processing
2. Electronic spreadsheets
3. Data base management
4. Graphics
5. Communication

Your personal microcomputer productivity may be increased by the capability to move data between programs and to integrate the operation of different types of programs. Your company's microcomputer productivity may be increased by using a common data base and integrating the operation of such special application programs as:

1. General ledger
2. Inventory control
3. Accounts receivable
4. Accounts payable

Programs that you have studied that integrate the use of microcomputers include:

1. The disk operating system
2. Programs that communicate between microcomputers
3. Programs that transfer files between microcomputers
4. Data base management programs
5. LANs

Some additional solutions to the transfer of data and programs include:

1. **Data file transfer software,** between programs.
2. **Modular software:**
   General application programs;
   Specific application programs.
3. Integrated software:
   General application programs;
   Specific application programs.
4. **Overlay utility software.**
5. **System overlay software.**

Integrating programs have three general objectives:

1. To integrate data files for use in various applications.
2. To integrate operation of software.
3. To hide the complexities of the disk operating system.

There are multi-tasking programs that allow the user to have several windows open on the screen, with individual application programs running in each window at the same time. Data available in a program operating in any window may be transferred to a program operating in any other window easily.

Data transfer between applications may be performed by DOS, word processor, spreadsheet, data base, file transfer, modular, integrated, utility overlay, or system overlay programs. The best solution depends on the number of times such a transfer is required, the disk operating system, the specific program used, the programs available, and the data file structure used (see Table 11–1).

Data file transfer software:
Programs designed to read data in the format produced by one program and change it to a format needed by a second program.
Modular software:
Programs sold in individual modules that can be put together to form a system.
Overlay utility software:
Programs that provide selected routines to the user at all times.
System overlay software.
Programs that take over the disk operating system and add such capabilities as multi-tasking and file transfer between two programs operating concurrently.

TABLE 11–1   Objectives by Software Type

Type of Package	Data Integration	Program Integration	DOS Simplification
Data file transfer	x	some	
Modular	x	x	
Integrated	x	x	
Overlay utility	some	x	
System overlay	x	x	x

WHY THE BUSINESS USER SHOULD KNOW ABOUT INTEGRATED DATA FILES AND OPERATIONS

The combination of data files, and application program and system operation may make the business user more productive. As the number of programs used by an individual expands, the tasks of transferring data between programs and integrating the operation of programs become more important. It is frustrating to re-enter data that is already in the microcomputer. As the volume of data increases, the task of re-entry becomes more difficult and time consuming.

The first time many users encounter the need to move data between programs may be when the output of a spreadsheet or data base program is needed in a word processing text file for the preparation of a report. This capability is often available by using the operating system in combination with spreadsheet or data base programs. The transfer method, although effective, is not efficient.

The steps in most systems to move the material from a spreadsheet program to a word processing program are:

1. Load the spreadsheet program.
2. Load the data file.
3. Print an ASCII file on disk from the spreadsheet program.
4. Exit the spreadsheet program.
5. Use the operating system to add the spreadsheet print file to a word processing ASCII file.
6. Load the word processing program.
7. Load the file created in step 5.

The software discussed in this chapter makes the transfer of data files between program applications easier, as shown in Table 11–2.

TABLE 11–2
The Capability to Transfer Data and Programs

Type of Program	Method of solution
Data File Transfer Software	Changing file formats.
Modular Software	Using the same format.
Integrated Software	Using the same format.
Overlay Utility Software	——
System Overlay Software	Allowing both programs to operate at the same time and providing between program block move routines.

The primary difference between overlay utility software and system overlay software is the capability for multi-tasking and file transfer. Some overlay programs may have similar capabilities.

The effort and time needed to learn a new program or routine can be reduced if the design and organization of the new routine are similar to one already learned. Modular and integrated programs are designed so each application looks similar to the other applications, and are relatively easier to learn than a series of different packages.

Overlay utilities and integrated programs may provide routines that are often needed, even in the middle of another task. For example, when creating a word processing document you may find the need to perform calculations. It is frustrating to have to use a pocket calculator when the full power of a microcomputer is available. Overlay utilities allow you to move a calculator routine onto the screen in front of the word processing program, perform the needed calculations, and then return to the word processor exactly where you left it.

Programs such as Framework and TopView which hide the complexities of the disk operating system often make it easier to learn to perform many tasks. These programs include routines to move data files, and to operate more than a single program at one time, even in an operating system without this capability.

The transfer of data files between the same program on two different microcomputers, even ones using different operating systems, may be easier than the transfer of data files between two programs on the same microcomputer. Usually programs operating on different systems use a consistent method of file storage, while different programs on the same microcomputer use unique methods of file storage.

In businesses with central computers, a common transfer cycle is often used (Figure 11–1). The data must be transferred in and out of the common data base constantly to get the updates from other sources that may be expected to continuously come in. If the central computer is a microcomputer central file server, the format conversion may be a conversion from the central data base format to one needed by the application program. If the central file server is a mainframe, the conversion may include a conversion in and out of ASCII.

DATA FILE TRANSFER SOFTWARE

Programs are needed to change the format created by one program so the data may be used in a different program. You should already know

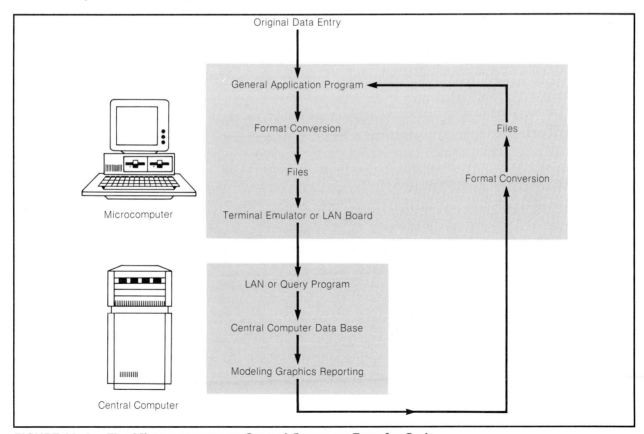

FIGURE 11–1   The Microcomputer-to-Central Computer Transfer Cycle

that there are many different types of data files used on a microcomputer. Among them are:

1. ASCII files
2. DIF, data interchange format files
3. Near ASCII files
4. Special custom files (some using all eight bits)
5   SYLK, symbolic link files

With the exception of some special custom files, the standard code used in each file is available from manuals or user groups. You can purchase programs that transfer material between these files. Some application programs include routines to transfer files between formats.

Special custom files sometimes use an eight-bit code rather than the seven-bit ASCII code. If data is contained in the "high" bit, converting such files to ASCII will result in the loss of data. The files using eight-bit codes may contain numbers from 000 to 255, and may be called binary files. Graphic files are often binary files.

It is easier to transfer into a word processor text file than into a spreadsheet program file. Spreadsheet files contain labels, formulas, and numbers, while text files contain text and numbers. Transferring formulas into a spreadsheet file is difficult unless you are using a DIF or SYLK type format.

The transfer of graphic files is also difficult due to the current lack of standards in this area. The trend is to develop standards, and it may be possible to import and export graphic files in the future. Figure 11–2 illustrates a software package with the capability to convert files from one type to another.

MODULAR AND INTEGRATED SOFTWARE

Routines may be purchased as an integrated package or one at a time as a series of modules. Program sets created by one organization may be controlled so the transfer of data between routines is easy. These programs may be designed to operate using similar menus and operating procedures so the user has an easier time using the software.

Modular programs are sold one routine at a time. You may purchase the word processor and then add spreadsheet or data base at some future

Converts standard ASCII text files to "native" files for:

1. Lotus 1-2-3
2. VisiCalc
3. Multiplan
4. dBase II
5. DIF
6. "Card" image format for mainframes

date when you have a need. Modules are operated from a menu or loaded from the disk operating system. Each module is called as needed. Upon instructions from the user, the program returns to the menu for the next module.

Integrated programs are purchased as a unit and usually operate from a common menu. Some integrated programs, such as Lotus Symphony, have windows (see Figure 11–3) in which different parts of the program may be executed at the same time, and between which data may be tranferred.

Integrated and modular programs usually combine general application routines such as:

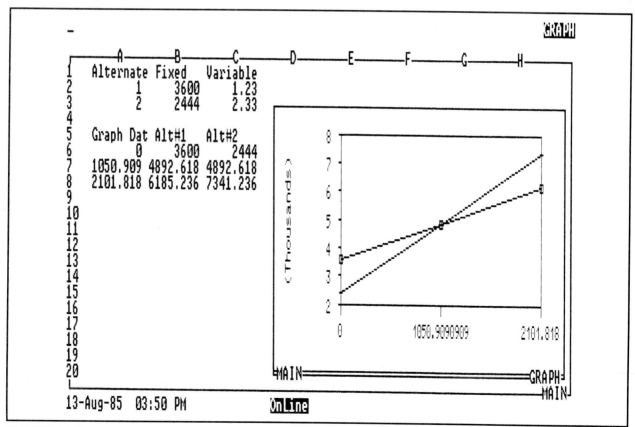

FIGURE 11–3   Lotus Symphony Windows

1. Word processing
2. Spreadsheet
3. Data base
4. Graphics
5. Communications

Integrated and modular software are available for such special applications as:

1. General ledger
2. Job costing
3. Project control
4. Time management
5. Billing/accounts receivables
6. Accounts payable
7. School administration
8. Banking applications

Some packages combine both general and special applications. Many available software products use general application programs as their base. Accounting, real estate, and statistical templates may be purchased for popular spreadsheet programs, making them ready to solve specific applications and giving the business user a starting point for custom applications.

Table 11–3 lists some of the more popular modular and integrated programs.

TABLE 11–3
Popular Modular and Integrated Programs

Modular Programs	Integrated Programs
pfs: Series	Corporate MBA
Visi: Series	Framework *
	JAZZ
	Lotus 1-2-3
	Symphony
	SuperCalc 3

*Framework has many featues of an integrated program as well as features of a system overlay program.

Integrated programs do not solve all the problems of creating a business environment for problem solving. In general, the biggest complaint about integrated programs is that they tend to be dominated by the base routine upon which the program is built. For example, Lotus 1–2–3 and Symphony are built on a spreadsheet file system, and this file structure tends to dominate the other aspects of these packages.

OVERLAY UTILITY SOFTWARE

Overlay utility software may be purchased that adds a variety of capabilities readily available to the user. Overlay utilities give you the capability of stopping what you are doing and calling up a second program to perform some necessary function. Checking the time or date, making calculations, looking up a telephone number, and writing a simple note are examples of the type of utilities added. Table 11–4 provides a list of some popular programs and some of their characteristics.

TABLE 11–4 Utility Programs

Common Feature	Homebase	MYDESK	Poly-Windows	Sidekick	Spotlight
ASCII table				x	
Autodialer	x	x		x	
Calculator	x	x	x	x	x
Calendar			x	x	x
Cut/paste	x				
Data base	x	x			
Data transfer	x				
DOS control	x			x	
Game			x		
Notepad	x	x	x	x	x
Rolodex	x			x	x
Price	$49.95	$199.99	$49.95	$49.95	$149.95

The features of these programs do not tell the whole story. Some are easy to use, while others are slow and cumbersome.

SYSTEM OVERLAY SOFTWARE

Programs have been created to hide the complexities of the disk operating system and to add features. There have been a number of attempts to develop shells around operating systems that make them easier to use. The early shells were aimed at making the operating system friendly, rather than trying to integrate operations or data files between applications.

The shells available today not only control the capabilities of the operating system, but also add some of their own in a manner similar to the overlay utility programs and allow the transfer of data between applications. Often, the utility programs cannot be operated at the same time as an operating system overlay program because they fight with each other for control of the microcomputer.

Among the features added by many operating system overlay programs are multi-tasking and windows. Concurrent operation of word processing, data base, and graphics is possible in some shells. Some shells use windows allowing the operation of more than one program to be viewed at one time. Text may be transferred between windows in a manner similar to moving blocks of text in word processing.

COMPARING INTEGRATED PROGRAMS

Integrated programs have a mix of capabilities depending on which modules are selected. Some of the features of a selected group of integrated programs are compared in Table 11–5.

TABLE 11–5   Comparing Integrated Programs

General Features	Framework	Lotus 1-2-3	Symphony	SuperCalc 3
Memory required	384K	192K	320K with expansion board	96K
Maximum memory used	Unlimited	3Megabytes	3Megabytes	640K
Hard disk subdirectories	yes	yes	yes	yes
Program backup	Limited	Limited	Limited	No limits
Modules				
Spreadsheet	yes	yes	yes	yes
Data management	yes	yes	yes	yes
Word processing	yes	no	yes	no
Graphics	yes	yes	yes	yes
Communication	yes	no	yes	no
Data Formats				
ASCII	x	x	x	x
dBase II	x	x	x	x
DIF	x	x	x	x
WordStar	x		x	x
1-2-3	x	x	x	x

SUMMARY

The task of managing data on a microcomputer goes beyond the capabilities of the disk operating system. The programs discussed in this chapter give you a number of additional routines to be used. The key points in this chapter include:

1. There are a number of software packages available to aid the user in integrating operations, data files, and improving disk operations.

2. The combination of data files and application program and system operation may make the business user more productive.

3. Programs are needed to change the format created by one program so the data may be used in a different program.

4. Routines may be purchased as an integrated package or one at a time as a series of modules.

5. Overlay utility software adds a variety of capabilities readily available to the user.

6. Programs have been created to hide the complexities of the disk operating system and to add features.

KEY TERMS

Data file transfer software
Integrated software
Modular software

Overlay utility software
System overlay software

REVIEW QUESTIONS

1. What programs give the user the initial increase in personal productivity?

2. Name programs studied in earlier chapters that integrate the use of microcomputers.

3. Name some additional programs that integrate the use of the microcomputer.

4. Identify the similarity and difference in the following terms:

Data file transfer software, between programs
Modular software
Integrated software
Overlay utility software
System overlay software

5. What are the three objectives of integrating software?

6. When is usually the first time a user encounters the need to transfer material between programs?

7. What steps are needed on most systems to move material from a spreadsheet program to a word processing program?

8. Describe the microcomputer-to-central-computer transfer cycle.

9. Identify the different types of data files.

10. What is the advantage to the business user of purchasing a prepared template?

11. What is the general complaint about integrated programs?

DISCUSSION AND APPLICATION QUESTIONS

1. Examine microcomputer magazine advertisements for data file transfer software between programs. What programs are available, how much do they cost, and what features do they have?

2. Examine microcomputer magazine advertisements for modular software. What programs are available, how much do they cost, and what features do they have?

3. Examine microcomputer magazine advertisements for integrated software. What programs are available, how much do they cost, and what features do they have?

4. Examine microcomputer magazine advertisements for overlay utility software. What programs are available, how much do they cost, and what features do they have?

5. Examine microcomputer magazine advertisements for system overlay software. What programs are available, how much do they cost, and what features do they have?

LABORATORY ASSIGNMENTS

1. With the programs available in your laboratory determine the number of ways you can transfer data files between programs. Use as many of these methods as possible to move data files. Report on the results.

2. If available in your laboratory use a modular program set and an integrate program set to solve the problems outlined in the earlier chapters of this text and report on the difference between these programs.

3. If available, use a utility program and report on its features.

4. If available, use a system utility program and report on its features.

SELECTED REFERENCES

Bell, Don. *The DIF File*. Prentice-Hall, 1983.
Clark, Roger E. *Executive SuperCalc 3*. Addison-Wesley, 1984.
Cobb, David and Geoffrey LeBlond. *Using 1-2-3*. Que Corporation, 1983.
Ewing, David P. *Using Lotus Symphony*. Que Corporation, 1984.
Graff, Lois. *Financial Analysis with Lotus 1–2–3*. Prentice-Hall, 1984.
Harris, David. *Lotus 1-2-3 Mastery w/Disk*. Prentice-Hall, 1984.
Harrison, Bill. *Framework: An Introduction*. Ashton-Tate, 1984.
Miller, David. *IBM Data Files—A Basic Tutorial*. Prentice-Hall, 1983.
"New Solutions to the Micro-to-Mainframe Puzzle." *Business Computer Systems*.
   April 1985, pp. 42, 46–48.

12

Chapter Outline

Chapter Goals

Upon completion of this chapter you will able to:

Understand how the microcomputer needs of a business are identified and purchase justified.

Understand how the knowledge gained in earlier chapters is combined with the identification of business needs to develop a set of specifications.

HOW TO SELECT
MICROCOMPUTERS

Flautt and Mann Properties, Inc. of Memphis, Tennessee is a large motel/restaurant investment and management firm. They own and manage properties in the Southeastern part of the United States between Florida and Texas.

Over the years Flautt and Mann Properties, Inc. have developed a number of evaluation procedures for the selection and evaluation of properties. They specialize in purchasing properties which have the potential for growth under their special management style.

The microcomputer can save dollars only if it is carefully selected to fill specific business needs. The microcomputer concepts and applications learned in earlier chapters must be integrated with the needs of a business. The microcomputer is a low-cost method of solving business problems but it can solve problems only if it is fitted for, and accepted into, your overall business system. You must learn how to identify the needs of your business that might be solved with microcomputers.

The business professional has computer options beyond microcomputers. Some of these options can better satisfy specific business needs.

WHY THE BUSINESS PROFESSIONAL MUST KNOW THE BUSINESS NEEDS

The professional must analyze the business to determine its needs before purchasing a microcomputer to fill the needs. The business professional is in a position to determine what a businesses current and potential needs are now and in the future, and to identify where a microcomputer system may be used to meet these needs. The business professional's background may combine:

1. Microcomputer training
2. Business training
3. Company experience

A microcomputer purchase requires a detailed business plan and analysis, which is the job of the professional.

BUSINESS PLANNING AND ANALYSIS

The steps in the analysis of a business-microcomputer needs are the idea, the objective, the plan, the analysis, and the installation. The steps to be taken in determining if a micrcomputer is needed or desirable include:

1. An IDEA (dream)
2. An OBJECTIVE, which is measurable, feasible, and has limitations including a time limit

3. The PLAN, with priorities and phases
   IDENTIFICATION of where you are
   Identification of LIMITATIONS, constraints
4. ANALYSIS and the decision to go ahead or stop
5. IMPLEMENTATION of the plan—usually running old and new systems in parallel

The Idea

A business problem or opportunity is identified by an **idea.** A human being must evaluate all the facts available and come up with an idea. The idea is the recognition that there may be a problem or opportunity in need of study. The idea precedes all other steps because it is the recognition of need.

Brainstorming sessions, a good night's sleep, a passing sight, or the occurrence of a problem might trigger the idea. Only people can create ideas or dreams. One of these ideas can be the use of microcomputers to solve some of your business problems.

Idea:
Recognition of a business need or opportunity.

The Objective

For an idea to become a business **objective** it needs to have several characteristics:

1. It must be feasible
2. It must be measurable
3. It must have a time limit
4. Its limitations must be recognized

Objective:
A business goal that is feasible, measurable, has a time limit, has recognized limitations, and has a plan for its accomplishment.

Feasibility A business cannot be led off into impossible situations. A feasible objective is one that can be accomplished. It is a meaningless dream of earning $10 million this year if you are starting at a base of $1,000. It is better to set realistic objectives and then to modify the goals as the company's capabilities grow.

There is a lower limit to the price of any system. What if you charged the purchasing department with obtaining a new microcomputer system with:

1. 256K of RAM
2. A 20Megabyte hard disk
3. A 360K floppy disk

4. MS/PC-DOS
5. A high-resolution card and color graphics
6. A color monitor

With a budget of $300.00 you would have an objective that is not feasible. No matter how hard and long the purchasing department worked, the objective could not be realized with the possible exception of the purchase of a stolen microcomputer system.

Measurable If you cannot measure the completion of a goal, there is no way to tell if you have completed it. To be rich is meaningless. To earn a million dollars can be measured and accomplished.

The goal "To improve the operation of this office" does not mean anything and cannot be measured. The word improve does not have a precise meaning. If there is a 2% increase in the output of the office, is this an improvement? If the lighting is replaced and the employees find the office an easier place to work, is this an improvement? If a microcomputer with a word processing program is purchased to replace a typewriter, is this an improvement? A restatement of the objective as: "To increase the number of letters produced by 20% with no increase of personnel" gives the manager a goal that can be measured.

Time Limit A time limit means a task must be completed by a specified date. If a business objective does not have a time limit, you can never fail to reach it. For example, "To computerize your business some day" is a dream, while "To replace 90% of the typewriters being used with microcomputers in the next twelve months" is an objective, if it is feasible.

Other Limitations Examples of business limitations are:

1. Limited number of trained persons
2. The availability of cash or credit
3. Floor space or storage room
4. Legal and moral limits

Limitations are restrictions that inhibit the ability of management to make decisions. With the exception of legal and moral limits, limitations may exist only in the short run. Trained people can be hired, cash can be obtained, floor space can be rented or purchased. The time limit is what makes these limits real in any given decision-making situation.

You may wish to purchase a microcomputer system, but if you do not have the cash or credit to make the purchase you will have to delay your purchase until the limitation can be eliminated.

Plan:
A series of steps detailing what must be done to move a business from where it is to where management has decided it is to go.

The Plan

A **plan** details how to get from where you are to where you want to go. If the objective is to replace ten typist/typewriters with three typist/word processors, then a plan could be:

1. Management evaluation: Ms. Mai Tran will determine the cost of using typewriters and the cost of using word processors. She will develop a plan of action and report to the manager's committee on June 3.

A decision will be made to complete the project or stop it.

2. Accounting: Ms. Carla Juarez will determine if cash or credit is available to complete the project and report to the manager's committee on July 6. The manager's committee will decide on the project's status.

3. Purchasing: Mrs. Freda Flippo will:
Write the final specifications with the aid of Ms. Mai Tran by June 30.
Select vendor by July 23.
Place order for delivery on September 12.

4. Personnel: Mr. Steven Lombard will:
Determine personnel transfers by September 5.
Determine training needs by September 5.
Setup and organize training program by September 12.
Report on any problem relative to the re- location of people by January 1.

5. Supervision: Miss. Betty Schilling will:
Supervise the installation and training with the aid of the Personnel Department.
Report on level of performance October 1, November 1, and December 1.

6. Final analysis of project by manager's committee on January 1.

Levels It is common to have several levels to a plan. Different levels of management are responsible for different types of decisions. Each level in the overall plan may have a detailed plan of its own. You have learned in this book that the task of writing a set of microcomputer purchasing specifications is time-consuming and complex.

Milestones Milestones are simply steps on the way to the completion of a plan. They are used to aide a company in staying on course. If a milestone is missed, management must investigate to see why and how to get the project back on plan.

Identification of Options An option represents a choice that management can make. One of the objectives of this book was to help you learn what microcomputers can do. With this knowledge you have a collection of solutions. Now it is necessary to match the problems with candidate solutions.

The general application programs covered give the microcomputer capabilities for electronic spreadsheets, word processing, data base management, graphics, and communications. Most businesses have some applications for all these capabilities. In addition, custom programs cover accounting, production management, project management, quality control, real estate management, and almost any other topic you can think of. Business details, needs, and opportunities are known only to the owner or manager. The task of matching needs with solutions falls on the business manager.

Special application software has a "single" use. Accounting programs can produce general ledgers, control accounts payable or receivables, or perform some other specific function.

A good starting place for the business manager seeking to purchase a microcomputer is the form shown in Figure 12–1. This form forces the manager to identify those activities in his or her business where the microcomputer is to be used. The form identifies the problems the microcomputer can solve.

Included on the form in Figure 12–1 is a place to indicate the timing of the application. Microcomputers are not difficult to use, but they do take time to learn. You cannot install all the capabilities of the microcomputer overnight. You must allow for learning and adjustment time. The form forces the manager to identify the beginning and ending time of each business application. These are milestones in the task of introducing the microcomputer into your business.

The form is designed with a thirty-six month planning horizon. The field of microcomputers is changing so fast that a longer planning hori-

FIGURE 12–1
Microcomputer Purchase Check List

Microcomputer Purchase Check List

Name _____ Date _____

Department _____

Company _____

Street _____

City _____

State ____   Zip _____

Overall Business Objective

Microcomputer Applications	Identify the beginning and ending				
	Start	6 Months	12 Months	24 Months	36 Months
1					
2					
3					
4					
5					
6					

zon is not recommended. With the low cost of microcomputers, if their applications cannot be justified in less than three years you may not need one.

Another advantage of a time plan is that you may not need to purchase all your equipment at the beginning. The cost of microcomputer hardware is steadily decreasing, or at least the capabilities that may be purchased are increasing while the price remains constant. A piece of equipment should not be purchased until it is needed.

The microcomputer may be the correct computer for many applications, but aquiring microcomputers is not the only answer. You may hire a service bureau to perform computerized tasks for you. Many banks offer accounting services. If you have no interest in having your own computer, or if your needs are limited, this may be an answer for you. The cost of service bureaus includes the labor for operating the computer as well as an overhead cost for the equipment.

Detailing the Plan A business plan starts with an idea and the identification of the problems to be solved. The exact equipment needed in the initial purchase, in six months, in a year, etc., can then be identified. For example, if you start with word processing a daisy wheel printer is usually required immediately. If graphics are added after six months, a dot matrix printer or printer plotter may be purchased then. The price and capabilities of dot matrix printers can be expected to change over the six months.

The layout of potential needs is shown in Figure 12–2.

It is easy to identify the beginning of a microcomputer application. It is more difficult to identify when the training period is over and the technique is being used. The basics of word processing may be learned in an hour. Employees may never learn to use all the capabilities of the word processor. They may never need all the capabilities. The measure of completeness is a function of the application, and is left to you as the business manager.

The plan for applications helps us determine our hardware and software needs. To do word processing, you need a microcomputer with one or two disk drives, the word processing program, a daisy wheel printer, and the cables necessary to connect the units together. Table 12–1 outlines the hardware needed by the system. Some of the later needs make

Microcomputer Applications	Identify the beginning and ending				
	Start	6 Months	12 Months	24 Months	36 Months
1 Word Process.	Start	Comp			
2 Graphics_____	Start		Comp		
3 Spreadsheets	____	Start		Comp	
4 Data base	____	Start			Comp
5 _____	____	_____	_____	_____	_____
6 _____	____	_____	_____	_____	_____

FIGURE 12–2
The Planning of Microcomputer Needs

TABLE 12–1   The Milestones of Your Plan

Microcomputer Needs	Start	6 Months	12 Months	24 Months	36 Months
Microcomputer	X				
Furniture	X				
Single Disk Drive	X				
Second Disk Drive	X				
Daisy Wheel Printer	X				
Cables	X				
Word Processor Prog.	X				
Dot Matrix Printer		X(80 Column)			
Printer Switch/Cables		X			
Graphics Program		X			
Dot Matrix Printer			X(132 or 200+ Column)		
Spreadsheet Program		X			
Data Base Program		X			
Hard Disk 10 Megabytes				X	

the earlier purchases obsolete. You will have to decide whether it pays to purchase the wide carriage originally to avoid the need to purchase a third printer later.

When a 10 Megabyte hard disk is purchased for the data base program, the second disk drive will be of little value. You may want to purchase the hard disk drive initially rather than wait until it is needed. Using the information in a table as the one in Table 12–1 can help you develop an intelligent plan.

Capacity Planning The maximum amount of RAM needed is usually a function of the software program that uses the largest amount, and the RAM used for needs such as a RAM disk or spooler. A RAM disk is a part of RAM that acts like a disk drive. RAM drives avoid slow and sometimes noisy disk I/O. They are like regular disk drives, but all information is lost when the power is shut off.

A spooler is the simplest multi-tasking operation of the microcomputer. A segment of RAM is set aside for information sent to the printer. The data is placed in the spooler at a rate faster than any printer can operate. Once all the data is stored in the spooler, the microcomputer is free to be used for another purpose. The printer continues to produce output as the microcomputer is used.

Spreadsheet, data base, and integrated programs tend to use the most RAM. Programs designed for CP/M, TRS-DOS, Apple DOS, and other eight-bit systems are designed to operate within the limitations of these systems, that is usually 64K of RAM. MS/PC-DOS programs often use up to 256K of RAM or more, because of added program features.

To size the RAM requires that specific programs be identified to perform each of the capabilities needed. Since RAM cost is low, we recommend you buy more than you need because as your skill in using the microcomputer grows you will find it is needed.

A hard disk drive adds speed and storage capacity to a microcomputer system. The speed is convenient to have for many different programs. The storage capacity is extremely convenient when many applications are needed on short notice, and when a data base system is established.

Data bases for inventory control, personnel, customer identification, credit, club membership, and data analysis may require large amounts of data storage room. There are ways you can estimate the amount of storage needed.

In the data base discussion in chapter 7, you learned what a field, record, and file were. Capacity planning starts with determining the size of a record, then estimating the number of records needed. Growth estimates are added, and the size is rounded off to the next largest hard disk system available. It is usually cost effective to purchase a little more than you need than to add additional storage by replacing one hard disk drive system with another at some future time.

Another factor that will affect the selection of a hard disk drive is how it is organized. There are ways to partition the hard disk between different applications and different operating systems used on the same microcomputer.

It is useful to develop checklists for your business needs. Figures 12–3 and 12–4 are two lists to use as starting points.

Application #
RAM On-Line Storage Printer(s)

FIGURE 12–3
Factors to be Sized-Checklist

Vendor Selection The price of a microcomputer is only one of the factors upon which the selection of a microcomputer should be based. A business selling in a local market must expect to make some of its purchases in the local market. You cannot expect a business professional to buy from you unless you give them the opportunity to sell to you.

USER WINDOW

The insurance salesman brags to a salesperson from a local microcomputer store that his local insurance office purchased a microcomputer through its home office. The insurance man claims the price of the unit was better than the local market could offer.

The insurance salesman then talks about making an appointment to talk about insurance. The computer salesperson says, "I'm sorry, I already bought through my home office."

FIGURE 12–4
Factors to Be
Specified-Checklist

Application #

Monitor type
  Color
  Monochrome
 	
Printer Type
  Dot matrix
  Daisy wheel
  Laser
  Ink jet
  Plotter
 	
Special Boards
  Graphics
  Communication
  Speech recognition
  Speech synthesis
  Special interfaces
  Additional memory
  Network
 	
Other Devices
  Mouse
  Joy sticks
  Koala Pad
  Paddles
  Bar code reader
  Digitizer pad
  Touch sensitive screen

A microcomputer, once installed, rapidly becomes an important part of your business. The ability of your vendor to repair, service, and upgrade your microcomputer is important. A loss of several days' work for equipment repair may be costly in terms of the lost employee time and effort and customer inconvenience.

You may purchase different types of service plans from many vendors. You may have on-site service, carry-in service, or take the chance and just pay for service as needed. Remember, a microcomputer is like any other piece of equipment; when used by a large number of individuals, it will require more maintenance than the same unit operated by a single user.

Training takes time and costs dollars. Training needs include startup and personnel replacement and retraining. When additional capabilities are added, you will again need more training . You must evaluate the ability of a vendor to provide such training, and what the cost is expected to be. A retail store often provides introductory-level training for new programs, but little more. Further training from an additional source or the hiring of a consultant is often necessary.

Many individuals learn how to use a program by reading the documentation. If you do not have the time or background to understand the documentation, you should consider hiring someone to help.

Some firms with centralized purchasing procedures often prepare a bid request form when purchasing equipment. A bid request is part of the computer use and purchase plan. You must know what your microcomputer is to do before its configuration can be determined. Whether you prepare a formal bid request or not, you should identify the required capabilities of your system.

If you have a business problem and do not wish to spend the time finding out how to solve the problem, it is often advisable to hire a consultant to do the job for you. Developing microcomputer specifications is a time-consuming task. You or one of your employees must spend the time to learn your microcomputer needs, or you must spend your dollars hiring an outsider to do the job. If you spend neither the time nor money doing the job right, you are likely to make costly errors by purchasing the wrong equipment. A good, reputable vendor may also be able to help.

Analysis

The **analysis** of alternative methods is based on the **productivity** of the company, office, or individual business professionals. The productivity is output divided by input, equation is:

$$\text{Productivity} = \frac{\text{Output}}{\text{Input}}$$

Analysis:
Comparison of alternate management actions.
Productivity:
Output divided by input.

The business professional must identify and measure the input and output.

Input Input includes all the factors of production:

1. Land (raw materials)
2. Labor (the women and men who do the work)

3. Capital (the dollars and equipment that the dollars may purchase
4. The Business Enterprise (management and other aspects of the organization)

The subsitution principle of the factors of production says if one factor becomes expensive, it should be replaced by another factor so the lowest cost balance is maintained. In a like manner, if one factor becomes less expensive it should replace the other factors.

Microcomputers with application programs are a part of the capital factor. The capital factor as applied to microcomputers is decreasing. As the capabilities of microcomputers and the effectiveness of their programs improve, the cost of using this equipment decreases.

You, as a business professional, have learned what a microcomputer can do.

Output Output is the goods and services produced by a company. The output of each company, office, or individual is a function of the job that must be done. The business professional is in a good position to determine what this output is.

Each person or work station in a business adds to the overall business objective by producing some contribution. Figure 12–5 shows the possible priority of some objectives in a local car dealership.

FIGURE 12–5
Hierarchy of Some Objectives

Level	Objective
Business enterprise	To make a profit
Sales department	To sell vehicles
Individual salesperson	To sell vehicles
	To set up and maintain a data base of all contacts.
Secretary	To product contracts, letters, and other documents.
	To set up and maintain a data base of all buyers.
Repair and maintenance	...

Simply writing down the objectives and output of specific positions brings to light some possible uses for microcomputers.

Measuring Input and Output Dollars and time are the most common measurements for input (factors of production). Each of the input factors must be identified and then measured.

Output measurement involves counting. In general, for a specific output you must:

1. Count the amount of material or power used
2. Count the number of hours of labor used
3. Count the number of capital dollars or amount of hours of capital equipment used
4. Count the dollar and time of management input.

The key word is "count." There is no substitution for hard work and counting. After counting you must record the results. Table 12–2 shows a "Work Sampling" report used to measure the labor activities in a typing group.

Activity	Percent of observations
Talking on phone	20%
Typing	65%
Talking to individuals	10%
Out of area	7%
Other	3%
	100%

TABLE 12–2
Work Sampling Report on a Typing Group

Once the input has been measured the output must be measured. The output of a typing group might be documents. If the mix of large documents (contracts) and small documents (letters) is constant then just counting documents may be satisfactory. If the mix changes, then a more detailed measure of output is needed. When the study is complete you will have a productivity equation:

$$\text{Productivity} = \frac{\text{Documents}}{\text{Power and supplies} + \text{labor hours} + \text{equipment cost} + \text{management costs}}$$

Finding a combined measure of input is difficult and often not necessary. If the cost of power, supplies (land), and management (business enterprise) does not change, you need not be concerned about measuring them.

When replacing a typist-typewriter with a typist-microcomputer/word processor you need to be concerned with labor hours input, equipment costs, and document output. The objective is to compare the productivity of the old method with the productivity of the new method to determine if the investment in the microcomputer system is justified.

Justifying a Microcomputer There are number of investment justification techniques. Among them are:

1. Breakeven analysis
2. Payback period analysis
3. Present worth analysis

All techniques depend on the measurements made in determining productivity. The breakeven and payback period analyses are simple and will be covered. Present worth analysis is better, but requires a background in finance. An ideal method of solving breakeven, payback, and present worth problems is with the use of a electronic spreadsheet and microcomputer graphics.

Breakeven Analysis The objective of breakeven analysis is to determine the number of units of output when the total cost of one method is equal to the total cost of another method.

MICROS IN ACTION

Flautt and Mann Properties, Inc. uses a number of different evaluation and analysis methods including breakeven, gross multipliers, and calculations of average daily rates combined with occupancies ratios in the case of motel and hotel investments. These simpler techniques are used as the initial pass to determine if it pays to spend additional time and effort making a detail period-by-period income and expense analysis.

The analysis procedures apply to the purchase of investment properties, the bidding on management service contracts, and the investment in equipment including trucks and microcomputers.

Assume one method is using a typist with typewriter and the other is a typist with word processor, and that the cost and time data are as shown in Figure 12–6.

FIGURE 12–6
Breakeven Analysis

Factor	Typist with Typewriter	Typist with Word Processor
New Investment	None	$3,000
Pages per hour	4.1	8.3
At $8.00/hour		
Cost per page	$1.95	$0.96

Estimates based on 45 character per minute average including the time required to load and unload the typewriter, 10 characters per line and 66 lines per page. The result is 14.7 minutes per page or 4.1 pages per hour.

The word processing cost per page assumes one original and two copies. The time to correct and print a copy is 25% of the time to create an original. The result is 7.252 minutes per page or 8.3 pages per hour.

The increased output of the word processor is due to its editing capability especially when doing corrections for second and third drafts. It is assumed that the document would be typed once, and two additional edited copies produced.

The breakeven equation is:

$$\text{Breakeven} = \frac{\begin{array}{c}\text{Capital cost} \quad \text{Capital cost}\\ \text{new method} - \text{old method}\end{array}}{\begin{array}{c}\text{Old cost} - \text{New cost}\\ \text{per unit} \quad \text{per unit}\end{array}}$$

$$= \frac{\$3,000 - \$0.00}{1.95 - 0.96 \text{ documents}} = 3,030.3030$$

The breakeven equation may be used to compare any two alternatives. You may replace new method by method #1 and old method by method #2 in the formula.

It may also be used to compare a revenue with a total cost. The revenue is considered an alternative with no capital cost in the formula.

This means that it is more economical to use the typewriter until 3,030 documents are produced. Above 3,030 the word processor becomes more economical.

Payback Period A payback period analysis is a breakeven analysis with the scale in terms of time rather than in pieces. Assuming that enough work exists to keep the typist word processing system operating at full speed, the output per day would be 8.3 times 8 or 66.4 pages per day. Dividing 3,030 by 66.4 the result is approximately 46 days for the payback period.

The mathematical results tell us that if full output is maintained for 46 days then it pays to purchase the microcomputer with a word processor.

Using Spreadsheets and Graphics The breakeven and payback analysis may be performed using a spreadsheet and graphics program. Figure 12–7 is a Lotus 1-2-3 spreadsheet with formulas to solve this program. The total cost at breakeven for the two alternatives should be equal. The spreadsheet shows the values to be: Typewriter = 5939.393, and Word Processor = 5909.090. The difference is 0.5% due to round-off.

Figures 12–8 and 12–9 are graphical analyses of the problem pro-

```
        A          B         C        D        E        F
1   Breakeven and Payback Analysis
2
3
4
5   Alternative           Fixed Cost      Variable Cost
6   Typewriter                 0              1.96
7   Word Processor          3000              0.96
8
9   Breakeven             3030.303
10
11  Payback Period         45.63709
12
13  For Graph:
14  Pieces       Days    Typewriter      Word Processor
15      0          0          0               3000
16    3030         46     5939.393         5909.090
17    6061         91     11878.78         8818.181
18
19

/////////////////////////////////////////

Cell          Formula
C9            (C6-C7)/(E7-E6)
C11           +C9/66.4
E15           +C7

A16           +C9
A17           +2*C9

B16           +C9/66.4
B17           +A17/66.4

C16           +1.96*A16
C17           +1.96*A17

E16           +0.96*A16+E15
E17           +0.96*A17+E15
```

FIGURE 12–7
Lotus 1-2-3 Analysis of Breakeven and Payback

FIGURE 12–8
Graph of Breakeven Analysis

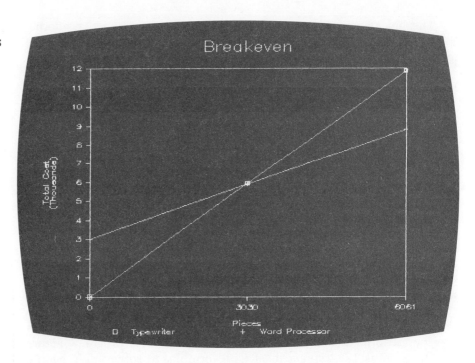

duced on Lotus 1-2-3. The differences between these two graphs are the labels and specification of the x scale. Figure 12–10 shows a spreadsheet combined with an overlay program which is also valuable in this type of analysis.

FIGURE 12–9
Graph of Payback Analysis

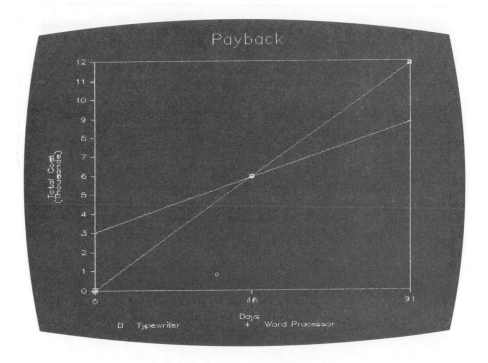

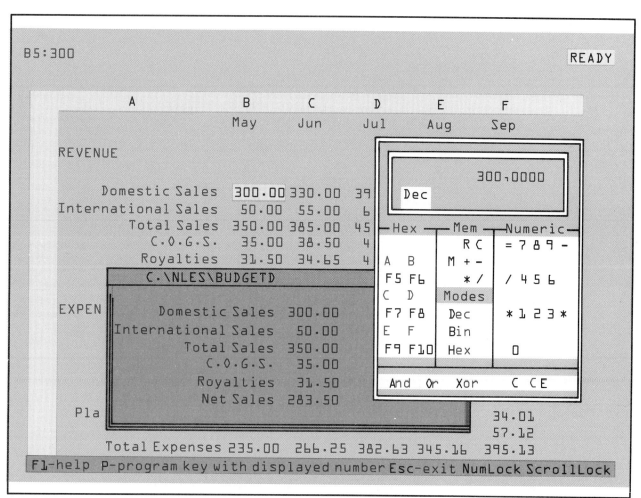

FIGURE 12–10   A Spreadsheet and a Sidekick

Both graphs tell the same story. The total cost of the old method (use of typewriters) is less than the total cost of word processors until the breakeven point (3,030 documents) or the end of the payback period (46 days).

Current Versus Future Demand In an actual study you will be concerned with how to administrate the introduction of the new equipment. If you currently have three typists it may be necessary to lay off two of them in order to justify the word processor. If you expect growth in demand for documents, you may be able to introduce the new equipment without any layoffs by simply not hiring additional people as the growth occurs.

Implementation

The last step is **implementation.** The plan details the steps to be followed in the implementation. The decision to go ahead is management's. The reports of accomplishments are returned to management.

Implementation:

Putting a method or microcomputer to work in a company.

SUMMARY

A microcomputer is a business investment and must be justified using the same methods used to justify all other business investments. You have learned how to identify the needs for a microcomputer and how they are justified. You have seen how the knowledge gained in earlier chapters must be used to help identify and develop specifications for a microcomputer system. The key points in this chapter are:

1. The microcomputer saves dollars only if it is carefully selected to fill specific business need(s).
2. The business professional must analyze the business to determine its needs before purchasing a microcomputer to fill the needs.
3. All business planning and analysis starts with an idea.
4. The objective is an idea with a plan detailing how it may be accomplished.
5. A plan identifies the steps necessary to complete a defined business objective.
6. The business professional must justify the purchase of a microcomputer with careful analysis.
7. The final test of a microcomputer is its installation into the workplace.

KEY TERMS

Analysis	Objective
Idea	Plan
Implementation	Productivity

REVIEW QUESTIONS

1. Why is the professional who has had a course in microcomputers in a good position to evaluate microcomputer acquisition?

2. What are the steps in the analysis of a microcomputer application?

3. What is a business idea?

4. What is a business objective? When does an idea need to become a business objective?

5. What are some of the limitations you may expect to be imposed on a business decision?

6. What is a business plan?

7. What are milestones?

8. Identify a computer option to microcomputer ownership?

9. What is productivity?

10. What is a business analysis?

11. What are the factors of production?

12. What is output?

13. How is output measured?

14. Name three commonly used investment analysis techniques and identify the objective of one.

15. Detail and explain the breakeven formula.

16. What is the last step in the purchase of a microcomputer?

DISCUSSION AND APPLICATION QUESTIONS

1. Use the forms developed in this chapter to configure a system for your remaining college years.

2. Develop a short outline of the needs for microcomputers in your school. Use the forms in this chapter to configure a system.

3. If you are working, configure a system through the idea, objective, and planning steps.

4. Study the needs of your religious organization and configure a system for them.

PROBLEM

1. There are two microcomputer systems being considered. The purchase price and operating costs are given below:

Purchase Price	Cost Per Document
$3,600	$1.23
2,444	2.33

   a. Solve by calculator or the use of an electronic spreadsheet program to determine the breakeven point.
   b. Draw the breakeven chart by microcomputer or manually.
   c. If the yearly volume in document output is 1500 what is the payback period.

SELECTED REFERENCES

Cohn, Jules A. and Catherine S. McKinney. *How to Micro-computerize Your Business.* Spectrum Book, Prentice-Hall, 1983.

Barden, Jr., William. *How to Buy & Use Minicomputers & Microcomputers.* Howard W. Sams & Co., Inc., 1976.

Dologite, D.G. *Using Small Business Computers.* Prentice-Hall, 1984.

Harold, Fred G. *Introduction to Computers.* West Publishing Company, 1984.

Mandell, Steven L. *Computers and Data Processing Today with BASIC.* West Publishing Company, 1983.

Veit, Stanley S. *Using Microcomputers in Business.* Hayden Book Company, 1983.

Zimmerman, Steven M., and Leo M. Conrad. *Business Applications for the IBM Personal Computer* . Brady Publishing Company, 1983.

Zimmerman, Steven M., Leo M. Conrad, and Donald R. Smith. *Business Applications for the Apple II & IIe under CP/M.* Brady Publishing Company, 1985.

Appendix A

CASES

CASE #1

William Barton is setting up a real estate office for himself and two sales associates. Among other things needed in the office is a copy machine.

The estimated number of copies is between a low of 500 and a high of 2000 per month. The options include:

1. Using a machine down the hall.
2. Purchasing a low-speed cartridge copier.
3. Purchasing a high-speed copier.

The secretary's wage is $8.50 per hour. Figures 1–1 and 1–2 list some of the detailed cost and performance information.

Alternative	Purchase Price	Single Copy Time	Monthly Recommended Capacity
Down the hall	0	38 seconds	no limit
Low speed unit	1,300	10 seconds	1,000
High speed unit	3,000	7 seconds	15,000

Figure 1–1   Purchase Price and Performance

The time required to produce a single copy on the machine down the hall is 38 seconds. This includes the walking time, and the amount of time required to produce a copy.

Down the hall	Paper	Cartridge	Toner	Developer	Drum
Cost	0.15				
Copies	each				
Low speed unit					
Cost	8.00	60.00			
Copies	500	2500			
High speed unit					
Cost	8.00		25.00	26.00	90.00
Copies	500		5000	10000	20000

Figure 1–2   Operating Cost

The low-speed unit requires a cartridge that includes the toner, developer, and drum maintenance cost. There are no additional costs other than paper. The high-speed unit does not use a cartridge but requires a toner, developer, and drum maintenance cost.

The power cost for operating each machine is approximately $0.50 per day. All calculations are to be based on 1,000 copies per month and an assumption of single copies being made.

Assignment

Make an analysis of the cost of each alternative. Use a breakeven and payback analysis to compare the different methods. Use a spreadsheet to make the analysis and produce the graphics. Use a word processor to prepare a letter or memo detailing the results obtained and make a recommendation on which alternative is better and why.

Examine the costs carefully. What would happen if the monthly volume estimate was 500 copies, 1,500 copies, or 3,000 copies? Assume that one cartridge copier will handle the 1,500 copies per month, but two are needed for 3,000 per month. The reason for the second machine is that maintenance costs become excessive when the monthly volume increases to 3,000.

CASE #2

An analysis of the selling price of hard disk systems with tape backup resulted in the data shown in Figure 2–1.

Assignment #1

You are employed by a firm that is marketing hard disk drives for microcomputers. Because of your background in microcomputers you have been asked to prepare a report on what is a hard disk drive, what is a tape backup, and who might possibly be customers for microcomputers with these types of on-line storage systems.

You must prepare message(s) for the:

- Stockholders
- Management Groups
  - Central Management
  - Marketing department.

All messages must contain three paragraphs. The objective of each paragraph is:

1. To identify what is a hard disk, tape backup.
2. To identify the need for and use of tape backup.
3. To identify potential users of these systems.

Figure 2–1   A Data Set

Data Capacity Megabytes	Prices (in dollars)
7.9	3290
10	2795, 3995, 3599, 2995, 3295
11	3135
12	2895
15	4345
16	4295, 4595, 3275, 3990
16.6	3790
20	4495, 4695, 4099, 3759, 3799, 2995, 3995, 3295
21	3195, 4290
25.3	4290
32	4395, 5700
33	5245, 5390
33.5	3995
35	6350, 5595, 5745, 4995
40	5699
41	5995, 6295
41.8	5890
42	5899
43	4995, 6090
43.5	5400
45	1495, 1595
56	7950
57	6699
60	7895
65.6	6590
67	6995, 7295, 7499
70	7495
71.3	6400
75	8995
81	7090
91.8	7990
92	8390
119	10950
141	9290
150	10900
160	10995
238	17450
441	15900

Assignment #2

Your task is to organize the data for presentation to management as a table and as a graph. You must determine what information is needed by management and how the data is best organized to provide this information. A memo is to be prepared for management detailing your results.

You will be expected to use pie charts, bar charts, line, and XY charts to help analyze the data.

CASE #3

Juanita Anderson, president of T-P Manufactuing Co, Inc., (T-P Mfg. Co.), founded the company in 1982. The company began business with limited capital. Although they have enjoyed a profit in the last three years, they constantly found themselves short of the working capital needed to purchase raw materials such as canvas, rope, and other supplies, as well as wages.

Currently, T-P Mfg. Co. produces four tent styles in two weights. The tents are 1, 2, 4, and 8-person models. The canvas weights are 10 and 12 ounces. All canvas is flame resistant as per current government regulations.

The tents are marketed through mail order houses, local retail dealers, and selected youth organizations. All retail dealers sell the tents under the brand name T-P. Mail order houses use house brand names, and the youth groups sell the tents under their own names.

During the first four years of the company's history, sales have been 65% to mail order outlets, 25% to retail stores, and 10% to youth groups.

The company has been contacted by a large retail discount chain about supplying them with tents. The volume (20,000 per year) required by this discount chain is equal to twice the current volume. No change in tent design or mix of sizes is expected. However, manufacturing procedures will have to be automated and the number of employees, the in-process inventory, and the investment in raw material inventory are expected to double.

Assignment #1

You must prepare message(s) for the:

- Stockholders
- Management
- Employees
- Local bank that provides short term funds.

All messages must contain three paragraphs. The objective of each paragraph is:

1. To identify the opportunity and to communicate to all concerned that no decision has been made.
2. To outline the steps of the decision making process.
3. To tell each specific department what has to be done.

Assignment #2

Your task is to organize the current sales, revenues, and costs data into a spreadsheet format for the first four years of operation. The final value needed is the gross profit per year. The initial analysis is to be performed assuming no tax obligation.

The average prices paid by the three types of buyers are shown in Figure 3–1.

Figure 3–1   Average Prices
Paid by Buyers

		Year		
	1982	1983	1984	1985
Ten Oz.				
Number of Units				
Sales by Type				
1-Person	900	1241	1544	1466
2-Person	1217	1402	1744	1656
4-Person	633	1149	1430	1357
8-person	260	560	697	662
Price per Unit by Year				
1-Person	20.75	22.83	25.11	27.62
2-Person	31.36	35.12	39.33	44.05
4-Person	38.78	43.43	48.64	54.48
8-Person	72.72	79.99	87.99	96.79
Twelve Oz.				
Number of Units				
Sales by Type				
1-Person	200	655	706	645
2-Person	652	740	797	728
4-Person	534	606	653	596
8-Person	486	296	318	291
Price per Unit by Year				
1-Person	23.25	25.58	28.14	30.95
2-Person	36.87	41.29	46.24	51.79
4-Person	43.96	49.24	55.15	61.77
8-Person	89.30	98.23	108.05	118.86

In Figure 3–1 you will find the sales volume and selling price per unit for both the 10 and 12 ounce fabrics for the four types of tents. You will need to combine the information in Figure 3–1 to determine the revenue earned by T-P Mfg. Co. for each fabric type during the time period given.

The direct manufacturing costs depend on the type of tent being manufactured and the fabric used. In a 1-person tent 3.5 yards of canvas, 4 yards of line, 12 grommets, and a yard of belting for tie downs are needed. The material cost is determined by the cost per yard times the amount of canvas needed. The cost for a 10-oz. 1-person tent was $6.72 in 1982 and it increased to $8.94 by 1984. The material costs other than canvas started at $2.76 in 1982 and increased to $3.67 by 1984. In a 2-person tent 4.5 yards, in a 4-person tent 6 yards, and in an 8-person tent 12 yards are required.

The tent is manufactured by laborers working exclusively on piece-work. Under a piecework payment scale the employee receives no dollars except on the number of units produced. The employer does not have to maintain a fixed payroll for employees under this payment plan.

The labor cost for a 1-person tent, regardless of fabric, was $4.81 in 1982 and increased to $6.40 by 1984.

The raw material shipping costs represent the allocated costs of shipping to each tent type. This cost started at $0.12 in 1982 and increased to $0.15 by 1984. These costs are shown in Figure 3–2.

Figure 3–2   Cost of Tent Manufacturing

		Year		
Costs	1982	1983	1984	1985
Direct Cost 10 oz.				
1-Person				
10 oz. Canvas	6.72	7.39	8.13	8.94
Other material	2.76	3.04	3.34	3.67
Direct labor	4.81	5.29	5.82	6.40
Raw mat'l ship	0.12	0.13	0.14	0.15
2-Person				
10 oz. canvas	8.64	9.50	10.45	11.50
Other material	3.54	3.89	4.28	4.71
Direct labor	5.61	6.17	6.79	7.47
Raw mat'l ship	0.13	0.14	0.15	0.17
4-Person				
10 oz. canvas	11.52	12.67	13.94	15.33
Other material	3.87	4.26	4.69	5.16
Direct labor	6.55	7.21	7.93	8.72
Raw mat'l ship	0.22	0.24	0.26	0.29
8-person				
10 oz. canvas	23.04	25.34	27.87	30.66
Other material	4.21	4.63	5.09	5.60
Direct labor	7.05	7.76	8.54	9.39
Raw mat'l ship	0.33	0.36	0.40	0.44
Direct cost 12 oz.				
1-Person				
12 oz. canvas	8.44	9.28	10.21	11.23
Other material	2.76	3.04	3.34	3.67
Direct labor	4.81	5.29	5.82	6.40
Raw mat'l ship	0.14	0.15	0.17	0.19
2-Person				
12 oz. canvas	10.85	11.94	13.13	14.44
Other material	4.45	4.90	5.39	5.93
Direct labor	5.61	6.17	6.79	7.47
Raw mat'l ship	0.16	0.18	0.20	0.22
4-Person				
12 oz. canvas	14.46	15.91	17.5	19.25
Other material	3.87	4.26	4.69	5.16
Direct labor	6.55	7.21	7.93	8.72
Raw mat'l ship	0.24	0.26	0.29	0.32
8-Person				
12-oz. canvas	28.92	31.81	34.99	38.49
Other material	4.21	4.63	5.09	5.60
Direct labor	7.05	7.76	8.54	9.39
Raw mat'l ship	0.41	0.45	0.50	0.55

In addition to direct costs, T-P Mfg. Co. incurs a number of indirect costs. The factory overhead costs include the cost of rent, maintenance of the building, and supervision costs, among others. The administrative overhead costs include salaries for the corporation managers and office employees, supplies, and similar items. The utilities costs are for heat, light, phone, and water. The interest expense is for payments on the loans for working capital currently outstanding. The insurance expense is for workman's compensation, product liability, and fire, theft, and other liability. These costs are shown in Figure 3–3.

	Year			
	1982	*1983*	*1984*	*1985*
Factory overhead	30000	33000	36300	39930
Adm overhead	32000	34560	37325	40311
Utilities	13000	14300	15730	17303
Interest exp	5000	5000	5000	5000
Insurance	5430	6082	6811	7629

Figure 3–3   Indirect Costs

T-P Mfg. Co. has some additional selling and distribution costs in the form of selling and advertising expenses. These costs include visits to individual retail outlets, phone calls, radio, newspaper, and TV ads. The costs are shown in Figure 3–4.

	Year			
	1982	*1983*	*1984*	*1985*
Selling expense	9792.94	13924.54	18266.93	19025.56
Adv exp.	5875.76	8354.72	10960.16	11415.33

Figure 3–4   Selling and Distribution Costs

With the information in Figures 3–1 through 3–4 you will be able to make an analysis of the profit performance of T-P Mfg. Co. over the past four years.

Assignment #3

You are an expert (accountant, computer, financial, personal, management, etc.) hired to help T-P Mfg. Co. solve its growth problems. Your job is to identify the most critical problem in your area of expertise, identify the current position of T-P Mfg., identify the goals they should set, develop a plan to accomplish the goals, and determine what information is needed to solve the problem.

A memo is to be prepared for the president detailing your opinion on what is T-P Mfg. Co.'s most critical problem.

1. Expansion needs: Equipment
2. Expansion needs: Marketing team
3. Expansion needs: Plant square footage
4. Expansion needs: Personnel (management, shop supervision, shop floor)
5. Expansion needs: Training
6. Expansion needs: Financial
7. Expansion needs: Inventory plan
8. Expansion needs: Accounting system
9. Expansion needs: Microcomputers
10. Determine price of company if sold
11. Investigate question: Should company expand?

THE IMPORTANCE OF SOFTWARE DOCUMENTATION

Laura B. Ruff
Mary K. Weitzer

There is an old saying which teachers are fond of quoting. It goes as follows, "Give me a fish and you have fed me for a day, teach me to fish and you have fed me for a lifetime." That quote came to mind as we were writing this piece on documentation research. Most software comes with some sort of written directions commonly referred to as documentation. Learning to use documentation is the key to realizing the capabilities and power of the accompanying software. Much documentation, however, is written by technical people using technical terms and can be rather intimidating, especially to the novice. But with a table of contents, an index, some of the pages in between, and a good measure of determination and fortitude, even the beginner can learn a software package by correctly using the documentation.

Unfortunately, some people never learn to use the documentation. Employers are dismayed to find that an employee who is trained in the use of one software package often cannot transfer that knowledge to another software package without additional training. It seems that many employees depend on learning a package from someone else and never learn to look things up for themselves. Several problems ensue from this lack of independence. This type of employee never learns to solve the unexpected problems that can arise when using software and never develops the tools needed to learn more about either the package currently being used, an update of that same package, or even a totally new package. Of course, in this rapidly changing field, new packages and updates of old packages are a fact of life with which all microcomputer users must deal.

Another problem results from not using the documentation. A user can learn only so much at any training session or in any course. Initially, a user is content with just the simplest functions of the software as opposed to the alternative of doing the tasks manually. Over a period of time, the novice becomes more comfortable with the software and starts looking for ways to increase productivity by doing the same tasks more efficiently and by adding applications that formerly were accomplished manually. "I wonder if I could do that with my software . . ." many times can be answered affirmatively simply by referring to the documentation.

It is easy to say that a user should "simply" read the documentation. For the first time user, however, this can be a frustrating experience. Documentation has become easier to read, better organized and more error free than it has been in the past. With anything new, though, there is a need to learn how to use this source of reference efficiently. The more often a person uses documentation, the more proficient that person will become at interpreting any type of software manual. Most software documentation does have several things in common. In order to gain microcomputing independence, look for the following items in software documentation. Happy fishing!

LICENSING INFORMATION

The licensing agreement will be of most immediate concern to you. Find out what the copyright will allow—how many backup copies (if any) are permitted? Is the software licensed to the user for use on any machine or licensed for use on only one machine? Can the software be used by more than one user at one time or by only one user without exception, or used by a variety of users as long as only the one copy is in use at any one time? The licensing agreement is usually fully visible before you even remove the wrapping. The terms of the agreement should be carefully followed.

As part of the licensing agreement, you will usually find a user registration card that will register you as a user of the software with the software publisher. Some software publishers issue a serial number for each package sold. If it is your responsibility, be sure to fill out the registration immediately and mail it to the publisher so that you will be entitled to receive any technical support, update information, or newsletters that may be provided to registered users.

PACKAGING

Documentation can be found in all shapes, weights, and forms. It may be contained in one or more three-ring binders, spiral bound book(s), a single sheet of paper, or simply as part of the program disk. If the documentation is in hardcopy form, one of the first things you will want to do when you open your documentation is to find out how the documentation is organized. If it is bound as one manual, does the manual have divider tabs? If there are two or more books that make up the documentation, which one should be examined first? Which one will be used most often? Sometimes when there is more than one book included as the documentation, there will be one manual for the novice microcomputer user (usually in tutorial form), one for day-to-day reference, one for the more technical or less frequently used functions, and so on. There may be separate quick reference cards and/or a keyboard layout chart or template. If you happen to be the first person to use the software you will find that the disks themselves will be somewhere within the documentation package. After you have examined the documentation as described here, you will be ready to more closely peruse its contents.

TABLE OF CONTENTS

A good Table of Contents will give you the first picture of the software and its functions. This section would be one of the first referral areas with which you would want to become familiar. The Table of Contents will help you to find out if the documentation has the other sections we are mentioning here and help you to discover any other special features and aids that may be available within the documentation.

INTRODUCTION (OR "READ ME FIRST")

All good software will offer some sort of introductory section that will explain the overall capabilities of the package, what tutorial materials are included with the software (if any), and possibly the hardware requirements of the software package. Even before you purchase a software package, this section of the documentation is a good guide to help you decide whether the software is appropriate for your applications. Usually documentation is available for examination before you purchase it at a retail computer software store. If so, you can check the hardware requirements so you will know if your machine has enough memory to support the software, for instance, or if a hard disk is required, or if your printer is supported by the software. Through the use of documentation at the point of purchase, you are already taking a step towards independence by not having to rely solely on what a sales representative tells you. You can read it for yourself.

If you are in a situation where you are responsible for selecting software, you definitely want to check the clarity and completeness of the documentation. The documentation is an important feature to consider when purchasing software. The Table of Contents and Introduction are good places to begin your evaluation. In addition to the documentation manual that comes with the software, check to see what other types of training aids, such as a tutorial disk or sample data disk, may be available for the software. Such training aids are excellent for the first time user, especially if used in conjunction with the documentation.

In a new software package, the actual program disks may come to you in a nice shrink-wrapped package. These disks must be "set-up", "installed" or in some way prepared to be used on your microcomputer system. Each package must be set up differently and even the same package may need to be prepared differently depending on the configuration of your machine. These directions are usually found in the introductory section of the documentation. If the information that you think should be found in the Introduction is not there, just check the Table of Contents to find out where the information is located. The warranty information is likely to be in this section as well as the license agreement. The number of backup copies (if any) of a program will be stated in the license agreement as well as the policy on updates.

Other information you might look for in the introductory sections includes an explanation of the keyboard layout that defines all keys as they will be used with the specific software, an explanation of the cursor movement keys and edit keys, descriptions of the screen layouts, an explanation of the help function, if available, and so on.

ADDRESS AND PHONE FOR TECHNICAL SUPPORT (HELP)

Another important part of the introductory information should include the address and phone number that can be used for technical support or at least some information regarding the software publisher's user assistance services. Most companies offer at least short term phone assistance that can later be extended for a fee. Others will offer free technical support indefinitely. What type of technical support is available for the software you are using or plan to buy? If you read the documentation you will find the answer.

REFERENCE SECTIONS

The most frequently used sections of the documentation will be those containing the actual description of how to use the capabilities and functions of the software. The number of reference sections contained within the documentation will directly depend upon the complexity of the software program and possibly the structure of the documentation layout. Become familiar with the arrangement of the reference sections. Are they arranged according to functions? Are they alphabetically arranged? Those two arrangements seem to be the most popular and logical but logic does not always seem to be the criterion for arrangement. The time you take to investigate and to become familiar with the reference section(s) will be time well spent.

SUMMARY SECTIONS

Much of the software documentation offers summary or quick reference sections that become increasingly helpful as you gain expertise. These sections will serve as a "tickler" to remind you of the procedures that you have already learned and used.

APPENDIXES

As with all other sections described in this appendix, the information found in the Appendixes will vary from software package to software package. In general, however, you might look for information on the error messages that are used by the program, printer configuration information (how to set up the program so that it works with your printer), printer codes (so that you can send special messages to the printer), explanation of menus used within the program, glossary of terminology, shortcuts for the advanced user (even software publishers realize that a lot of the knowledge acquired while using one type of software package can be transferred to make learning a different software package easier), and so on.

GLOSSARY

Some documentation includes a Glossary, which is an alphabetical listing of terms along with their definitions. Some of the terminology and definitions may be specific to the particular software package while others are more general terms that are not software specific. The Glossary is usually located right before the Index.

INDEX

The Index found in most documentation can help you find more detailed information than is contained in the Table of Contents. Alphabetically arranged, you can find the page number for an explanation of specific procedures, functions, capabilities and so forth. If you know that the software is capable of performing a function, you might check the Glossary to find out what term is used for the specific function and then look up the page number for a description of the function in the Index. Just taking the time to slowly go through the Index can reward you with quite a bit of information about a software package and its capabilities.

Appendix C

Types of Index Organization

The schemes used for indexing include:

1. Binary search methods
   a. B-Tree
   b. Inverted B-Tree
   c. Modified B-Tree
2. Hashed
3. Index entry
4. Inverted file (keyed)
5. Sequential
6. ISAM-Index sequential access method
7. Key words
8. Pointer.

The binary search technique works only on data that is in sequence. It is a technique for locating an item by continuously dividing the file into groups by two. This is a simple but effective method for making a rapid search for data in a file. The B-Tree, inverted B-Tree, and modified B-Tree are variations of the binary search concept.

Hashing is most commonly used in multi-user data base systems. Hashing uses a **nonlinear** rather than **linear algorithm** for storing data in and retrieving it quickly from a data base.

An index entry is an individual line or item of data contained in an index. It is similar to an entry in a dictionary.

An inverted file is a file indexed on characteristics. All individuals in the scout master list who are trained have a marker to indicate the level of training. A key number is maintained to tell the system the meaning of the code used.

A sequential or **ordered file** is one where the data has been ordered. Such sorting is slow but necessary for binary searching. When it is necessary to sort on more than one field, individual indexes for each field are often more effective. This is referred to as ISAM, index sequential access method. The records may then be left in random order.

Key words are used to retrieve data from libraries and other data bases. A set of key words for searching is entered. The key word list of each record is searched. When a complete match is made, the record is flagged. Key word search is often combined with some other indexing scheme.

The pointer method is a table look-up technique that permits each data set to be stored with a pointer pointing to a list of associated data.

Linear:
A straight line. Nonlinear is a mathematical relationship that is not a straight line.

Algorithm:
A sequence of mathematical rules used to obtain a desired result.

Nonlinear algorithm:
A sequence of mathematical rules based on nonlinear mathematical relationships for obtaining a desired result, the rapid storing and retrieving of data in a multi-user data base.

Ordered file:
A file stored in the data base in numeric, alphabetic, or ASCII code number order relative to a specific field.

GLOSSARY

Absolute reference (spreadsheet): The indication of where specific data are found in a fixed column/row location. When cells are moved or copied absolute references do not change. 138

Access method: The scheme used by the operating system to control communication between work stations in a LAN. 270

Acoustical coupler modem: A modem that connects directly to the telephone system using acoustical cups to hold the telephone. 222

Analog devices: Devices used to monitor real-world conditions such as temperature, sound, and movement. These devices use continuous voltage rather than the binary coding system of the microcomputer. 227

Analysis: Comparison of alternate management actions. 301

ANSI: American National Standards Institute. Develops and maintains standards on many aspects of microcomputers. 25

Answer: Modem setting in asynchronous communication. One partner must answer, the other originate. 231

Apple-DOS: Disk operating system used on Apple computers. 68

Application programs: A program designed for the business professional to perform a specific business function. 2

Architecture: The design of the microcomputer. How the parts are put together. Also called design architecture. 35

ASCII: American Standard Code for Information Interchange. This is a seven-bit binary code. Numbers from 00 to 127 can be produced with a seven-bit binary number. The decimal number 90 is 1011010. Each number in ASCII stands for a character or control instruction. 82, 230, 253

ASM: CP/M Utility used to create a machine language file from assembly language code. 85

Assembly language: A language that is close to machine language and easily converted using a special program called an assembler. 25

Asynchronous communication: Communication that requires timing only when a bit is being transmitted. 229, 254

Attribute: A particular characteristic of interest about an entity. 169

Backup: A copy of a disk, diskette or file. 69

BAK: Extender used to indicate a file is a backup file. 81

BAS: Extender used to indicate a file is a BASIC program file. 81

Baseband coaxial cable: Similar to television cable, for medium-speed local area networks. Can handle one transmission at a time. 269

BASIC: Beginners All-purpose Symbolic Instructional Code. 25

Batch run: A scheduling system which requires computer tasks be collected and given to a central controller who then runs them as a single job batched together. 255

Baud rate: Usually refers to the transmission rate. 1200 baud means 120 characters per second. 222

Binary file: Programs stored in machine language form. A binary file may be directly executed by the microcomputer. 82

Binary number: A number consisting of 0 and 1. Each 0 or 1 is a bit. The decimal numbers 0 to 126 require 7 bits. To add the decimal numbers 127 to 255 require the 8th bit. 82

Binary search: For ordered records. An item is located by continuously dividing the file into groups by two.

Bit: A binary digit. The microcomputer uses a binary number system consisting of 0 and 1. A bit is a 0 or a 1. 37

Bit map: Picture represented by dots, digitizing. 196

Block: A collection of characters with beginning and ending markers that must be entered by the user. 99

Boards: See cards. 13, 40

Booting: Starting the system. 39

Boot strap: Program that starts the system. 39

Breakeven analysis: An evaluation technique that calculates the amount of output when the total cost of one method is the same as the total cost of a second method. 303, 304

Briefcase microcomputer: A microcomputer that fits in a briefcase and/or may be used on an individual lap. 17

Broadband coaxial cable: Cable that may handle many transmissions at one time for local area networks. 269

Bubble memory: A memory device that uses no power. Uses a thin magnetic recording film that looks like bubbles. 40

Bus: Pathway or channel for data and instruction between hardware devices. 84, 270

Business graphics: Pictorial representation of business data. 194

Business graphics programs: Programs with the capability of producing bar charts, pie charts, line type graphs. 6

Business professional (as used in this book): An "end user" of a microcomputer who uses it to solve his/her own problems, and who is assumed to have little or no computer training—in other words, not a programmer. 2

Byte: A sequence of binary digits taken as a unit. Eight binary digits per byte microcomputers are currently the most common. Seven or eight bits are used to create characters. 37

C: A microcomputer and computer language that uses structured programming and can perform many tasks that would normally require the use of assembly language. 26

CAD: Computer aided design. 2

CADD: Computer aided design and drafting. 2

CAE: Computer aided engineering. 2

Cards: Flat pieces of material with printed circuits and electronic components to add special capabilities to the microcomputer. Often called PC (Printed Circuit) boards. 13, 40

CAT: The name of the directory in (Apple) PRO-DOS. See DIR. 74

CATALOG: The name of the directory in Apple-DOS. See DIR. 74

Cells: Column (vertical division) and row (horizontal division) location on screen and in spreadsheets. 3, 132

Central file server (program): Program that controls the access to files by individual work stations in a LAN. 268

Central switching station: The central microcomputer connected to a series of stations in a LAN. 270

Centronics connection: The name of the standard parallel connector. Centronic was the first printer company to make this connection popular. 75

Character size: The number of bits per character byte. 231

CMOS: Memory that uses little power, complementary metal oxide semiconductor. 40

COBOL: COmmon Business Oriented Language. A mainframe computer language that is available on microcomputers. 26

Code: The use of symbols or numbers to represent letters, numbers, or special meanings. 25, 82

Cold boot: Starting the system from the beginning when the system is first turned on. 70

Collector: An interface that collects messages from a number of devices, organizes the messages, and then forwards them to the central computer. 255

Column: Vertical division of screen and spreadsheet. 3, 132

COM files: Files in machine language ready to operate on a specific microcomputer. 81

Communication Bus (Layout of LAN): A LAN layout around a bus which serves as a channel for communication. 270

Communication program: A program that allows computers to communicate with each other. 8

Communication ring or circle: Layout of LAN where the stations are connected in a ring or circle. 270

Compatibility: Capability of microcomputers to work together as a system and to exchange physical parts. 34

Compiler: A translator program that takes near English code and translates it into a set of machine language codes all at one time. 25

Composite monitor: Type of color monitor. 44

Compressed mode: Printer that produces small letters to increase the characters per line of output. 45

Condensed mode: See compressed mode. 45

Configuration: Matching the hardware, software, and operating systems settings so that all the parts work and communicate with all the other parts of a system. 34

Conventions: The standard and accepted abbreviations, symbols, and their meanings for users of microcomputers. 70

Copy (block): To duplicate an image of a block at a new location (in word processing). 111

Copy protected (program): Programs sold with a limit placed on the number of copies a user may produce. 54

CP/M: Operating system, Control Program/Microcomputer. One of the first operating systems developed for microcomputers. 25

CPU: Central Processing Unit. 13

CRT: Cathode Ray Tube, screen, monitor. 13

CSMA/CD: Carrier Sense Multiple Access/Collision Detect, a communication system that operates like a telephone party line. 272

Cursor: A symbol on the monitor that indicates where text will be typed. The cursor is often a line (_) or a box. It may be steady or blinking. 103

Data: Facts that have been collected, organized, and stored. 5, 164

Data base: A collection of data stored in your microcomputer, that is used for a variety of business purposes. 5, 164

Data base management programs: Programs designed to store, update, and retrieve business data. These programs are not limited to any particular type of application. 5, 164

Data file transfer software: Programs designed to read data in the format produced by one program and change it to a format needed by a second program. 279

DDT: CP/M Utility used to debug an assembly language file. 85

Debug: To remove errors from a program. 85

Default drive: The disk drive from which data and programs are read unless the microcomputer is instructed otherwise. The default drive is the logged drive if no additional instructions are given. 55, 71

Delete: An instruction to remove a character, block or file. When characters are removed, the text closes up. 103

Desktop microcomputer: A microcomputer that has the greatest capabilities, most expansion room, and requires a part of a desk for its work area. 16

DIF: Data Interchange Format. An ASCII file in a specific format developed for VisiCalc used for both spreadsheet and data file interchange. 174

Digitize: To convert a picture or other data to numbers, that are then recorded in the microcomputer. 196

DIP: Dual Inline Package, housing to hold a chip or other items to printed circuit board. 41

DIP switches: A series of toggle switches built into a DIP, that are mounted on a pc-board. The switches are used for system configuration. 41

DIR: Directory. Instruction that tells what files are on a storage media. Name used in CP/M, TRS-DOS, and MS-DOS. 73

Direct-connect modem: A modem that connects directly to the telephone system using telephone line. 222

Disk: An eight inch flat, round piece of plastic coated with magnetic material and placed in a protective cover. The disk is used to record microcomputer programs and data. 14

Diskette: A five and a quarter inch flat, round piece of plastic coated with magnetic material and placed in a protective cover. The diskette is used to record microcomputer programs and data. Often called a floppy disk. 14

Document assembly programs: Programs that create documents from prerecorded paragraphs. 3

Documentation: Narrative supplied with programs to help the user operate the software. 2

DOS: Disk Operating System. See operating system. 68

Dot matrix printer: Printer that produces characters using dots rather than whole letters. 45

Download: To transfer a file from another computer into yours. 181, 236, 237

DSDD: Double Sided and Double Density diskette or disk drive. 56

Dumb terminal: Terminal that communicates only under the control of an individual. 8, 235

EBCDIC: Extended Binary Coded Decimal Interchange Code. The standard code developed and used by IBM for its mainframe computers. It is a binary code made up of eight-bits that allows 256 characters. 253

ED: CP/M utility used to edit a file. 85

Editing: Making corrections to spreadsheets, word processor, and other files. 145

Electronic mail: The transmission of letters, memos, and other messages by one microcomputer to another computer. 246

Electronic spreadsheet: See spreadsheet programs. 128

Emulators: A printed circuit board that fits into a microcomputer and gives it the capability to act like a special purpose terminal. 253

End user: See Business Professional. 2

Engineering/scientific graphics: Includes CAD, computer aided design; CAM, computer aided manufacturing; CADD, computer aided design and drafting. 6

Entity: Something that has separate and distinct existence. 169

EOF: End Of File. A code placed at the end of a file to indicate the end has been reached. 73

EPROM: Erasable Programmable Read Only Memory chips. This type of chip makes it easy for individuals to produce custom programs. 39

Erase: To remove a block. 111

Esc.: Key found in the upper left of most keyboards. Used as a control type key. 81

Extra capabilities: State of the art features. 11

Facts: Something that exists and must be taken into consideration. 164

Families: Groups of microcomputers that use the same or similar microprocessor and the same or similar operating system. These groups have similar capabilities. 68

Field: A unit of data about an attribute of an entity. 169

File: A collection of related material. May be data or programs or both. 68, 171

File maintenance: The entering and updating of data in a data base. 165

File management programs: Programs designed to store, update, and retrieve business data. These programs are limited to managing simple files with narrow objectives. 5

File management-report generators: See File management programs. 171

File server: The computer which controls the storage and retrieval of files from a common disk or hard disk when a number of computers are connected together to form a system. 253, 268

Filename: Name given to a data or program file. 81

Filespec: Includes name of disk drive, colon, path (if

any), filename, decimal point, and extender. 81

Floppy disk drive: Data storage devices; stores data, programs and other computer files. 14

Font: A style of letter or character such as Italic, Courier, or Prestige. 96

Footprint: The amount of space taken on a desk by a microcomputer. 17

Format: Defines how code is saved on a diskette. It also defines how characters are placed on a piece of paper and how the characters are displayed on the screen. 77

FORMAT: Instruction used to tell the microcomputer to prepare a diskette or disk for use. Magnetic marks are made on the media to identify tracks and sectors where data is to be stored. 73

Formula: Rules defining the relationship (outcome) between numbers used in the spreadsheet. Electronic spreadsheet formulas often use cell references as variables. 131

FORTH: FOuRTH generation language. A microcomputer language used for business, scientific, process control, and robotics. Contains a resident assembly language. 26

FORTRAN: FORmula TRANslator. A mainframe computer language now available on microcomputers. Used for engineering and science application. 26

Free format data bases: Data bases that combine different forms of data entry including text, lists, tables, charts, and graphs. 173

Full-duplex: Both communication partners can send and receive at the same time. 232

Full-featured microcomputer: A microcomputer system that includes most of the accessories available at a given time. 11

Function key: Keys found on the left side of the IBM PC keyboard, or the top of some look-alikes that send custom instructions to the microcomputers. In some programs the user may define the instructions sent by the function keys. 99

Functions (operating system): Routines built into the operating system. These routines provide the user with the capability to perform needed tasks. Functions are loaded into RAM with the operating system and remain there. 68

Functions of management: Planning (including goal setting), organizing, directing, and controlling. 175

Gigabyte: One billion bytes, 1,000,000,000 or 10^9. 56

Graphics: Pictorial representation of data. 194

Hacker: An individual working alone who developed both the hardware and software of the microcomputer. A person who may or may not be trained for the task (hobbyist). 19

Half-duplex: One communication partner can send and the other receive at any given time. 232

Hard copy: Text printed on paper. 3

Hard disk drive: Data storage devices, may be fixed or removable. Stores data, programs, and other computer files, 14

Hardware: The part of the microcomputer you can see and feel. 11

Hex: Hexadecimal. A Hex file is a file stored using numbers based on 16 digits. 85

Hierarchical data bases: A data base organized from the top down. 172

Hierarchical files: A file structure consisting of a top down organization. Files are organized in what is often referred to as a tree structure. Some operating systems allow sophisticated security to be established for hierarchical files. 73

Hierarchy: Classification or grading of a group or set from high to low. 23

High bit: The last bit in a binary number. High bit numbers are the decimal numbers that can only be created when the last bit is used. The decimal numbers 00 to 126 may be created by seven-bit binary numbers. The addition of the eighth-bit allows the creation of decimal numbers 127 to 255. 231

High-level language: A computer language near English. 25

Idea (business): Recognition of a business need or opportunity. 293

IEEE-488: Port specification. Used for laboratory type devices. 75

Implementation: Putting a method or microcomputer to work in a company. 307

Index hole: Hole on disk and diskette used to index the reading operating in some operating systems. 54

Indexing: The manner in which a program orders the records in a file. 174

Information: Data that has been processed and recalled from a data base in an organized manner. 164

Ink-Jet printers: Printers that use jets of ink to produce characters. 48

Input: see I/O

Input (factors of production): The factors of production, land, labor, capital, and the business enterprise used to produce goods and services. 301

Input devices: A device connected to the microcomputer through which data and instructions are entered. 13, 42

Insert: When a word is typed into existing text, the text that follows it moves over to make room. 103

Instruction set: Instructions built into the computer. The instruction set is contained in the microprocessor. 82

Integrated programs: Programs that combine the capabilities of two or more general or specific application programs. 9, 279

Interface: A common boundary between independent systems; in the field of microcomputers the connection between two parts of the system; the programs and hardware that make it possible for two parts of the microcomputer system or two computers to work together. 68, 255

Interpreter: A program that translates a line of near English code into machine language, executes the line of code, translates the next line, etc. until all instructions have been completed. 25

I/O: Input and output devices or methods. 14

Join command: A command that allows searching all records with a given characteristic in a specified field, and combining in a variety of ways the data pertaining to that characteristic. 172

Justified: Lining up of type on a page or in a cell. Left justified means lined up evenly on the left side of page or cell, while right justified means lined up on the right. 143

K: see kilobyte. 39

Kilobyte: 1024 bytes, or 2^{10}. 39

Knowledge: The assignment of meaning to information by a human being. 164

Labels: Words identifying columns, rows, or overall titles. 131

LAN: Local Area Networks. A series of microcomputers connected together sharing peripherals, files, and programs. 266

LAN topology: The relative physical and logical arrangement of stations in the network. Types include central switching station, communication bus, communication ring, and point-to-point. 270

Language: See Programming language. 5

Lap microcomputer: See briefcase microcomputer. 17

Laser printer: Printers that use technology similar to that of some copying machines. They produce quality results at relatively high speeds. 47

LCD: Liquid Crystal Display microcomputer output device. 44

Letter quality printer: Printers that use thimbles, balls, daisy wheels, or other impact devices. 46

Limitations: Restrictions on the decision making process. 294

Linear: Relating to a straight line. Nonlinear is a mathematical relationship that is not related to a straight line.

Load: To transfer a file from an on-line storage media into the RAM of a computer so it can be used. 68

LOAD: CP/M utility used to convert Hex files to COM files. 85

Logged drive: The disk drive from which data and programs are read. 71

LOGO: A microcomputer educational language that uses graphics for programming. 26

Low-level language: A computer language near machine language. 25

Machine language: A formal system of signs and symbols including rules for their use that convey instructions to a computer. 25

Macros: Custom routines which substitute a few keystrokes for many. They may be created by the user and saved on disk as routines that are recalled with a few keystrokes when needed in spreadsheets or similar programs. 149

Magnetic tape: Data storage media. 14

Mainframe: A large computer. Originally all computers were mainframe computers. Most require technical expertise to operate. 246

Master diskette: Diskette upon which data or programs are stored for safekeeping. A copy of the master diskette is made to be used as the working diskette. 57

Mathematical operators: Symbol that indicates a mathematical process such as addition ($+$), subtraction ($-$), multiplication (*), division (/), and raising to a power (^). 138

Measurable: An activity or item which can be measured. If a goal cannot be measured there is no way of knowing when the goal has been accomplished. 294

Megabyte: One million bytes. 40

Menu: A list of microcomputer actions displayed on the screen from which the user selects the one wanted. 84

Microprocessor: An integrated circuit on a silicon chip, usually less than two inches long and a half inch wide, that contains the arithmetic, logic, control, and memory units. The remaining hardware supports this chip. 13, 37

Milestones: Steps on the way to the completion of a plan. 295

Minicomputer: Medium-size computer, larger and more expensive than a microcomputer, but smaller than a mainframe. 246

Modem: A device to connect the microcomputer to the telephone. It changes binary codes to sound for telephone transmission and then back again. 8, 222

Modular software: Programs sold in individual modules that can be put together to form a system. The user has the option of purchasing only those modules desired. 14, 279

Monitor: see CRT, VDT. 14

Monochrome monitor: A green, amber, or black and white monitor. 44

Mother board: A printed circuit board or card containing the microprocessor, computer memory, and selected controller circuits to direct the signals that are received from external connectors. 35

Move: To relocate a block. 111

MOVECPM: CP/M utility used to relocate the system to make room for special programs. 85

MS/PC-DOS: Microsoft disk operating system; Personal Computer Disk Operating System used on the IBM PC and look-alike family of microcomputer. 25

Multi-tasking: The capability of the microcomputer to perform more than one task at the same time. 40, 268

Multi-user: Microcomputers and programs that allow more than one user to share the same microprocessor. 40, 268

Multi-user data bases: A data base program that allows more than a single user access at the same time. 173

National electronic data bases: Dynamic libraries that are used by connecting a microcomputer to a telephone. Current information about economics, business, and other specialized topics are available using such data bases. 248

Near ASCII file: A file that uses the ASCII codes, has some additional control codes, and may be edited to an ASCII file without excessive effort. 115

Network data base: A hierarchical data base that allows for multiple relationships among levels. 173

Non-procedural language: A programming language that does not require programming techniques to be used. It allows the user to send instructions to the computer in English-like statements. 165

Null-modem: Device that makes the computer behave as if it is connected to a telephone to allow communication between computers. 8, 223

Numbers: Mathematical values, business data. 131

Objective: A business goal that is feasible, measurable, has a time limit, has recognized limitations, and has a plan for its accomplishment. 293

OCR: Optical Character Reader. 42

On/off-line: The operation of computer equipment at the same time as other equipment under the control of the microprocessor (on-line.) Independent operation is called off-line. 49

On-line devices: Devices connected electronically through controller circuits. They may or may not be physically part of the microcomputer. 14

On-line storage devices: Devices available to the microcomputer through communication cables. 49

On-line storage media: Media used to store microcomputer files. 52

Operating system: The program that directs the flow of data among the parts of the microcomputer, the user, and application programs, often called the disk operating system (DOS or OS). 2, 68

Operational compatibility: The capability of microcomputers to work together as a system. 57

Originate: Modem setting in asynchronous communication. One partner must originate, the other answer. 231

Output (business): The goods and services produced by a company. 301

Output devices: A device connected to the microcomputer through which data and instructions are communicated to the user or other devices. 14, 44

Overflow (cell): More characters are entered than the cell can contain. The additional characters appear in the next cell. (See also Truncated.) 142

Overlay utility software: Programs that provide selected routines to the user at all times. 279

Overwrite: When a character is typed, it replaces the character formerly at the location of the cursor. 103

Parallel communication port: Connection to communicate over a number of "parallel" wires at the same time. 41

Parameter: A variable value. Parameters are values that must be set before communication can occur. 231

Parity bit: The error checking bit. 230

Pascal: A simple and structured microcomputer language for general use. 26

Path: Used on a hard disk divided into subdirectory to locate a file. 75

Payback period: The amount of time until the total cost of one method is the same as a second method. 303

PC-boards: See cards. 13, 40

PC-DOS: See MS/PC-DOS. 25

Peripheral: A device such as a printer, bar code reader, or modem connected to a microcomputer to give it special capabilities. 16

Phase I: See Pre-microprocessor phase. 19

Phase II: See Hardware hacker phase. 19

Phase III: See Software hacker phase. 19

Phase IV: Use of the microcomputer by the business professional in all sizes and types of organizations. 19

Physical compatibility: The capability to exchange physical parts with other microcomputers. 41

PIP: CP/M utility, Peripheral Interchange Program, used to transfer files from one diskette to another. 85

Pixels: The dots on a microcomputer's screen used to create numbers, graphics, and other characters (letters, numbers, and symbols). 44, 194

Plan: A series of steps detailing what must be done to move a business from where it is to where management has decided it is to go. 294

Plotter printer: Printer that uses lines to create graphic type output. 48

Pocket microcomputer: Computer small enough to fit in a pocket. 19

Point-to-point LAN: Layout of LAN topology where each station is connected directly to other stations, 270

Portable microcomputers: Often refers to transportables, and at other times to all computers smaller than transportables. 16

Ports: Outlets or connections that allow the microcomputer to communicate with peripherals and other computers. 75

Powerful (programs): Programs that have many capabilities to accomplish a variety of business objectives. 2

Precedence (Math): The order in which mathematical operations are executed. The standard order is parentheses, power, multiplication and division, and addition and subtraction. 138

Pre-microprocessor phase: Phase I of the history of microcomputers before the development of the microprocessor. 19

Print spooler: A program that sets aside part of the RAM or disk to receive text to be sent to the printer. 116

Printer controllers: Programs or routines that take a text file and produce a hard copy. 115

Productivity: Output divided by input. 301

Programming language: A language used by programmers to create, store, recall, and edit instructions to computers. 5

Programs: See Software. 2

PROM: Programmable Read Only Memory chips. 39

Proportional spacing: Allows for differences in letter size to make the document look like typeset material. 116

Protected cell: A cell that has been protected from change by the spreadsheet designer. It is good practice to "protect" the cells with labels when a standard form is created. 136

RAM: Random Access Memory. Memory used for data and program storage by the user. The user can read and write data in RAM. 13, 38

Range (spreadsheet): The identification of the cells in a spreadsheet by the specification of the cell in the upper left position and the cell in the lower right position. 136

Raster graphics: Graphics using a bit map. 196

Real time processing: To process data and instructions as they are transmitted to the computer. The user works interactively with the computer. 255

Record: A collection of facts about an entity. 169

Relational data bases: A data base with the capability to combine the data from a series of records that has a field with a matching relationship. 171, 172

Relative reference (spreadsheet): The indication of where specific data are found in terms of a fixed number of columns and rows from the cell where the data are needed. When cells are moved or copied the relative references are changed to maintain their relative position. 138

Report generation: The creation of a formatted report to output information from the data base. 165

Resolution: The sharpness of the image produced by a monitor. 44

RGB: Type of color monitor (Red, Green, Blue) for microcomputers. 44

Right justification: When the text is lined up evenly on the right margin. 107–108

ROM: Read Only Memory. Memory with instructions (programs) needed when operating the microcomputer. The user cannot write data into ROM. Sometimes called firmware. 13, 38

Rotation hole: Hole in the middle of diskette or disk. 54

Routine: A part of a program that performs specific tasks. 68

Row: Horizontal division of screen and spreadsheet. 3, 132

RS-232, RS-232C: The standard serial port for input and output communication with peripherals and other computers. 75

RS-422: A serial port. 75

Screen: See CRT, VDT. 14

Scroll: Text is moved up or down to display text that cannot be shown on the monitor at one time. 103

Sector (of diskette): A division of a track on a disk. 54

Sequential search: A search of a file starting at the beginning and examining each record in turn seeking a particular record. 174

Serial communication port: Connection to communicate sending one bit after another in series. 41

Smart terminal: Terminal that can be used to transfer data files between computers. 8, 236

Software: Programs, instructions that tell the microcomputer how to perform. 2

Spreadsheet: A method for organizing, calculating, and presenting financial, statistical, and other business data for managerial decision making, 128

Spreadsheet programs: Programs used for calculation (formula oriented) and presentation. 3

SSDD: Single-Sided and Double-Density diskette or disk drive. 56

SSSD: Single-Sided and Single-Density diskette or disk drive. 56

Stand-alone: Programs that operate independently of other programs. 40

Start bit: The bit (in asynchronous communication)

that tells the second microcomputer a character is being sent. 230

STAT: CP/M utility used to check the status of disks and system. 85

Stop bit: The bit (in asynchronous communication) that tells the second microcomputer the character is complete. 230

String: A character or characters. Strings may be one or more characters in length. 108

SYLK: Symbolic Link. An ASCII file is a specific format developed for MultiLink used for both spreadsheet and data file interchange. 174

Synchronous communication: Communication that requires continuous timing. 229, 254

Syntax: The manner in which code must be put together for the computer to understand, including spelling. 26

SYSGEN: CP/M utility used to generate a CP/M operating system on a new diskette. 85

System overlay software: Programs that take over the disk operating system and add such capabilities as multi-tasking and file transfer between two programs operating concurrently. 279

Template: A spreadsheet or other model saved on disk to be recalled into a spreadsheet or other program as a pattern for future applications. Templates may be purchased on disk or copied out of books for many business applications. 148

Terminal: A computer work station, input/output device. It may consist of a keyboard and a monitor or be a microcomputer. 76

Text: Characters found on paper, on the screen, or stored in a microcomputer text file. Text may be a letter or a manuscript length book. 94

Text editor: A program that makes possible creating, changing, storage, and retrieval of text in the file. 103

Text file: A computer file that contains words and characters. Such files are commonly created during word processing. 94

Thermal printers: Printers that use a heating element to make a letter or character on either heat-sensitive paper or regular paper with a heat-sensitive ribbon. 48

Time limit: A date or time of day by which a task must be completed. 294

Timesharing: More than one terminal may be connected to and operated at one time on the same computer. 76

Token-passing: Transmission control system when a circle is used. Each station checks to see if a transmission is for them, and if it is not, passes it along to the next station. 272

Tracks (of diskette): A magnetic circle on a diskette or disk for storing data. 54

Transportable microcomputers: Microcomputers that

are packaged with most of the features of a desktop, including a monitor. 16

TRS-DOS: Tandy Radio Shack Disk Operating System used in various forms on the many Radio Shack microcomputers. 25

Truncated (cell): More characters are entered than the cell can contain. The additional characters are cut off at the end of the cell. 143

Twisted-pairs: Telephone wires used for some local area networks. 269

UNIX: The multi-user operating system of AT&T. 68

Upload: To transfer a file from your computer or terminal to another computer. 181, 236, 237

User friendly: Microcomputers and programs that are easy to use. 2

Utilities: Programs that support the operation of the operating system by adding capabilities. 23, 68

Variable: A quantity that may assume any one of a set of values. There are two types of variables: Independent—variables that change by themselves, such as time; Dependent—variables that depend on a second variable(s), such as sales per month, that depend on the month of the year. 201

VDT: Video Display Tube. 14

Vertical market: A narrow market that is limited to a specific professional area. 9

VisiCalc: First electronic spreadsheet program. 23

Warm boot: Starting the system from the beginning when the system is already operating. 70

What if?: The investigation of economic and business consequences assuming that changes in business decisions are to be made, and the conditions under which the decisions are made. 132

Windowing: The capability to divide a monitor into parts. In each part a different task or program may be operated. 76

Word processing program: A program designed to aid an individual in the creation, editing, printing, storing and retrieving of text. 3, 94

Word size: Microcomputers commonly process 8, 16, and 32 bits at one time. A 16 bit microcomputer may process two eight-bit bytes (characters) at one time. The overall speed of a microcomputer is a function of the number of bits per word, word size.

In microcomputer communication the bits per character is also referred to as word size. 37

Word wrap: The moving of the last word in a line to the next line when there is no room between margins. 100

Write protect notch: Notch on disk that is covered to make write, only on five and one quarter diskette and uncovered on eight inch disk. 54

<CR>: Press the return or enter keys. 69

^n: ^means press the control key at the same time as n, where n is another key. 81

INDEX

Registered Trademarks (continued)

pfs:Write are trademarks of Software Publishing Corporation, **Senior Partner** is a trademark of Panasonic, Inc., **Sidekick** is a trademark of Borland International, Inc., **Sideways** is a trademark of Funk Software, **Smartcom II,** and **Smartmodem 1200B** are trademarks of Hayes Microcomputer Products, Inc., **Smartlin II** is a trademark of Business Computer Net, **Spotlight** is a trademark of Software Arts, **Supercalc** is a trademark of Sorcim/IUS, **Telenet** is a trademark of GTE Corporation, **The Source** is a trademark of Source Telecomputing Corporation, a subsidiary of the Reader's Digest, **TRS-80 Model I, II, III, 4, 12, 100, 200, 1000, 1200, 2000, 6000, Daisy Wheel II Printer,** and **PC-4** are trademarks of Tandy Corporation, Radio Shack, **Unix** is a trademark of Bell Laboratories, **Visicalc** is a trademark of Visicorp, a subsidiary of Lotus Development Corporation, **Volksmodem 12** is a trademark of Anchor Automation, **Volkswriter** is a trademark of Lifetree Software, **Westlaw** is a trademark of West Publishing Company, **Z80** is a trademark of Zilog, Inc.

Chapter Opening Photos

Chapter 1 Courtesy of International Business Machines Corporation, **Chapter 2** Courtesy of International Business Machines Corporation, **Chapter 3** Courtesy of AT&T Information Systems, **Chapter 4** Courtesy of International Business Machines Corporation, **Chapter 5** Courtesy of International Business Machines Corporation, **Chapter 7** Chorus Data Systems, a manufacturer of image acquisition and data management products for P.C.'s, **Chapter 8** Courtesy of Radio Shack, a division of Tandy Corporation, **Chapter 9** Courtesy of Radio Shack, a division of Tandy Corporation, **Chapter 10** Courtesy of Hayes Microcomputer Products, Inc., **Chapter 11** Courtesy of Hewlett-Packard Company, **Chapter 12** Courtesy of International Business Machines Corporation

Intext Photo Credits

Fig. 1–1 Courtesy of Hewlett-Packard Company, **Fig. 1–4** Princeton Graphic Systems, An Intelligent Systems Company, **Fig. 1–5** Micro Technology, Inc., **Fig. 1–6** Princeton Graphic Systems, An Intelligent Systems Company, **Fig. 1–7** MicroTouch Systems, Inc., **Fig. 1–8** Courtesy of Hewlett-Packard Company, **Fig. 1–10** Courtesy of AT&T Information Systems, **Fig. 1–11** Courtesy of Compaq Computer Corporation, **Fig. 1–12** Courtesy of Hewlett-Packard Company, **Fig. 1–14** Princeton Graphic Systems, An Intelligent Systems Comany, **Fig. 1–15** Courtesy Interface, Inc., **Fig. 1–16** Courtesy Interface, Inc., **Fig. 1–17** Courtesy AT&T Information Systems, **Fig. 1–18** Courtesy of Hewlett-Packard Company, **Fig. 1–19** Courtesy of Epson America, **Fig. 1–20** Courtesy of Radio Shack, a division of Tandy Corporation, **Fig. 2–1** Courtesy of NEC Information Systems, Inc., **Fig. 2–2** Micron Technology Systems Group, Boise, Idaho, **Fig. 2–6** Courtesy of International Business Machines Corporations, **Fig. 2–7** Courtesy of the Voice Connection, Irvine, California, **Fig. 2–8** (a) Courtesy of Apple Computer, Inc., (b) Courtesy of Koala Technologies Corp., (c) Courtesy FTG Data Systems, (d) Courtesy of Hewlett-Packard Company, **Fig. 2–9** Courtesy of NEC Information Systems, Inc., **Fig. 2–10** Courtesy of NEC Information Systems, Inc., **Fig. 2–11** Courtesy of NEC Information Systems, Inc., **Fig. 2–12** Courtesy of Hewlett-Packard Company, **Fig. 2–13** Courtesy of Hewlett-Packard Company, **Fig. 2–14** Courtesy of Hewlett-Packard Company, **Fig. 2–15** Courtesy of NEC Information Systems, Inc., **Fig. 2–16** Courtesy of Epson America, **Fig. 2–17** Courtesy of NEC Information Systems, Inc., **Fig. 2–18** Courtesy of Radio Shack, a division of Tandy Corporation, **Fig. 2–19** Courtesy of Apple Computer, Inc., **Fig. 2–20** Courtesy of NEC Information Systems, Inc., **Fig. 3–3** Courtesy of NEC Information Systems, Inc., **Fig. 7–1** Photo Courtesy Polaroid Corporation, **Fig. 7–2** Photo Courtesy Polaroid Corporation, **Fig. 7–3** Princeton Graphic Systems, An Intelligent Systems Company, **Fig. 7–4** Photo Courtesy Polaroid Corporation, **Fig. 7–5** Courtesy of Epson America, **Fig. 7–6** Courtesy of Alpha Merics, Inc., **Fig. 7–7** Chorus Data Systems, a manufacturer of image acquisition and data management products for P.C.'s, **Fig. 7–23** Chorus Data Systems, a manufacturer of image acquisition and data management products for P.C.'s, **Fig. 8–2** Courtesy of Radio Shack, a division of Tandy Corporation, **Fig. 8–3** Courtesy of Radio Shack, a division of Tandy Corporation, **Fig. 8–4** Courtesy of Radio Shack, a division of Tandy Corporation, **Fig. 10–1** Courtesy of Hewlett-Packard Company